# MOTIVATIONAL INTERVIEWING

## FOR HEALTH CARE PROFESSIONALS

### A SENSIBLE APPROACH

# MOTIVATIONAL INTERVIEWING

## FOR HEALTH CARE PROFESSIONALS

### A SENSIBLE APPROACH

**Bruce A. Berger**

Professor Emeritus
Harrison School of Pharmacy
Auburn University
President, Berger Consulting, LLC
Auburn, Alabama

**William A. Villaume**

Professor Emeritus
Harrison School of Pharmacy
Auburn University
Auburn, Alabama

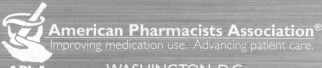

**American Pharmacists Association®**
Improving medication use. Advancing patient care.

APhA          WASHINGTON, D.C.

Editor: Nancy Tarleton Landis
Acquisition Editor: Sandra J. Cannon
Cover Design: Richard Muringer, APhA Creative Services
Design and Composition: Circle Graphics
Proofreading: Kathleen K. Wolter
Indexing: Suzanne Peake

Published by the American Pharmacists Association
2215 Constitution Avenue, N.W.
Washington, DC 20037-2985

To comment on this book via e-mail, send your message to the publisher at aphabooks@aphanet.org.

**Library of Congress Cataloging-in-Publication Data**
Berger, Bruce A.
  Motivational interviewing for health care professionals : a sensible approach / Bruce A. Berger, William A. Villaume.
      p. ; cm.
  Includes bibliographical references and index.
  ISBN 978-1-58212-180-2
  I. Villaume, William A. II. American Pharmacists Association. III. Title.
  [DNLM: 1. Motivational Interviewing. 2. Disease—psychology. 3. Health Behavior. 4. Professional-Patient Relations. WM 55]
  RC480.5
  616.89'1—dc23
                                    2013016381

**How to Order This book**
Online: www.pharmacist.com/shop
By phone: 800-878-0729 (770-280-0085 from outside the United States)
VISA®, MasterCard®, and American Express® cards accepted

# Contents

# Preface

This book is the product of its coauthors' varied career paths and their eventual collaboration on an approach to helping patients with health-related behavior change.

Bruce Berger practiced pharmacy before returning to graduate school to earn a PhD in social and behavioral pharmacy that focused on health psychology and health communication. While practicing pharmacy, Bruce noticed that the way health care professionals (HCPs) talked to patients affected whether patients were willing to consider and discuss their medications and their illnesses. Bruce was struck by how critical it is in patient care to build rapport with patients. This observation led him back to graduate school at The Ohio State University College of Pharmacy. Since then, Bruce's research has continued to focus on how HCPs talk to patients and how their talk affects patient outcomes such as treatment adherence. HCPs never stop having influence on their patients. With motivational interviewing (MI), we increase the probability that the influence will be positive.

In the late 1980s and early 1990s, Bruce's research on improving treatment adherence led him to Miller and Rollnick's work on MI. He knew immediately that this caring, compassionate, and genuine way of being with the patient would improve adherence and treatment outcomes. It was then that he brought MI into health care and began to teach it as a faculty member at the Auburn University Harrison School of Pharmacy, where MI is now a required part of the core curriculum.

Bill Villaume was a Lutheran minister who went to graduate school at The Ohio State University and received a PhD in speech communication. Bill has always been fascinated by how people use language to build relationships and to influence each other. His studies in communication theory, linguistics, discourse/conversation analysis, and interaction analysis gave him a breadth of theoretical perspectives and research methods to apply in studying how MI works in professional–patient interaction.

Fortuitously, Bill was a graduate teaching assistant in a PhD-level course in human communication theory at Ohio State that Bruce was taking as a student. It was there that they met. In 1982, shortly after Bruce arrived at Auburn University to take a faculty position in the Harrison School of Pharmacy, he looked for faculty members in psychology and communication with whom he could collaborate. Lo and behold, there was a faculty member in the Department of Speech Communication named William Villaume—how many could there be? The two made contact and have worked together ever since.

Bill has used his background in communication theory to contribute several major concepts to our theoretical description of MI. First, he identified how a patient's losing face triggers resistance on the part of the patient. Then, the classic distinction between the content and relational dimensions of messages led to his identification of two types of resistance in patients: issue resistance ("I don't like taking medicine because I am worried about side effects"; "I'm under too much stress to quit smoking now") and relational resistance ("Look, I told you . . . I am just not ready to quit! Stop nagging me!"). Finally, the theory of practical reasoning led to an understanding of how to address the patient's issue resistance without creating more relational resistance. These concepts are important both theoretically and practically, because integrating the management of both types of resistance is critical to optimizing the power of MI to facilitate patients' consideration of health behavior change.

Bruce brought a distinctive psychodynamic approach to our conception of MI. Bill often notes that Bruce has an uncanny ability to understand the nature and essence of emotions experienced by both patients and professionals during their interaction. Bruce has also provided deep insight into how empathy with the patient allows the patient's issues to be addressed in a nonthreatening manner. Finally, Bruce's insight into the nature and impact of emotions has allowed him to identify the nature of several major impasses experienced by HCPs as they learn MI.

The collaboration between the two of us has produced a tremendous synergy that has spurred the development of our own theoretical description of MI. As a team, we are deeply committed to the proposition that the optimal use of MI can facilitate major health behavior change by patients.

We have taught MI to thousands of physicians, nurses, pharmacists, social workers, dietitians, and psychologists who work in various health care settings. We have taught thousands of students at the Auburn University Harrison School of Pharmacy. To understand how to teach MI more effectively, we have studied hundreds of hours of videotapes of our students interacting with standardized patients. We have also listened to countless hours of audiotapes of HCPs with patients (de-identified to meet federal privacy requirements) to better understand where and why success is occurring and where and why problems are consistently occurring. Ultimately, our study of these successes and problems led to our own theoretical description of MI, which improved our teaching of MI. Subsequently, HCPs seemed to grasp the heart of MI more quickly and to have more success at laying aside their controlling patterns of talk to listen to the patient and address the patient's core concerns. This book is a response to requests from HCPs that we describe our approach to MI in a book they can use as a resource.

# CHAPTER 1

# Why Another Book on Motivational Interviewing?

Motivational interviewing (MI) is a powerful patient-centered counseling approach that optimizes the possibility that patients will consider and implement health behavior change. In many organizations, it is the centerpiece in the implementation of the patient-centered medical home. MI requires that we attempt, in a caring, nonthreatening, nonjudgmental way, to understand and explore how patients make sense of health and illness. MI views the patient as a collaborative partner with expertise every bit as valuable as our own. As health care professionals (HCPs), we act as a caring resource to assist patients in making better decisions about their health. Ultimately, it is not we but the patient who decides.

The literature is replete with examples of studies demonstrating the effectiveness of MI in increasing patient and provider satisfaction and producing better outcomes. We conducted one such study for Biogen Idec involving its interferon beta-1a product Avonex for multiple sclerosis.[1] In a randomized, controlled clinical trial, a significantly lower proportion of patients in the MI intervention group (1.2%) than in the standard care group (8.7%) discontinued treatment with the drug. In addition, movement toward continuation of therapy was significantly higher in the intervention group. Given that the drug was a weekly injection that at the time of the study cost approximately $200 a dose, 9000 fewer dropouts from treatment with the drug represented a $93,600,000 cost recovery per year (9000 patients × $200/dose × 52 weeks/year = $93,600,000). These powerful results demonstrate our belief that MI can bring about major health behavior change by patients.

Given the extensive literature on MI, we begin by answering the question, "Why another book on MI?" We believe we have unique experiences and expertise in health care that will make this book especially useful for physicians, pharmacists, nurses, physical therapists, dietitians, social workers, and other professionals who work with patients. We will present a new and exciting theoretical basis for MI that will help HCPs understand why MI, when fully implemented, is so powerful. We believe that knowing this theoretical basis will help HCPs understand how to better respond to their patients and to positively influence their patients' decision making. The book will provide HCPs with insights into what kind of talk behaviors and introspective reflection are needed to assist patients in moving forward with health behavior change.

We would be remiss if we did not acknowledge our gratitude to the landmark work and thinking of William Miller and Stephen Rollnick in developing and refining the concepts and principles of MI. Their initial conception of MI and their ongoing commitment to compassionate care for patients and clients have inspired thousands of disciples of MI, including us. Without these foundations, this book would not have been possible.

## Teaching MI in health care

The book is the culmination of our more than 20 years of teaching and research on MI with HCPs. We describe what we have learned about teaching MI to HCPs and health professional students. We believe there are three fundamental differences between teaching MI in health care and teaching MI as originally conceptualized for substance abuse: (1) the training of HCPs, (2) the nature of the patient or client, and (3) the context of treatment. The relationship between an HCP and a patient is often vastly different from the relationship between a counselor or psychologist and a client.

First, the training of counselors is vastly different from that of HCPs. Counselors are taught to talk differently to patients. They are taught that their role is to explore patients' problems and that the patients must eventually draw their own conclusions if change is to occur. Counselors see their role as being supportive and caring and providing insight. The patient is in charge, because it is the patient's life and therefore the patient's decision.

HCPs are taught that they are the experts and that they are in charge. This orientation creates many problems for HCPs in adopting patient-centered approaches. HCPs have to learn an entirely different way of talking, which counselors have already learned before they are exposed to MI. When learning MI, HCPs must learn that they are *not* in control and that they are *not* the only expert in the room. Patients are experts, too. They are experts on their lives, their goals, and their aspirations. Equally important, they are experts on their sense making. How do patients make sense of what is happening to them? What is their understanding of diabetes, or high cholesterol, or hypertension? What is their understanding of what can happen if these illnesses are not treated? How does the way patients make sense of their illness and treatment affect their motivation for change and their emotional responses to the diagnosis and treatment? Generally speaking, patients will develop their own theories and lines of reasoning about all of these things.

Before our expertise can be useful, we need to understand what the patient knows, understands, and believes. And we must respectfully acknowledge these things at the outset. Without understanding how patients construct their ideas about illness and risk, HCPs really cannot know what information or education might be useful or meaningful to the patient. Unfortunately, the medical model (implemented as a clinical workup) often is mechanical and formulaic and does not thoroughly take into account the patient's perspective. The clinical workup is quite linear: Do this, then this, and finally this. But patients are not linear. They may not be ready to be "worked up," and it is folly to skip to the workup without first finding out how patients are making sense of what is happening to them. It is their story, not ours. In many ways, MI must undo and replace the medical model in which the clinician is the sole expert and in control. This is no easy task. HCPs have been used to giving directions, telling patients what to do, and then blaming patients when there is "failure." The approach taken by MI is one of guiding patients, not dictating to them. It is about providing patients with options that fit the patient's larger goals. This requires learning how managing asthma or diabetes or cholesterol, for example, aligns with the patient's broader aspirations.

Another profoundly important distinction between HCP training and the training of counseling and clinical psychologists is the issue of introspection. Counseling and clinical psychologists are trained to be introspective and conscious of how their own needs or issues could affect or contaminate the relationship. Through practicums and mentoring in their training, they are made aware of these needs so that they do not interfere. Interestingly, despite the fact that HCPs are going to work directly with patients concerning their health and critical decisions about their health, the curricula experienced by many HCPs now in practice did not in any appreciable way broach the subject of introspection, consciousness, and transference and countertransference. Current curricula do focus on reflective practice; however, the focus is often on decision making, knowledge, and skills. Greater emphasis is needed on personal and introspective reflection by HCPs to assess how one's self-concept affects interactions with patients. Moreover, personal reflection of this nature must be guided and mentored by someone with expertise at identifying and resolving these issues in practitioners and students. Any training of HCPs must address this subject. It is simply too important to ignore—especially in learning MI.

A simple example should help: After intensive training in MI a nurse expressed her frustration with many of her patients. She said, "I'm a doer. I get things done. Many of them just don't want to move forward, and then I find myself getting frustrated and I forget what I have learned about MI." The nurse was asked the following questions: "When your patients don't move forward as fast as you would like, what rewards that you get as a doer have to be suspended? How does that affect how you see yourself and your success with the patient? In other words, can you see a time when you will be able to bear not defining your success through your patients' decisions? Can you suspend being a doer?" These questions had a profound impact on this nurse, and she began to see how her definitions of success and self were actually undermining her ability to be fully present (caring, nonjudgmental, and patient). So, in addition to having to learn and master the skills and spirit of MI (which fly in the face of the standard medical expert model), HCPs also must learn to become introspective and aware of how their personal assumptions and issues can interfere with their ability to influence patient decision making in a positive and nonthreatening way. This makes learning and mastering MI even more difficult for HCPs.

In addition to issues surrounding HCP training, patients with chronic illness are different from clients struggling with substance abuse or marital discord. Traditional MI assumes that patients have everything they need internally to make changes. The role of the counselor is to help patients discover and activate those resources and come to better conclusions about their behaviors. Keep in mind that MI was developed in work with patients with substance abuse problems. We agree that at some level patients with personal or substance abuse problems often know all the pros and cons associated with their behavior. On the other hand, although patients managing chronic illness have the same set of internal psychological resources, they often do not have everything they need to manage an illness (e.g., diabetes). Patients often have misconceptions about the illness and its severity, especially if it is left untreated. This is particularly true if the illness is asymptomatic. Sometimes patients don't see the point in treating their illness because they "feel fine." A well-trained HCP, using MI, can assist the patient in making healthier decisions by filling in gaps in the patient's understanding or knowledge and then inviting the patient to respond to this new information. A well-trained HCP using MI is aware that without a strong foundation of rapport with the patient, information provided by the HCP can be interpreted by patients as a way of putting them in their place or correcting them, rather than as an extension of the caring provided by the HCP.

Finally, HCPs often use MI in a different treatment context than substance abuse counselors, because HCPs often do not have the luxury of repeated 50–60 minute encounters. Many times, the HCP may have only one chance to make an impact on the patient, because continuity of care is not where it needs to be in health care. Therefore, the approach taken here leans toward brief MI in the form of 5–30 minute encounters.

We have made the argument that training HCPs in MI is different from and often more difficult than training counseling or clinical psychologists. The previous training of HCPs often is in opposition to MI principles. In addition, patients with chronic illness often lack knowledge or information to make good decisions; they need to be presented with new information to reformulate their sense making before they can make a decision to engage in behavior change. And the context of the patient–client relationship in health care makes brief encounters even more critical.

Having realized these differences, we attempted to improve our teaching of MI to HCPs. We quickly found that we had to recast the basic explanation of MI in order for HCPs to understand what was happening in the course of their interaction with patients. What was self-evident to counselors was thoroughly puzzling to HCPs. For example, counselors could be presented with a simple description of basic MI tools (summarized in the form of the READS or OARS acronyms, which we discuss in later chapters) and could envision how these tools might be used with the patient. In contrast, HCPs struggled with where, when, and how to use these tools. They struggled to be able to see the smooth flow of MI that develops when MI tools are used appropriately to respond to the issues and concerns expressed by the patient. So, we started to use communicative and psychological concepts familiar to us to explain and illustrate the flow of MI. Slowly, over time we have developed a theoretical description of MI that helps HCPs to grasp the profundity of what is happening in MI. In our theoretical description of MI we are not only describing the heart of MI in a different way but also starting to specify two underlying dimensions of MI that are essential for its optimal implementation. In this sense, we view our theoretical formulation of MI as a response to the call by Miller and Rose[2] for a more developed theory of MI.

## Relational resistance and rapport building

Recently, in the latest edition of their classic work on MI,[3] Miller and Rollnick have refocused the theory of MI on how to work with ambivalence in the patient. In doing so, they no longer discuss the READS principle of "roll with resistance," and they postpone the discussion of resistance until late in the book. We have taken the opposite direction in our theoretical description of MI, by highlighting resistance over ambivalence. Although we concur that ambivalence is alive and well in patients who have chronic illness, we also believe that resistance is active in many patients. Furthermore, HCPs are much more inclined to think of patients as being resistant rather than ambivalent. Consequently, we have focused on how to use MI to address resistance in patients. We have distinguished two kinds of resistance: issue resistance and relational resistance. Issue resistance (or ambivalence) resides in the patient's reasoning or sense making about a behavior: "I'm not ready to quit smoking right now, because I just have too much stress in my life"; "I feel fine, and I don't see why I need this medicine"; "I'll take the medicine, but I am not changing my eating habits." Relational resistance concerns *how* we respond to the patient about issue resistance. When we fail to build rapport with the patient and disrespect the patient's thoughts and concerns, the patient suffers loss of face and may react with resistance to any possibility of change. Chapter 4 details our formulation of this dynamic and how it can affect health outcomes. Although we concur with Miller and Rollnick that importance and confidence on the part of the client are critical to behavior change, we have found that

1. The interaction between rapport and addressing the patient's judgments of importance and confidence is more than additive; it is synergistic, and
2. This synergy energizes the possibility of change.

When HCPs accurately empathize with the core concerns and lines of reasoning at the heart of the patient's sense making, the resulting rapport gives HCPs the leverage to use their expertise in a way that allows the patient to see that expertise as an extension of caring rather than as a way of putting the patient down. This has been a critical discovery that we will present as the heart of our approach to MI.

## REFERENCES

1. Berger BA, Hudmon KS, Liang H. Predicting discontinuation of treatment among patients with multiple sclerosis: an application of the transtheoretical model of change. *J Am Pharm Assoc.* 2004;45:1–7.
2. Miller WR, Rose GS. Toward a theory of motivational interviewing. *Am Psychol.* 2009;64:527–37.
3. Miller WR, Rollnick S. *Motivational Interviewing: Helping People Change.* 3rd ed. New York: Guilford Press; 2013.

# CHAPTER 2

# Preparing to Be Patient Centered

Nonadherence to health behaviors costs the U.S. health care system billions of dollars each year. The New England Healthcare Institute conservatively estimates that nonadherence to medication regimens alone costs this country more than $290 billion per year in unnecessary physician visits, emergency room visits, and surgeries.[1] It is estimated that nearly 50% of all patients with a chronic illness do not take their medications appropriately.[2,3] Nonadherence to lifestyle changes (e.g., weight loss, more physical activity, healthier eating habits) is even worse.

Traditionally, patients have been relegated to a relatively passive role in health care. Professionals diagnose a problem and then prescribe a treatment plan that often is imposed on the patient with little or no patient input. Patients are often discouraged (either subtly or not so subtly) from voicing their concerns and questions about the diagnosis and treatment plan. It should not be surprising that many patients wind up ambivalent about or resistant to implementing these plans. Nonadherence to health behaviors, and its associated costs, often occurs because passive, uninvolved patients may not express their concerns or questions about their treatment plans. To address the enormous costs and poor outcomes associated with nonadherence to prescribed health behavior changes, the health care system has been slowly moving toward patient-centered care and the patient-centered medical home (PCMH). The assumption is that if patients are moved from the passive periphery of medical care to become active participants involved at the heart of decision making, they will be more committed to implementing a treatment plan they helped formulate.

Conceptually, the PCMH is a way of organizing and delivering medical care to patients in a collaborative practice marked by continuity of care. Health care professionals (HCPs) work together to coordinate the primary care of *patients who are actively involved in their own care*. Ideally, PCMH is a partnership between the patient and the primary care physician and a coordinated team of HCPs (nurse, physician assistant, pharmacist, social worker, and psychologist) to provide high quality, continuous patient-centered care. Because patients get to know the team members on a more personal basis, the practice feels like "home" to them.

Numerous managed care organizations are using the principles of PCMH to reorganize the way care is effectively delivered to patients so that adherence is increased and better outcomes are produced. The military has been actively engaged in developing this kind of care for active duty personnel and veterans. While PCMH is a philosophy and mechanism for organizing patient-centered care, the centerpiece has been motivational interviewing (MI), which is evidence based and patient centered. MI is *how* HCPs communicate with patients to create caring, collaborative relationships. MI is both a patient-centered way of being and an associated skill set. It is one thing to say you will be patient centered; it is another to skillfully and genuinely communicate this to the patient.

This chapter explores important considerations in preparing to move from provider-centered to patient-centered relationships. We discuss characteristics of patient-centered relationships, what it means to be patient centered, and examples of how MI forms the foundation of patient-centered care.

MI involves a set of skills and a way of being with patients that requires respect, genuineness, and caring. We have learned through experience that it is almost impossible for professionals who fundamentally want to remain provider centered to learn MI by acquiring a set of patient-centered techniques. Inevitably, being provider centered leaks through when they talk with patients. When MI is learned as a set of techniques in a provider-centered context, it simply becomes a new way to manipulate patients. MI requires a desire to see the world as the patient sees it and to respect patients even when their beliefs and ideas about health may be in error. Miller and Rollnick call this "the spirit of MI."[4] Fundamentally then, MI requires a substantial change from how HCPs traditionally see themselves in relationship to the patient.

# Provider-centered relationships and problems

What happens when HCPs are provider centered instead of patient centered? How do essential problems manifest themselves in relationships with patients? What types of things do HCPs say when they are experiencing the effects of being provider centered or professionally privileged? The following paragraphs discuss common problems that arise when the relationship is provider centered, as often described in comments by professionals. If you find yourself identifying with any of these comments, you might consider adopting a more patient-centered perspective.

**"I just need to tell my patients what to do."** To understand why this kind of limited thinking is problematic, consider the following story about Adam and Eve. (This is not meant as a religious sermon or lesson, but the story is nonetheless instructive.) As you recall, God (the source of all truth and knowledge) told Adam and Eve not to eat from the fruit of the tree in the Garden of Eden. Nevertheless, both Adam and Eve ate from the tree. In essence, Adam and Eve were noncompliant . . . even though it was God who had told them what to do! And we are certainly not God. Why would we as HCPs believe that patients will do whatever we tell them to do when Adam and Eve would not even listen to God? People make their own choices, even if these choices may be unhealthy or against their best interests.

Patients will do what they believe is necessary (or what makes sense) in their individual lives, not necessarily what is healthiest for most people. Patients' decisions are based on what they believe is *important* to them and what they are *confident* they can achieve. We must discard the notion that we or our patients are totally rational decision makers. Patients do what they think is necessary, not necessarily what is healthiest. Patients do not always operate with accurate information. In addition, as we explain in greater detail in a later chapter, the way information is given to patients can affect whether it is accepted. People do what they think is important or what they have confidence in achieving. This is often a balance between the benefits and downsides of the choice from the perspective of the individual. The sad fact is that HCPs often severely underestimate their own patients' degree of nonadherence: "Yeah, lots of patients are noncompliant. But that's not a problem with my patients. They do what I tell them." Such blindness relieves HCPs of the need to consider how they may be contributing to the problem of nonadherence.

Our job as HCPs is to help our patients understand their medical situation and what options they have, and then help them decide what they want to do. We facilitate change, not direct it. When patients make their own decisions about what they need to do, they are more committed to implementing the decision than if the decision is imposed on them.

**"I just need to educate my patients."** We must discard the notion that knowing is enough. That is, the idea that if we educate patients enough by explaining what's good for them and telling them what to do, then they'll do it. While awareness and education are prerequisite to behavior change, they do not predict it. If knowing were enough, no one would smoke. One would have to be living under a rock to not have heard that smoking is bad for your health. Yet, people continue to smoke. The extreme case is posed by HCPs who, in spite of knowing and believing just how bad smoking is for their health, continue to smoke. The same holds true for HCPs who are overweight and continue to overeat and not exercise. They know the risks, but that is not enough.

We do need to educate our patients about healthy choices and options, but just educating and telling our patients what to do is not enough. We need to explore what matters to each patient. What would make quitting smoking, losing weight, taking the medicine, or engaging in more physical activity more important to the patient? What is getting in the way of these changes? What are the barriers? We need to explore each patient's thinking to find the answers to these questions, because the answers will be different for every patient. One patient with high cholesterol states, "I want to bring my cholesterol down. I don't want to have a stroke or heart attack," while another says, "I'll take the medicine, but don't count on me changing my diet or exercising—that's not happening," while another says, "Look, everyone in my family has had high cholesterol and they ate what they wanted and lived a long life—no strokes, no heart attacks . . . cholesterol is overrated." Each of these patients needs to be responded to differently. Each of them deserves caring and respect, but one size does not fit all. Population data do not provide us with what to do at the individual patient level. Education and intervention strategies must be tailored to the needs and understanding of the patient. Consequently, we have to give patients the opportunity to educate *us* about what matters most to them as individuals.

**"I need to empower my patients."** The idea that we empower our patients is part of the problem. To empower means to give power or authority to another. Patients already have the power and authority. It is their lives . . . their decisions. It is arrogant and self-centered for HCPs to believe that they give power to patients. To use an analogy, many HCPs think we are driving the bus and the patient is going along for the ride. In reality, the patient is driving the bus and we are simply trying to influence the route. We can help patients use the power they already have, and we can provide sincere encouragement, but we do not give power to them. If anything, they give us permission to use our power and authority to help them. When HCPs believe they empower rather than encourage their patients, it puts the HCP, not the patient, at the center of the relationship. From this viewpoint, the patient is passive until activated by the HCP. This simply is counterproductive.

**"It is my job to motivate my patients."** MI is not about motivating patients. It is concerned with assessing patients' motivation and exploring their ambivalence or resistance so that they are better equipped to make their own decisions. If you think your job is to motivate patients, you have an impossible job. The burden that HCPs often carry to motivate their patients to lose weight, take their medicine, or make other changes leads to frustration, blaming, shaming, and feelings of failure and inadequacy for both the patient and the HCP. It creates a great deal of anxiety for the HCP that often results in feelings of failure for both the HCP and the patient. The realization that despite the best care, concern, and information, patients may still not quit smoking, take their medications properly, or make other needed changes can be freeing for the HCP. When HCPs finally shift from being in charge and responsible for what the patient does to becoming a caring and safe resource for the patient, change can happen. When this shift takes place, it is possible to become fully available to the patient and respond with care and concern, not anxiety and fear.

Related to this is the declaration by many HCPs that "My patients are not motivated." We have found, more often than not, that the HCPs are really saying their patients are not motivated to do what the HCP is asking them to do. That does not mean the patients are not motivated. For example, a physician wanted his patient to start taking a statin for his high cholesterol. The patient unenthusiastically agreed and then was nonadherent to the medication regimen. The physician asserted that this patient was unmotivated. In reality, the patient wanted to change his eating habits and get more physical activity *before* trying medication for his high cholesterol; he just wasn't motivated to take the medicine. Even the patient who does not want to take medicine or make any lifestyle changes is motivated and not lazy; he is motivated to maintain his current lifestyle.

**"I need to fix or save my patients."** Unfortunately, when we believe that we motivate and empower patients, we often believe that we also have to fix and save patients. Professionals may treat patients in very paternalistic and condescending ways.

But patients need to fix and save themselves. When we try to fix or save patients, we are saying we know better than they do about how to conduct their lives. We certainly may know more about treating an illness and the health risks if it is not treated, but patients must ultimately decide and implement the treatment they consider to be best for them.

HCPs may say that they are motivated to fix their patients because they care. In reality, they are responding to anxiety about feeling that they themselves are failing in some way, as we discuss in a later chapter. For HCPs, the focus needs to be on providing caring, resources, and insight so that patients can make better decisions.

**"I do disease management."** We are living in an era of extreme specialization. Specialties in health care, such as cardiology, pulmonology, and endocrinology, can be further divided into subspecialties. There are physicians, nurses, and pharmacists who specialize in these areas. These specialists will consistently tell you they do disease management in their specialty areas (by the way, generalist practitioners will tell you the same thing). We have to constantly remind them that *they* do not do disease management—*patients* do disease management.

Both of us authors have high cholesterol (and both effectively treat it differently). There is not an HCP who treats our cholesterol; *we* treat our cholesterol (or *we* don't). HCPs do not manage anyone's illness except their own. Patients manage illness, despite what HCPs believe or have been taught.

What HCPs do is provide information and support to assist patients in managing illness and making better health choices. HCPs can certainly create an environment in which patients feel safe and cared for so they can ask better questions, express their concerns and fears, and make better decisions about their health. HCPs can also create the opposite environment by ignoring what patients are thinking and feeling. We propose that HCPs always have some sort of influence, and we would like that influence to be positive rather than negative. HCPs have the greatest positive influence on patients when they make it safe for patients to express their feelings and thoughts.

It is ironic that many HCPs who say they do disease management often scold or blame their patients when they do not comply with the HCP's instructions or orders. The extreme outcome of this is that there are HCPs who fire their patients. They may warn patients that if they do not take their medications properly, the HCP will no longer be their provider. Of course, this extreme (and possibly unethical) behavior assumes that the problem is the patient, not the way the HCP communicates with the patient. In such situations, HCPs assume that they are in charge and that they have the right to fire the patient, not the reverse. This approach is entirely provider centered.

**"My patients lie to me."** In our training programs HCPs make various comments and ask a lot of great questions. One comment they make is that "My patients lie to me (about their health behaviors)." Our response is "Of course they do." In provider-centered relationships, patients are often treated like children. For example, when asked, "How are you taking your medication?" a patient may initially respond honestly, "Well, I feel OK, so I might miss a few days a week." The HCP might then chastise the patient: "How many times have we been over this? You need to take your blood pressure medicine every day if you want to get your blood pressure down. You don't want to have a stroke, do you?" Several observations are relevant here. First, this response implies that the patient is stupid. Second, it does not address the patient's core concern (and the implied sense making) that if she feels OK she must be OK. Even if the HCP had addressed this concern in a very parental and condescending manner by saying, "Look, just because you feel OK doesn't mean you are OK—you need to take the medicine," it would have been hard for the patient to hear the truth in this response because it does not sound at all caring. Finally, once the patient has been chastised for telling the truth about how she takes her blood pressure medicine, she will very likely be reluctant to tell the truth again. The truth was simply not respected, encouraged, or explored. When asked in the future, "How are you taking your medication?" this patient is likely to answer, "Every day as prescribed" even if she is not taking it every day, and regardless of who asks.

HCPs need to make it safe for patients to tell the truth. In response to the patient saying, "Well, I feel OK, so I might miss a few days a week," the HCP could have said in a calm voice, "So because you feel OK, you haven't taken the medicine every day and you're wondering if that's really necessary." This MI response would have shown respect for the patient, demonstrated caring and understanding, and encouraged a dialogue. The patient would have felt understood and not judged.

**"I feel like I'm wrestling with my patients."** Do you ever feel like you are wrestling with your patients? If you do, you are probably communicating in a way that is increasing the patient's resistance about an issue (e.g., doesn't want to quit smoking, lose weight, take the medication) and now you are creating more resistance because you are pushing too hard (persuading) rather than exploring the resistance. With this additional resistance, the patient not only does not want to work on the issue but also does not want to work with you on any other issues. This feels like wrestling and should be an indicator that this is a provider-centered relationship.

**"I am the expert here."** Far too often, HCPs have been taught that they are the experts and should tell their patients what they need to know and what they need to do to have better health. Such a characterization of expertise means that HCPs really do not have to listen to their patients, since the patients are not experts. It also means that HCPs can be defensive and threatened when their expertise is questioned by a patient. This defensiveness and the resultant anxiety often produce provider-centered judgmental and paternalistic responses to the patient. Patients then either dig in even more or withdraw in any number of ways. Both patients and HCPs stop listening to each other.

We characterize MI as an *exchange* of expertise. Patients are experts, too—about how they make sense of their illness and treatment, what risks they think they are facing, what they are willing to do, what is getting in the way, and what would make treating the illness important to them. We simply cannot know what aspects of our expertise we should use until we have explored what the patient knows and understands. It does not make a lot of sense to go into a long-winded discussion of diabetes and the risks of complications when the patient already understands. It also doesn't make a lot of sense to talk about how to treat diabetes when the patient does not believe that it is really a problem anyway because he feels "just fine." Giving the same information to each patient is neither efficient nor tailored to the needs of the patient. Again, one size does not fit all.

To illustrate this point, we encourage HCPs to ask patients to describe in their own words what their illness means to them. For example, in response to the question, "What does your diabetes mean to you?" one patient with an A1c of 9 responds, "The doctor told me my sugar is very high. He said that if it stays high I could have serious eye problems, including blindness, circulation problems, kidney failure, and more. I don't want that to happen." This patient's "expertise" informs us that he understands the seriousness of the diagnosis and the risk of complications. An appropriate response would be "You understand how serious untreated diabetes can be. Those complications are all preventable. Would it be OK if we talk about how you can take steps to prevent those complications from occurring?" If the patient says, "Sure," we would say, "There are three things you can do to get your diabetes under control and reduce the risk of complications. They are taking your medication as prescribed, increasing your physical activity, and making healthy, low-sugar food choices. They work best in combination. What would you like to work on first?" Notice that after hearing the "patient's expertise," we provide our expertise, and the patient is then asked what he would like to do.

In response to the same question, "What does your diabetes mean to you?" another patient with an A1c of 9 says, "I don't know. The doctor said I have sugar, but I feel fine." This patient's response informs us that he may not understand a lot about diabetes. What we said to the patient in the previous example would not be a fruitful response. This patient is probably not going to work on anything if he doesn't believe that diabetes is important enough to treat. A better response would be "So you were told your sugar is elevated, but because you feel fine, you're wondering, 'What's the big deal about having diabetes?'" The patient would probably say, "Right," and you could respond, "That's a great question. Would you mind if I give you some information to address your question and you let me know what you think?" After the patient says OK, you could respond, "One of the things that makes diabetes or high blood sugar so dangerous is that many times it does not have any symptoms until some serious complication occurs such as damage to the eyes or kidneys or circulation. Our body needs a certain amount of sugar for energy and normal function. When the body cannot use all of the sugar in the blood, which is the case in diabetes, and too much sugar stays in the blood, then the blood becomes like syrup. It soaks all the organs, nerves, and blood vessels in syrup, and then they deteriorate. When this deterioration gets bad enough, symptoms appear quite suddenly. Where does this leave you now in managing your diabetes, even though you feel OK?" Notice that in this interchange the use of "you're wondering" allows us to provide an answer to a question. It also allows us to praise the patient for raising a reasonable question and encourages the patient to ask questions or "push back" in the future. In addition to asking permission to answer the question, we also let the patient know we want his feedback ("you let me know what you think"). All of this shows interest in and respect for the patient and says that ultimately he decides. The expertise we provide now fits the patient's expertise. That is, the patient is not sure why this is a big deal if he feels OK, and our information answers that question and then asks the patient how this new information affects his line of reasoning. This is an *exchange* of expertise.

A point related to the idea of an exchange of expertise is that we do not spend time identifying how patients make sense of their illness and treatment. What does the patient know about the illness? What does the patient understand about the treatment regimen or protocol? Although knowing does not predict success absolutely, it is a prerequisite. We need to find out what the patient knows and understands so that we know what information or education is needed. What are the patient's lines of reasoning about the illness that may be accurate or inaccurate? It does not make sense to give patients information they already know. Moreover, how patients make sense of their illness will often determine how motivated they are to treat it. How important is it to them to treat their illness? How confident are they that they can manage it?

In addition, what does the patient know and understand about the risk of not treating the illness? If patients do not understand the seriousness of the consequences of not treating the illness, chances are low that they will engage in the necessary health behaviors. Often, when patients feel "fine" they are expressing that they don't sense there is anything serious they need to be concerned about.

Therefore, it is very important to first assess the following:

1. In patients' own words, how are they making sense of the illness? What does it mean to them?
2. What do they think of the treatment? Do they believe it will work? Do they believe it is necessary?
3. What is their understanding of what can happen if they don't treat the illness?
4. If they are committed to treating the illness, especially a chronic illness, what will keep them on track and what might get in the way over the long term?

Asking these questions will give you a much better idea of what education and information may be needed to fill in gaps, what doubts patients may be having about treating the illness (this allows you to ask what would make treating the illness important to them), and finally, how to plan for change. Without knowing these things, you may provide information that does not address the patient's unique needs and concerns. It may be important to use some of these same questions to reassess patients who are not newly diagnosed. The questions may reveal sources of nonpersistence in treating the illness. And it is feasible that these questions were never asked in the first place and that patients went along even though their commitment was weak because of ambivalence or resistance.

**"My patients are difficult and often in denial."** Patients who are resistant or ambivalent are often labeled as difficult or in denial; their resistance may be seen as a character flaw: "They are the problem; it's not me. If only they were better patients and just did what I told them to do, then we would get the results we should be getting. They need to change; I don't."

Our position is that there is no such thing as a difficult patient. Why would a patient be considered difficult just because she doesn't want to quit smoking or lose weight or take her medicine? After all, it is her life, her decision. There certainly are difficult situations (explored later in the book), and there are patients who are angry, frustrated, or uninformed. But an HCP who focuses on a patient's being difficult is really struggling with not knowing what to do or how to "fix it," so the patient is labeled as "difficult." Even when patients state that they don't like how they are being treated, they are labeled as difficult or in denial.

Patients are not in denial simply because they don't evaluate the situation in the same way the HCP does. They often underestimate the risks of decisions they make. They often overestimate the benefits of what they do ("smoking relaxes me"), but they are not in denial. HCPs using MI understand this and try to help patients realistically appraise the risks and benefits of their behaviors so they can make better decisions.

Moreover, MI practitioners see resistance as a gift. Resistance is informative. If patients are willing to express their resistance, we then have an opportunity to honor it, respect it, and explore it. We may be able to identify where and how we can share some specific information that may allow patients to reconsider their actions or draw new conclusions about what they need to do. If patients resist in silence because they don't want to be shamed or blamed, the opportunity to influence their decision making may be lost. MI practitioners welcome the expression of resistance because of the opportunities it affords for caring influence.

The comments discussed above are representative of the frustrations felt by HCPs who use a provider-centered approach. You may be able to add other thoughts that you or your colleagues have had about patients. Of course, there is an equally long list of frustrations experienced by patients. When HCPs become ill and experience being patients, they may gain a new awareness of the problems involved in provider-centered care. Being treated like a child can be particularly vexing to an HCP accustomed to being the privileged expert. Will that HCP then make the connection between this experience as a patient and how the HCP himself habitually communicates with his patients?

# What does it mean to be patient centered?

Next, we consider what it means to be patient centered in health care. We describe the patient-centered tenets undergirding the principles of MI and how these tenets work. You may find these considerations to be very liberating. Don't be surprised, though, if it is difficult to unlearn provider-centered language habits that you have acquired over the years and used "on autopilot." Some of you may find these considerations of what it means to be patient centered somewhat troubling. You may feel some resistance or ambivalence. For example, you may not like the idea of having your expertise denied or overlooked by your patients. It's important that you let these thoughts surface, reflect on them, and explore how they fit into the practice of MI. We've often encountered such reservations in our workshops. Our aim is to allow you to see how MI can turn your reservations into opportunities. For example, if you are concerned about being viewed as an expert by your patients, the good news is that MI actually leads patients to value and trust your expertise rather than deny it. The next part of this chapter will provide opportunities to see your interaction with patients from a new perspective.

MI is derived in large measure from Carl Rogers's client-centered therapy[5] and hence is patient centered. Although there is a great deal of talk in health care about patient-centered care and the PCMH, these concepts often are discussed without a good understanding of what they entail. Some of the characteristics of patient-centered relationships are discussed in the following paragraphs.

**Respecting the patient as a whole person.** The patient is not an abstract diagnostic problem or an object to be manipulated. The patient is a person whose thoughts and feelings matter, who has a right to be heard and understood—a person who deserves our care and our unconditional positive regard. This does not mean we can't disagree with patients' decisions (and express our concerns), but in all cases we value the patient as a person. Patients must know that we care for them as individuals and want to help them. Such respect and care must be expressed genuinely and congruently; formulaic expressions of care and empathy quickly expose the incongruence between our words and our feelings.

**Honoring the patient's right to decide.** The patient ultimately has the power to veto any aspect of treatment by simply not implementing that treatment; therefore, it is much wiser and more effective to honor that right by involving patients in the decision-making process: What are they willing to do? What can they do?

What do they want to do? This means providing options and choice to the extent possible.

**Individualizing care.** What is the patient willing to do? For example, to control cholesterol, patients may take their medication, reduce the fat in their diet, and increase their physical activity to burn more fat. These behaviors in combination may have the biggest impact on lowering cholesterol, but one patient may choose to do all three while another patient may say, "I'll take the medicine, but don't expect me to do anything else." To the first individual, we would respond, "I'm glad you are so committed to lowering your cholesterol. These three things in combination can have a major impact on lowering your risks of stroke and heart attack. Which would you like to talk about first?"

To the second patient, we might respond, "I'm glad to hear that you are committed to taking your medication. That is a really important step in getting your cholesterol under control. Would you mind if I give you some additional information and you tell me what you think?" If the patient agreed, we would then say, "I want you to know that the medication can lower your cholesterol by up to 50%. Your total cholesterol is 500. That means the medication could bring it down close to 250. We know that the risks of stroke and heart attack go down even more when the total cholesterol goes below 200. What are your thoughts about making any changes in your eating habits or physical activity to bring your cholesterol down below 200?" This response does several things. It provides information in a clear, simple, and objective manner. It respects the patient's choice. After providing information, we ask how this new information affects the patient's thinking (line of reasoning). This response also recognizes that the patient chooses. Finally, there is shared decision making; both of these patients are given a menu of options and choose what they want to do.

**Personalizing care.** Patient-centered care includes finding out what is meaningful to the patient. An approach is not chosen a priori; the approach has to match the needs and desires of the patient, regardless of your good intent. What would make this individual decide to take his medication, lose weight, or make another change? What would make the behavior important to this person? What would get in the way? Management of a patient's illness is personalized through discussing what is important in the patient's life. What goals are blocked or facilitated by engaging or not engaging in treatment? For example, we might use an MI skill called "a look over the fence" to ask a patient with poorly controlled asthma, "If you were to wake up tomorrow morning and you were using your chronic inhaler every day so that your asthma was well controlled, in what ways would your life be better? What things could you do that become difficult when your asthma is not controlled?"

**Facilitating the patient's experience instead of privileging the HCP's convenience.** We have become so regimented and information driven in health care that we often forget *why* we are collecting information. It is common for health plans to be "stuck" asking an hour's worth of questions to comply with quality standards before they establish any kind of relationship with the patient. Providers may say to the patient something like "I am required to ask you a bunch of questions and collect some information before we get started. It will take about 45 minutes. Is this a good time?" What does this communicate to the patient? Not only does it sound like drudgery for the HCP, it does not sound like anything the patient should even be interested in providing. How does it help the patient? In a patient-centered environment, getting acquainted with the patient should be the first priority. What are the patient's questions or concerns? What would the patient like to know?

We have asked health plans to think about what they actually want to tell patients about who they are in relationship to the patient. Why should patients be interested in being involved in a case management or disease management program? What is in it for them? What role will the HCP play? There is a big difference between "I need to ask you some questions" and "I'm here to be a resource and address any questions or concerns you may have so that you can make better decisions about your health. I will need to collect some information to become better acquainted with you and your family history. But first, I would like to know what questions or concerns you have."

Questions can be worked in throughout the process. Create a transition to the required questions and give some choice about when to answer. Engage patients' reasoning rather than measuring some patient attribute as an object to be plugged into a formula gauging progress and outcomes. In other words, how are patients making sense of all they have been told? How are they feeling? How important is all of this to them? Diagnostic and clinical reasoning should be processed in the background and not allowed to become the focus of the interaction. There should be no doubt as to why questions are being asked or information is being provided: The only reason the information is offered is to assist patients in reaching their decisions, not to put patients in their place.

**Respect.** Patient concerns, thoughts, and beliefs are not minimized but instead are accurately reflected and explored. When patients are angry or frustrated, they are respected by the HCP's ability to remain separate but fully available; the patient's anger is not taken personally. Patients' beliefs about their health and illness are respected even if the beliefs are factually inaccurate. This does not mean that we let the beliefs (line of reasoning) go uncorrected; it simply means that we recognize the validity and importance of those beliefs to the patient. We show respect and concern for the patient as we go about getting those beliefs corrected.

**Genuineness.** The HCP truly wants to help the patient. The HCP wants to understand the concerns of the patient and expresses this in a sincere manner.

**Congruence.** This is related to genuineness. We cannot simply say words that express care and concern. There must be congruence between our verbal and non-verbal communication. If you have ever been exposed to disingenuous empathy, you understand how problematic this can be in building rapport.

**Transparency.** Transparency should exist at several levels. Information provided should be clear, objective, thorough, and transparent to the patient. The only way we can know this is by asking patients what they think after new information is provided.

When we ask patients clinical questions, the reasons for asking these questions should be transparent to them. For example, if a patient has a complaint ("My medicine doesn't seem to be helping anymore") and we need to ask questions to determine what might be happening, we don't just jump into clinical cross-examination ("What have you been doing differently? Are you taking the medicine every day? When did the medicine stop working?"). All of these questions may be necessary, but we let the patient know *why* we need to ask questions: "To better understand why your medicine isn't helping and figure out what may be happening, I need to ask some questions. Would that be OK?" The patient then knows that we are asking questions to address the patient's issues, not to show that the patient has done something wrong. Without such transparency, clinical questions can make the patient feel like a witness being cross-examined.

It is important to be honest and truthful with patients so they can make informed choices. HCPs often withhold information or "soften" what they tell patients about lab results or conditions. For example, a patient newly diagnosed with diabetes with an A1c of 9.3 is told by his physician, "Your A1c is a little high." This statement is problematic for four reasons:

1. The patient may have no idea what an A1c is.
2. The A1c is not a little high, it is a lot high! If the patient feels OK and doesn't have symptoms, he may believe that this is not serious and may choose not to do anything about it. The HCP has contributed to the

patient's failure to perceive that there is a potentially serious problem. When we ask HCPs why they tell a patient with an A1c of 9.3 or blood pressure of 160/110 or total cholesterol above 400 that it is "a little high," they often respond that they don't want to frighten the patient. We ask, "Why not?" We don't want to paralyze patients with fear, but we do want to give them a realistic sense of the risks and complications if the illness is not treated.

3. The statement does not answer the question of "So what?" Why should the patient care about his A1c being high? What are the risks if his diabetes is not treated? If the patient does not perceive that failing to reduce his A1c carries serious risks, he is not likely to act.

4. The patient doesn't know what is OK and what is not OK—what A1c value is healthier or safer.

A more appropriate statement to this patient, using MI, would be "We just got your lab work back and your A1c, which is a measure of your blood sugar over time, is 9.3. This is very high. We know that when the A1c falls below 7.0 the risks of serious complications—such as circulation problems that can result in amputations, heart disease, kidney disease, and blindness—go way down. Your number is quite a bit higher than that, which puts you at much greater risk for these complications. Where does this leave you now in regard to wanting to treat your diabetes?"

Notice that this response provides the patient with honest information so he can make a better decision. The risk of complications is also stated honestly and realistically. In addition, a goal is not imposed on the patient; the patient is not told, "Your goal is to get your A1c below 7.0." The patient is given information about how risks drop with an A1c below 7.0 so that he can make a better decision. The same approach can be taken with cholesterol and blood pressure. Note that after the information is provided, the patient is not told what to do. That would be paternalistic and would place the HCP in the role of being the sole expert. Remember, this is an *exchange* of expertise.

Now that the HCP has provided this new information, she wants to find out how ready the patient is to control his diabetes. What does the patient think about this new information? The patient's responses could range from "I had no idea. I don't want that to happen" to "I feel fine. I'll take my chances." In the first case, the HCP is in a position to say to the patient, "It sounds like you want to do whatever you can to prevent those complications. There are basically three things you can do to decrease your blood sugar and your risks: Take the medication as prescribed, decrease the sugar and carbohydrates in your diet, and increase your physical activity, such as walking.

They work best in combination. What do you want to work on first?" In the second case, the patient is expressing resistance. This needs to be reflected and explored. An appropriate response would be "So because you feel OK, you really wonder 'What's all this fuss about diabetes, anyway?'" The HCP would then see what the patient says, offer information, and ask what the patient thinks. This might be a good place for the syrup analogy. If the patient continues to indicate that he doesn't want to do anything, the HCP could say, "You feel OK and you're willing to take your chances. It really is your decision. I'm wondering, is there anything you would need to know or find out that would make you decide that you really need to treat your diabetes? I would hate to see you have any of these complications when they are avoidable."

**Shared decision making.** The HCP's role is to be a resource and disclose to patients things they can do to manage their illness. This needs to be negotiated, not dictated. It includes sharing concerns for patients to consider. For example, a patient with diabetes is unwilling to change her eating habits and get any exercise. She takes her medication and believes that should take care of everything, yet her A1c is well over 9.0. The patient understands the complications of uncontrolled blood sugar and knows that an A1c over 9.0 is high. When she is informed that her A1c is over 9.0, she responds, "Just give me more medicine." The physician responds, "That certainly is one option, and I'm glad you are committed to taking medication. Could we discuss the pros and cons of that option, and then you let me know what you would like to do? I'm concerned that your A1c is so high." Notice that this physician expresses his concern and asks permission to look at pros and cons with the patient so the patient can make an informed decision.

**A sense of safety and care.** In a patient-centered relationship the patient feels respected, safe, and cared for by the HCP. The patient's sense is the following: "I am important to my doctor (or nurse, or pharmacist, or other HCP). She doesn't always agree with me and I don't always do what she says, but I always feel respected, listened to, and safe to ask questions or push back when I don't like something. My doctor doesn't scold me or judge me when I don't quit smoking or lose weight, but instead she asks me what would make this more important to me, shares her concerns with me, and then lets me decide what I want to do."

## MI as the foundation

The use of MI in health care grew out of a need to understand and respond appropriately to noncompliance with or nonadherence to health behaviors such as medication taking, weight loss, better eating habits, and smoking cessation. The goal was to assist patients in achieving better health outcomes. MI is crucial to the implementation of patient-centered health care. We cannot provide patient-centered care with provider-centered communication habits. Even when HCPs desire to provide patient-centered care, the skills of MI need to be learned and incorporated into practice. These skills are complex and are not intuitive.

So, when do we get good at MI? Practice makes a huge difference; in a later chapter we will talk about ways to practice and get feedback. However, the biggest changes we have seen in people we have trained do not come from simply assimilating new skills and having more practice. Equally important is developing the ability to reflect on our own responses and learning to give up the need for control. The patient really does decide. When this becomes clear, MI becomes easier and HCPs learn to help patients with choices rather than try to fix or save them.

## QUESTIONS FOR REFLECTION

1. Identify three to five fundamental differences between provider-centered and patient-centered relationships.
2. Discuss factors that make learning MI more difficult for HCPs than for counselors or psychologists.
3. Why has the movement toward patient-centered care and the PCMH grown so rapidly?

## REFERENCES

1. New England Healthcare Institute. *Thinking Outside the Pillbox: A System-wide Approach to Improving Patient Medication Adherence for Chronic Disease.* Cambridge, MA: New England Healthcare Institute; 2009.
2. Claxton AJ, Cramer J, Pierce C. A systematic review of the associations between dose regimens and medication compliance. *Clin Ther.* 2001;23:1296–310.
3. Krueger KP, Berger BA, Felkey BG. Medication adherence and persistence: a comprehensive review. *Adv Ther.* 2005;22:319–62.
4. Miller WR, Rollnick S. *Motivational Interviewing: Helping People Change.* 3rd ed. New York: Guilford Press; 2013.
5. Rogers C. *Client-Centered Psychotherapy.* Boston: Houghton Mifflin; 1951.

# CHAPTER 3

# What Is Motivational Interviewing? A Short History

The roots of motivational interviewing (MI) go back to Bill Miller's insightful reaction to the confrontational approach widely adopted in the field of addiction counseling in the 1980s. In that approach, substance abusers were portrayed as "pathological liars with formidable immature personality defenses, in denial and out of touch with reality."[1] Counselors were taught to confront this denial in order to establish what these substance abusers had to do to re-engage with reality and return to health. Miller's initial experience of these same patients during his early clinical training was quite different, however:

> Because I knew very little about alcoholism I relied heavily on listening to clients on the ward, learning from them and trying to understand their dilemma. I found them usually to be open, interesting, thoughtful people well aware of the chaos ensuing from their drinking. That's why, when I began reading clinical descriptions, I thought, "That doesn't sound at all like the same people I've been seeing!"[1]

With more experience and reflection, Miller came to the realization that a patient's openness to change is directly affected by how the counselor talks to the patient:

> Counsel in a way that evokes defensiveness and counterargument, and people are less likely to change. . . . I set out, then, to discover how to counsel in a way that evokes people's own motivation for change rather than putting them on the defensive. A simple principle that emerged from our earliest discussions was to have the client, not the counselor, voice the reasons for change.[1]

Thus began the development of MI as a thoroughly patient-centered form of counseling that helps patients reason their way to the conclusion that to achieve their goals they need to change their behaviors.

In seeking to correct the prevailing confrontational approach, with its disparagement of the patient, Miller embraced the client-centered counseling of Carl Rogers,[2] who stressed that the relationship with the patient had to be based on unconditional positive regard for the patient as a person and therefore had to avoid shaming and blaming the patient. It is only by valuing and supporting the patient as a person that the therapist allows the patient the freedom and safety to examine his own behaviors and their consequences for others.

While embracing the relational stance advocated by Rogers, Miller rejected Rogers's nondirective method of talking with the patient. Rogers believed that if the counselor accurately and consistently reflected back what the patient was saying, the patient would eventually achieve self-insight and start to see the need to change. Although this Rogerian approach to counseling can be very effective, it is notoriously slow and time-consuming. Miller sought a more directive way of addressing the patient that does not cause defensiveness and that helps the patient conclude that change is both needed and possible. Eventually, this more directive approach was characterized as a "guided" approach in the sense that personal guides (such as in hunting and fishing) use their expertise to acquaint the client with a range of possible options and then allow the client to choose which option to implement.

## Changing views on implementing MI

The history of MI is marked by a consistent commitment to respecting and caring for the patient. This relational commitment to the patient, known as "the spirit of

MI," has been central to every major formulation of MI through the years, even though "the spirit of MI" was not explicitly referenced until later.[3] What has changed is the explanation of how to implement this spirit through the use of specific verbal techniques that guide ambivalent or resistant patients to consider the possibility of change.

These specific verbal techniques—the technical component of MI in contrast to the spirit of MI[3]—have been summarized by acronyms such as READS, OARS, and DARN. Since many HCPs have learned MI through the use of these acronyms, in this chapter we will discuss the acronyms as part of a short history of how the technical aspect of MI has been explained. Then we will discuss the problems we have experienced in teaching HCPs this concept of how to do MI. In the next chapter, we will present our own explanation of how MI works to facilitate health behavior change in ambivalent and resistant patients. Although we are going to teach you MI using our own theoretical concept of MI, we believe it is important for MI practitioners to understand the original explanation of how to do MI.

By the early 1980s Bill Miller had worked out his new form of patient-centered counseling that guided ambivalent and resistant patients to consider the possibility of change. When Miller served as a visiting professor of counseling in Norway, his graduate students were so impressed by hearing MI in action that they asked Miller to explain what he was doing. Miller's early formulation of MI resonated with Stephen Rollnick in Great Britain, who recognized the tremendous value of this guided approach to counseling. Subsequently, Miller and Rollnick collaborated to publish in 1991 the first edition of their landmark work, *Motivational Interviewing*.[4]

## The READS principles

Miller and Rollnick[4] emphasized that MI requires the establishment of an interpersonal context that respects and honors the perspective of the patient. By not shaming and blaming the patient, the MI practitioner can create a sense of safety so the patient will be willing to discuss his thoughts about change. Miller and Rollnick then stressed that the MI practitioner needs to stay focused on helping the patient talk about the motivation for change that is already operative within the patient. Eliciting the patient's reasons for change helps to activate and reinforce the natural process of change. How this is to be achieved was spelled out by a set of five principles summarized by the acronym READS, explained in the following paragraphs.

**Roll with resistance.** In confrontational counseling, resistance by the patient is viewed as an entirely negative phenomenon that must be overcome. In contrast, Miller and Rollnick stressed that resistance and ambivalence are quite normal reactions to the prospect of change. Moreover, resistance provides information that helps the practitioner understand the patient's perspective on the possibility of change. So instead of trying to suppress the expression of resistance by the patient, the MI practitioner should explore resistance in order to understand the patient's questions and concerns. By providing relevant information to address those questions and concerns, the MI practitioner can pose new possibilities for the patient to consider—without coercing the patient in any sense. Thus, in MI, once the practitioner has explored the thrust of the patient's resistance, the patient

> is invited to consider new information and is offered new perspectives. "Take what you want and leave the rest" is the permissive kind of advice that pervades this approach. It's an approach that is hard to fight against.[5]

Rolling with resistance involves resisting the urge to push back at resistance expressed by the patient and instead exploring that resistance. If the patient has said, "I just don't see what all the fuss is about. A lot of people have high cholesterol," rolling with resistance would entail saying, "You're not certain whether you need to worry about high cholesterol. Tell me more about what having high cholesterol means to you," instead of saying, "You need to be a lot more concerned about the effects of high cholesterol." Pushing back at resistance only causes the patient to become more resistant and close the door to further discussion. Calmly accepting the patient's resistance and exploring it keeps the door open to further discussion of the serious consequences of allowing cholesterol to remain high.

**Express empathy.** When the patient expresses ambivalence or resistance to the prospect of health behavior change, it is important to reflect back the patient's perspective accurately and without judgment. Such empathy does not mean that the MI practitioner agrees with the patient's perspective. Rather, empathic responding lets the patient know that his perspective has been heard, understood, and respected on a deep level. When the MI practitioner empathizes with the patient, the practitioner is essentially saying to the patient, "How you are making sense of your situation matters very deeply to me." Then the patient no longer feels any need to defend his perspective by more forcefully reasserting his thoughts, concerns, and feelings. As a result, the patient is opened up to the possibility of engaging in dialogue with the MI practitioner and considering other ways to make sense of his health situation.

Expressing empathy with the patient's perspective is often called for when a patient has a profound emotional reaction to being newly diagnosed with a serious medical condition such as diabetes or heart disease. The patient's initial shock at the diagnosis can often be expressed as a matter of disbelief: "I just can't believe that I have high cholesterol. I've tried to live a healthy life and take pretty good care of myself." It's easy to hear this comment, on the surface level, as a statement that the patient does not believe the diagnosis; consequently, it's tempting to respond by saying, "Well, there's little doubt about the diagnosis, because your total cholesterol is well above 400." Such a response totally misses the patient's experience of shock. As a result, the patient feels even more isolated in his state of shock and may be closed to any further discussion of high cholesterol. Trying to initiate education about reducing cholesterol may be counterproductive at this point. Instead of arguing with the patient's statement of disbelief, expressing empathy with the patient's initial shock about the diagnosis might sound like this: "Because you've really worked at following a healthy lifestyle, you were caught completely off guard by being diagnosed with high cholesterol. In fact, you sound shocked at the prospect of having high cholesterol." Being heard on this deeper level helps the patient to engage in dialogue about the shock. For example, the patient may respond by saying, "I am shocked, because my father died of a sudden heart attack brought on by high cholesterol that he just couldn't get down." Because the patient felt understood and safe, he revealed another significant aspect of his experience that is central to the whole issue of how he will go about managing his cholesterol. By continuing to respond with empathy, the MI practitioner can help the patient focus on the heart of what has shocked him: "So, given what happened to your father, you're worried that you might not be able to reduce your cholesterol and avoid a heart attack or stroke." When the patient responds, "Yeah, I am worried, very worried. I want to be here for my children and grandchildren," the HCP can respond by saying, "You sound like you want to do everything you can do to reduce your high cholesterol so that you can avoid a heart attack or stroke. You want to be here for your family for many years to come. And I really want to help you achieve that goal. There are several very effective options for bringing your cholesterol down to much healthier levels. I want to help you figure out which options will work the best for you." By empathizing with the patient, the HCP has helped the patient to continue talking about how he is making sense of his situation and what his goals are. With all this new information that flowed from the patient, the HCP can weave together an account of how to help the patient as a partner in healing rather than as a dictator of healing.

**Avoid argumentation.** When practitioners fail to roll with resistance, they often wind up arguing with their patients. Arguing is an extremely counterproductive interaction that results in reinforcing the patient's resistance to change. Arguing forces the patient to defend his perspective by asserting why he cannot or need not change. The more vigorously the patient defends his position, the more his resistance has been reinforced and the less likely are the chances of any consideration of behavior change.

Such arguing is often triggered by the practitioner's use of a "yes, but" response because the practitioner considers it important to correct the patient's thinking. If the patient has said, "I just don't see what all the fuss is about. A lot of people have high cholesterol," the practitioner might say, "Yes, a lot of people have high cholesterol, but they are in just as bad a situation as you are. You all need to get your cholesterol down." In response, the patient might say, "Well, I doubt that. I have many friends who were told they have high cholesterol, and they are just fine." And so the arguing progresses as each participant resorts to "yes, but" responses. The only result is to reinforce the patient's resistance to any consideration of cholesterol reduction. MI avoids arguing with the patient in favor of helping the patient draw his own conclusions about what is best for his health.

**Develop discrepancy.** MI practitioners explore ambivalence and resistance in order to assess the possibilities for developing the patient's internal motivation to change. The most prominent possibility is to create a discrepancy between a goal the patient wants to achieve and the consequences of the patient's current behaviors. Recognizing such a discrepancy leaves the patient in an uncomfortable position that calls for a solution. Instead of the practitioner's having to impose a need to change, the patient is left to conclude that something must be done to achieve the goal. Developing discrepancy is a highly individualized process of thoroughly exploring the patient's perspective and hearing the patient's aspirations and concerns. It requires the MI practitioner to listen closely to what matters to this individual patient. Listening closely to the patient gives the MI practitioner the building blocks to develop a discrepancy that matters to the patient.

To our patient with high cholesterol, the HCP might be tempted to say, "Look, if you don't do something about reducing your cholesterol, you're not going to be able to teach your grandsons to hunt and fish." The HCP has identified a potentially powerful discrepancy for the patient to consider, but this discrepancy is being imposed in a demeaning, judgmental way rather than being posed with the respectful, caring spirit of MI. Instead, an MI practitioner might calmly say "So, on the one hand you really want to be healthy enough to teach your grandsons to hunt and fish. On the other hand you aren't certain you can reduce your cholesterol enough to lower your risk of stroke and heart attack. What are your thoughts about this?" Posing this discrepancy in a respectful and caring manner puts the problem squarely on the patient's shoulders. If the patient isn't ready to commit at this point to reducing his cholesterol, the discrepancy has been posed in a way the patient can hear. In the future, every time the patient thinks about hunting and fishing with his grandsons, he will also think about how the risk of a stroke or heart attack could prevent this from happening. The more often he dwells on this discrepancy, the more likely he is to consider stronger steps to reduce his cholesterol at some point in the future. Nurse case managers who interact with patients by phone report to us that patients often say something like this during a subsequent phone call: "You know, I've been thinking about what you said last time. I really want to have a lot of years hunting and fishing with my grandsons. I guess I might need to start doing something more than just taking cholesterol medicine." Using the spirit of MI to develop a discrepancy within the patient's sense making can trigger powerful motivation within the patient to implement health behavior change.

**Support self-efficacy.** Even though a patient has concluded that he needs to make a major behavior change to achieve better health, the patient may not attempt to make that change. Why? The patient may not believe he is capable of doing it, so to avoid the pain of failing he doesn't try to change. In psychology, Bandura[6,7] identified the crucial function played in the change process by self-efficacy—the belief that one can succeed in carrying out a task. Across a variety of contexts of change, self-efficacy is a significant predictor of successful change.[8] Consequently, Miller and Rollnick stressed supporting self-efficacy as a key principle of MI. Instead of focusing on talk about why the patient might fail, the MI practitioner works to support the ability of the patient to succeed in implementing change.

For example, our high-cholesterol patient might express low self-efficacy by saying, "I just cannot manage to maintain a diet. Once I stayed on a diet for about six weeks and then it became impossible. I might as well not even try again." The temptation is to respond by focusing on what caused the patient to give up the diet and telling the patient how to be successful. This type of response tends to confirm the patient's lack of self-efficacy with regard to staying on a diet. Instead of talking immediately about why the diet failed, an MI practitioner can first focus the patient on what he was doing during his successful six-week maintenance of the diet. So the MI practitioner might say, "It sounds like you were quite successful in maintaining the diet for six weeks. What were you doing during that time that contributed to your success in healthier eating?" As the patient explains how he successfully implemented a low fat and low cholesterol diet during that time, the MI practitioner listens for behaviors and strategies to affirm: "Healthy eating was manageable for you while you were basically eating at home and could plan your meals. But when you headed out on a long sales trip, you hadn't thought through your plans for how to eat on the road. It sounds like you might be quite successful at healthier eating if you also planned for how to eat on the road."

Miller and Rollnick explained these five READS principles to provide insight into the basic counseling stance of MI. They went on to describe a series of specific verbal strategies to use in MI to help elicit motivation from within the patient. These included the following:

- Using open-ended questions to explore the patient's perspective, because they encourage the patient to explain and elaborate on his thoughts, feelings, and goals;
- Listening closely to the patient and then reflecting back with appropriate emotion what the patient has said;
- Affirming and supporting positive aspects of the patient's thoughts, feelings, and behaviors;
- Summarizing the essence of what the patient has said and what the patient is struggling with; and
- Eliciting self-motivational statements that express the patient's positive reasons for change.

The goal of MI is to combine the use of these specific strategies to guide the patient toward making the argument for why he needs to change his behavior. How these strategies are to be used in combination was not explained in detail by Miller and Rollnick. Instead, they advocated using resistance in the patient as a "compass": If the patient starts to become more resistant, stop what you doing and try a different direction, one that is less directive and coercive. Such use of resistance as a relational compass was based on Miller and Rollnick's belief that all resistance is ultimately relational in nature. In their view, resistance is a sign that rapport and harmony in the relationship with the patient have been disturbed. Therefore, it is crucial for the MI practitioner to monitor constantly for signs of resistance in the patient to determine what specific verbal strategies are productive or counterproductive during the course of counseling that patient. The application of MI principles and strategies must be highly individualized through listening closely to each patient.

## MI formally defined

The response to the first edition of *Motivational Interviewing* was extremely positive and sparked much MI training and research. No longer was MI considered solely a method of addiction counseling. Increasingly, it was recognized across many health care settings as a method for facilitating any voluntary health behavior change by patients. As MI came to be embraced beyond the field of addiction counseling, Rollnick and Miller[3] felt constrained in 1995 to offer some corrective thoughts about MI, because they perceived that its diffusion was leading to dilution. They wanted to ensure that the widespread adoption of MI did not result in versions that no longer authentically expressed what they considered to be the heart of MI.

The first corrective step was to offer a formal definition of MI as "a directive, client-centred counseling style for eliciting behaviour change by helping clients to explore and resolve ambivalence."[3] This definition continues to stress the "guided" approach that derives from being both directive and client centered, but its focus is more explicitly on resolving ambivalence than on resolving resistance. This emphasis on ambivalence over resistance seems to derive from the difference between counseling patients with addictions and counseling patients with newly diagnosed chronic diseases. Patients with addictions are often aware of the whole range of reasons calling for a decision to stop drinking alcohol or stop using illicit drugs. Such patients are ambivalent because they are caught between continuing their addictive behavior and stopping it. On the other hand, a patient newly diagnosed with diabetes may not be well acquainted with the range of reasons for and against managing blood sugar. In fact, patients newly diagnosed with a major chronic disease often have mistaken ideas that beg for re-education by the HCP. For example, the patient may say, "I don't see the point in doing anything about my blood pressure. I feel just fine." Such patients are better characterized as resistant rather than as ambivalent.

As we continue with the history of MI, we will see further development of this emphasis on ambivalence over resistance in the writing of Miller and Rollnick.

This trend has negative implications for how easily MI (as formulated by Miller and Rollnick) can be implemented by HCPs such as physicians, nurses, and pharmacists.

## The spirit of MI

The second corrective step offered by Rollnick and Miller[3] was an explicit reminder that the skills of MI could not be implemented without the spirit of MI. They were concerned that once MI skills (such as the READS principles) are separated from the relational stance of MI, these skills become manipulative in intent and thereby can trigger increased resistance in the patient. It seems significant to us that even after Miller and Rollnick spelled out the relational stance of MI so eloquently, HCPs focused on adopting the specific skills of MI rather than on fundamentally reforming their relationships with patients. This separation of MI skills from the spirit of MI was possible because there was no clearly articulated theoretical explanation of how MI skills act synergistically with the spirit of MI to help patients resolve their ambivalence or resistance.

## Change talk and resistance/sustain talk

In 2002, Miller and Rollnick published the second edition of *Motivational Interviewing*.[9] The major change in this edition was the introduction of the concept of "change talk," which replaced the first edition's "self-motivational statements." Remember that for Miller and Rollnick the essence of MI is to assist the patient in voicing the case for why the patient needs to change. "Change talk" is defined as any talk by the patient that focuses on why the patient needs to change her behavior in order to achieve her goals. Change talk can range from an initial request for more information about the consequences of diabetes ("Uh, just how bad can those nerve problems become?") to the expression of relevant personal goals for the future ("I'm really looking forward to being active in my retirement") to an indirect behavioral commitment to change ("I guess I just need to start taking my diabetes medicine, much as I don't like the idea").

The opposite of change talk is resistance talk, defined as any talk focusing on why the patient doesn't want to or doesn't need to change. Such resistance talk can range from the expression of doubt about the physician and the diagnosis ("He just doesn't know what he's talking about. I feel fine. There's no way I have diabetes") to the assertion of other more important goals ("I'm just not giving up my pasta and desserts! I like eating way too much") to the expression of the inability to change ("Look, there's just no way that I can change what I'm eating. Any diet I've tried has always been a huge failure. I'm not trying again").

Given this distinction between change talk and resistance talk, the focus of MI in the second edition of *Motivational Interviewing* was to elicit as much change talk from the patient as possible and avoid stimulating more resistance talk. This is almost the opposite of what we do as HCPs when we are communicating "on autopilot." The automatic tendency for most HCPs is to minimally acknowledge any change talk, because that's what the patient ought to be saying anyway, and then to focus on refuting the resistance talk with extensive counterarguments. This argumentative tendency only creates more resistance in the patient. Miller and Rollnick stressed responding in ways that keep the patient focused on the change talk and allow the resistance talk to fade into the background. The more the patient engages in change talk and the less in resistance talk, the more likely the patient is to engage in health behavior change. Why? Because increased change talk and decreased resistance talk positively affect the decisional balance of pros versus cons. The more the patient talks about the reasons for change, the more these reasons are strengthened. When the patient finally voices the realization that the pros of behavior change outweigh the cons of behavior change, the heart of the decision has been made by the patient.

So, how did Miller and Rollnick recommend that an MI practitioner elicit change talk from the patient while not triggering more resistance talk? Their approach in the 2002 edition was to formalize and extend four skills that had been mentioned briefly in their first edition. These skills were summarized by the acronym OARS (open-ended questions, affirmations, reflective listening, and summarizing).

**Open-ended questions.** MI encourages patients to become comfortable in articulating their thoughts about the prospect of behavior change. This purpose is not served by asking closed-ended questions to which the patient can answer yes or no with little elaboration. Typically, when HCPs ask closed-ended questions, the HCP, not the patient, remains as the interactional focus. Closed-ended questions imply that the HCP is gathering information so that the HCP can solve the problem for the patient. This is the opposite of what is desired with MI, which relies almost exclusively on open-ended questions to get the patient talking more freely and openly.

However, according to Miller and Rollnick, not all open-ended questions are helpful in MI. For example, questions such as "What are the advantages of continuing to smoke?" and "What makes it difficult for you to consider trying to quit smoking one more time?" invite the patient to engage in resistance talk. By answering these open-ended questions, the patient will reinforce the reasons against quitting. Miller and Rollnick's approach is to ask open-ended questions that prompt change talk—that is, the voicing of positive reasons for the contemplated behavior change. They recommend asking four specific types of open-ended questions:[10]

1. Ask about the disadvantages of not changing:
   "What worries would you have if you continue to smoke?"
   "How might your continuing to smoke interfere with what you want to do in the future?"
2. Ask about the advantages of changing:
   "What would you like if you were able to stop smoking?"
   "How would your life be better if you were able to cut back on your smoking?"
3. Ask about being successful in changing:
   "How confident are you that you can stop smoking?"
   "What personal strengths can you rely upon to help you succeed in cutting back on your smoking?"
4. Ask about the intention to change:
   "You said that you need to quit smoking at some point in time. How will you know when that time has come?"
   "Of the three options that we've discussed for quitting smoking, which one do you feel the best about trying?"

All of these questions serve to get the patient engaged in voicing change talk while avoiding resistance talk.

**Reflective listening.** As a patient starts to express thoughts and feelings about the prospect of change, the MI practitioner needs to give the patient evidence that the practitioner has heard what the patient has been saying. Unfortunately, saying "Uh huh," "OK," or even "I understand" doesn't provide any evidence to the patient that you have really heard what the patient has said. Such formulaic phrases can be uttered even as you are obviously not listening to the patient. The principle is to reflect back to the patient what you heard the patient say.

Again, not every reflection is of equal value in MI. Often in the course of reflection it is more valuable for the MI practitioner to emphasize the patient's change talk and give less prominence to the patient's resistance talk. Consider an example in which the patient has just said, "It would be nice if I could quit smoking, but I know that's never going to happen as long as I'm under such stress at work. Smoking helps me to cope with all that stress." If you reflect back, "It sounds like you won't consider quitting smoking as long as you're still working your stressful job," the patient is likely to respond, "Right!" This reflection has served to reinforce a major reason against change instead of helping to affirm the possibility of change. A better MI reflection might be "It sounds like you would really like to quit smoking and would feel a lot more encouraged about the possibility of quitting if you could figure out a way to handle the stress at work." When the patient responds with "Right!" the patient has affirmed the possibility of change and will most likely be willing to discuss options for controlling stress at work that don't involve smoking. We will discuss reflection and empathy in much more detail in Chapter 6, Developing Rapport.

**Affirmations.** As a patient engages in change talk, it is helpful to support the patient through the use of affirmations. Remember that one of the READS principles is to support self-efficacy. Again, the selection of what to affirm is crucial; not all affirmations are equally helpful in MI. Sometimes, for example, affirming the patient's ability to change can be argumentative, especially if the patient has just expressed significant doubts about her ability to change. The MI practitioner has to be more circumspect in selecting what to affirm; the principle is to affirm things that naturally progress into more change talk.

Consider the patient's comment in the preceding section on reflective listening: "It would be nice if I could quit smoking, but I know that's never going to happen as long as I'm under such stress at work. Smoking helps me to cope with all that stress." Saying "I have faith that you can handle the stress at work without smoking" is an affirmation, but it functions on a deeper level as a rejection of the patient's expressed lack of confidence, and it is likely to cause the patient to defend that lack of confidence. Thus, this affirmation can trigger stronger resistance talk instead of prompting change talk. The MI practitioner has to be insightful in selecting what to affirm. In this case, a helpful MI affirmation might be "It's great that you have been able to identify how you use smoking to help you cope with the stress at work. This insight will help you figure out what other options you have for managing your stress at work." Affirmations should encourage the patient to engage in the next step in the process of change talk instead of pushing the HCP's vision of what the patient ought to do at the end of the process.

**Summaries.** If the patient has been engaging in freely flowing change talk, it is helpful to tie together the patient's thoughts, concerns, and feelings into a clear, coherent account. Miller and Rollnick liken the process to "collecting flowers one at a time and then giving them to the person in a little bouquet."[11] Offering the patient such a summary has several advantages. First, a summary helps create a sense that something significant has transpired. A summary can tell a compelling story about how much the patient has accomplished in the course of talking. Such a summary functions as an affirmation. Second, a summary can help the patient see how various thoughts, feelings, and concerns work together to form a very personal basis for change. Finally, a summary can provide closure to one line of discussion and allow transition to a second line of discussion. The key is to compose the summary to the extent possible out of positive elements that can help tilt the decisional balance in favor of change. An insightfully presented summary can set the context for an inquiry about where the patient is in terms of a decision to change. It can work as follows: "So, it sounds like you've come to a couple of major realizations that have encouraged you about the prospect of successfully quitting smoking. First, seeing your grandchildren over the summer convinced you of just how much you want to be involved with them when you retire. And then you watched your good friend stop smoking and stay quit even though he has a stressful job, too. So you're thinking that if he could stop smoking, you certainly can. These thoughts taken together pose the question of where you are in terms of making the decision to quit smoking."

In summary then, the OARS skills, when insightfully focused on eliciting the positive benefits of health behavior change, help the patient to engage in extended change talk. The more the patient engages in change talk and avoids resistance talk, the greater is the likelihood that the patient will decide in favor of making constructive changes in health behavior.

# Six themes in change talk

This emphasis on extending change talk by the patient was further developed by Rollnick, Miller, and Butler in their 2008 book titled *Motivational Interviewing in Health Care: Helping Patients Change Behavior*.[12] They recommended that HCPs listen for six major themes of change talk by patients, summarized by the acronym DARN (desire, ability, reasons, need) plus two additional themes (commitment, taking steps).

**Desire.** This theme involves the wants, likes, and desires of the patient. It would include statements such as

"I would give anything to be able to stop smoking."
"I love to exercise, especially if there's some competitive sport involved."
"I want to look at myself in the mirror and feel good about how I look."

Reflecting back and affirming such statements of desire by the patient can reinforce the patient's positive motivation for change.

**Ability.** This theme of change talk relates to what the patient feels capable of doing, as is evident in the following statements:

"I can cut back on my smoking without any help."
"I might be able to take my blood pressure medicine more regularly than I have been."
"Walking a mile every evening after dinner is something that I might be able to manage."

When responding to ability-related change talk, the MI practitioner needs to be sensitive to the degree of qualification involved. The first of these three statements is extremely straightforward and unqualified. It is a strong expression of confidence. The other two statements are qualified and express less confidence ("I might be able" instead of "I can"). When reflecting back ability talk, the MI practitioner has to be careful to match the level of ability expressed. Reflecting back greater ability than the patient feels can cause resistance in the patient.

**Reasons.** This theme involves answers to the question, "Why should I change my behavior?"

"I know that allowing my blood pressure to remain high is not good for me."
"I'm willing to listen to whatever you suggest if it will get rid of this pain."
"I want to teach my grandsons to hunt and fish."

Such reasons overlap with the theme of desire; a desire to achieve a meaningful personal goal can be a powerful reason for health behavior change. Whenever a patient expresses a reason for change, the MI practitioner should reflect back and affirm that reason for change.

**Need.** This theme involves the patient's sense of what is needed and calls for a way to meet that need.

"I really need to get back to watching what I eat."
"I guess I just have to make healthier choices."
"I need to get more sleep at night."

Reflecting back and affirming a statement of need allows the MI practitioner to reinforce the need identified by the patient and to elicit the patient's thoughts on how to go about meeting that need.

Miller, Rollnick, and Butler[12] identify these DARN themes as precommitment forms of change talk. The patient can express these themes in the course of exploring the reasons for or against change, but the expression of these themes does not guarantee that the patient will make any particular decision. More important, these themes can be expressed in opposition to each other, because desires, abilities, reasons, and needs are relevant to both sides of the decision. For example, the patient can say, "I don't want to suffer all those horrible consequences of diabetes. But I don't think that I can do everything that's needed to control my blood sugar." The first part of this patient utterance is an expression of the desire and reason themes. The second part is an expression of an inability theme. The positive desire to control the consequences of diabetes is canceled by the patient's perceived inability to do what is required. If the MI practitioner continues to reflect back and reinforce the desire and reason themes without addressing the inability theme, the patient will remain ambivalent. Although the DARN acronym has identified four prominent themes that may be woven through how a patient is making sense of health behavior change, the acronym provides no guidance about how these themes combine to form sufficient motivation for the patient to make a decision and publicly commit to that decision.

The last two themes of change talk identified by Miller, Rollnick, and Butler approach and may even constitute the decision to change.

**Commitment.** This theme relates to commitment by the patient to some sense of action. The ultimate decision for health behavior change may be expressed in a form of commitment such as

"I intend to watch what I eat a lot more closely."
"I'm ready to start getting more exercise into my life."

"You can count on me taking my blood pressure medication absolutely every day!"

The MI practitioner has to realize that commitment language can be involved at many points before the final decision for health behavior change. For example, the patient could say, "I'm going to think about that some more. I just am not ready to make a decision right now about starting insulin shots." Here, the patient has committed to thinking about the issue under discussion but has also expressed a lack of readiness to make a decision for or against insulin shots. Although this commitment is not the ultimate decision, it represents a significant step toward the ultimate decision, and it certainly needs to be reflected and affirmed by the MI practitioner. For example: "I'm glad to hear that you are going to think through what's the best way to get your blood sugar back under control. If I can help you get closer to the point of being ready to decide what's best for you, please let me know."

**Taking steps.** This theme relates to actions taken by a patient that point in the direction of change. The actions may amount to a major change, as in the case of a patient who has regularly been 10 to 15 days late in refilling a monthly prescription for diabetes medication at your pharmacy. The last time, you talked with the patient privately in a consultation area. This time, the patient picks up her prescription right on time and says, "I've decided to take my medication every day to see what it can do. I really want to avoid having to go on insulin." Like the other themes discussed above, this theme needs to be reflected, affirmed, and subtly extended, as in "Taking your diabetes medication every day as prescribed, along with healthy eating and increased physical activity, can be very effective in controlling your blood sugar and helping you avoid having to take insulin shots. I look forward to hearing how these steps work out for you."

Some such steps can be intermediate rather than final, as in "I talked for over a half hour the other day with a friend who has had diabetes for years and seems to handle it a lot more successfully than I have." Seeking out an experienced and trusted source of information such as this friend is a major self-initiated step that can be reflected, affirmed, and extended by the HCP: "Talking with your friend can be a great way to help you figure out how you can manage your blood sugar more successfully. Tell me more about what you learned from that conversation."

These six themes (DARN+C+T) represent a significant amount of the content of change talk that can be elicited from patients. The more patients talk about these themes, the more these themes are strengthened and reinforced. According to Miller,

Rollnick, and Butler, when the MI practitioner has helped the patient explore these themes sufficiently, the patient ultimately may construct a self-persuasive argument for why she needs to make one or more significant changes.

## Spirit plus skills—but how does it work?

As we have seen, MI has been explained both by its spirit and by its technical aspects (i.e., its techniques, skills, and methods). The spirit of MI is caring for and respecting patients as full persons who ultimately decide what they need to do to achieve their goals. The spirit of MI creates in patients a deep sense of interpersonal rapport with the HCP. This rapport allows patients to open up and express their thoughts, questions, and concerns about the prospect of health behavior change. When the professional responds using the techniques and skills of MI (as explained by the acronyms READS, OARS, and DARN+C+T), the professional elicits increased change talk from the patient. Somewhere in this mix of MI spirit and MI techniques resides the power of MI to help patients find their own internal motivation to make constructive health behavior changes.

Unfortunately, this dual approach of explaining MI as spirit plus technique has left many people less than clear about what is at the heart of MI. In 2009 Miller and Rollnick published an article titled "Ten Things that Motivational Interviewing Is Not."[13] They were trying to disavow the multiple misunderstandings that had arisen as people attempted to implement MI. For example, they took pains to establish that MI is not just a variant of other psychological approaches such as the transtheoretical model of change,[14] client-centered counseling,[2] cognitive-behavioral therapy,[15] and decisional balance therapy.[16] Although MI may have strong theoretical connections to these psychological approaches, Miller and Rollnick contend that the heart of MI goes considerably beyond these connections. MI is a form of guiding that allows the practitioner to have some positive influence on the patient while still respecting the patient's right to make the ultimate decision about what the patient needs to do. Exactly how this guiding works to facilitate patient decision making has yet to be specified in a theoretically accurate or practically adequate fashion.

The need for a more clearly specified theory of how MI works has been building slowly as scholars have attempted to validate the effectiveness of MI in facilitating voluntary health behavior change. Since 1983, well over 200 clinical trials of the effectiveness of MI have been conducted.[17] Systematic reviews of the results have shown MI to be generally more effective than various forms of treatment-as-usual but no

**FIGURE 3-1** Causal chain model of motivational interviewing (MI). (Adapted from reference 21.)

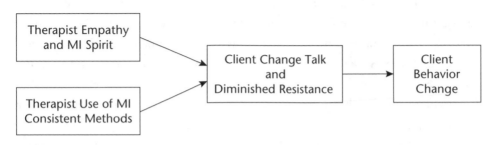

more effective than other systematic counseling approaches.[18-20] The authors of these systematic reviews concluded that the clinical trials of MI were hampered by the lack of a clearly specified theory of the nature and power of MI. In response, Miller and Rose took a first step toward a fully specified theory of MI by proposing a causal chain model of MI, the heart of which is shown in Figure 3-1.[21] This model is nothing more than a graphical representation of the spirit-plus-technique explanation that we have discussed. The MI spirit and the use of MI techniques exert independent effects to increase change talk by the patient and decrease resistance in the patient. The increased change talk and decreased resistance lead to behavior change. There is little theoretical explanation of why and how these effects occur.

## Helping HCPs make sense of MI

At about the same time as Miller and Rollnick's article on what MI is not[13] and Miller and Rose's model[21] were published, we were teaching MI to pharmacy students and to HCPs including physicians, nurses, pharmacists, social workers, and dietitians. We relied on the dual approach to MI that we have discussed here. We discovered very quickly that teaching MI to HCPs is quite different from teaching it to trained psychological counselors, and that the lack of theoretical clarity about the heart of MI is particularly troublesome to HCPs.

Psychological counselors are accustomed to being introduced to new counseling approaches and then practicing these approaches in role-played counseling sessions. They are also accustomed to examining in detail how their talk practices affect their clients. HCPs typically are far less sensitive to such issues in communicating with patients. Faced with having to use MI with a role-played patient, HCPs typically "implode." Therefore, with our colleague Jan Kavookjian, MBA, PhD, at the Auburn University Harrison School of Pharmacy, we created a series of intermediate exercises to help HCPs experience and assimilate MI in small, graduated steps. We found that these exercises were successful in helping HCPs to encounter the spirit of MI and to practice the individual techniques and skills summarized in the READS, OARS, and DARN+C+T acronyms. But the HCPs still experienced major problems when faced with integrating the spirit of MI with the skills of MI during role-played patient counseling.

One problem experienced by many HCPs during role play resulted from focusing on the letters of the acronyms to figure out what to say next. For example, HCPs might arbitrarily decide they needed to develop discrepancy because that's what the D in READS stands for. Then, having used this MI tool, they might decide it was time to use another READS tool, perhaps expressing empathy or supporting self-efficacy. Another problem we found was that the HCPs could use empathy fairly quickly, but they did not know where to go once they had empathized with the patient's feelings. The role-played counseling sessions felt disjointed because the HCPs were acronym centered and not patient centered. During discussion of this problem, HCPs consistently asked us how we knew which MI tool to use and when to use it. This question was a reflection of their being accustomed to fully understanding the theoretical justification for the sequence of steps in the clinical workup in a medical encounter. It did not help them when we responded with Miller and Rollnick's advice that if in the course of eliciting change talk you start to encounter resistance in the patient, you should back off and try a different approach or explore the resistance with open-ended questions.

We came to realize that we needed to explain MI to HCPs in a different way than Miller and Rollnick were explaining MI to psychological counselors. HCPs need a clear conception of the heart of MI that allows MI practitioners to know where, how, and why they can exert a positive influence on their patients' decisions about health behavior change. Chapter 4 will trace our journey of discovery as we developed a theoretical explanation of MI that would make sense to HCPs.

## Diverging theories

Before moving on, we need to address the recent third edition of Miller and Rollnick's *Motivational Interviewing: Helping People Change*.[1] The authors have extensively rewritten their previous edition, improving their description and explanation of MI. A primary thesis of this new edition is the belief that patients already have inside them everything they need to solve their own problems; it is the therapist's job to activate these internal resources. In other words, at some level, patients know what they need to do. In health care, however, this simply is not the case. In marriage counseling, both parties might really know deep down that they are contributing to the marital discord, even though they are blaming each other. The therapist can skillfully help each partner take appropriate responsibility. However, many patients really do not understand their illnesses. They do not know why they need medication if they feel OK (even though they have seriously elevated blood pressure). They do not understand why they need to change their eating habits or get more physical activity. They may even question how serious their illness is in the first place (even if it is very serious). Thus, one of the significant functions of the HCP using MI is to help patients better understand what is happening to them—for example, to help them make sense of how they can be at risk and still feel OK. Patients simply do not have inside themselves everything they need to know.

Some classic elements of MI have been almost entirely removed from Miller and Rollnick's new edition.[1] For example, the READS acronym is barely mentioned. We do not see rolling with resistance mentioned at all. Other elements have been given greater emphasis. For example, the OARS acronym, rather than the READS principles, is given a central position at the heart of the MI process. Some major distinctions have been reformulated or rephrased. Change talk remains a crucial concept, but it is now contrasted with "sustain talk" instead of with resistance talk. Change talk focuses on arguments leading to the conclusion that the patient should change; sustain talk focuses on arguments leading to the conclusion that the patient should sustain his present behaviors. Miller and Rollnick emphasize change talk almost to the exclusion of addressing sustain talk. This emphasis is problematic in health care. For example, when patients express such strong concerns about a medication's side effects that they do not want to take the medication, those concerns have to be addressed. Change talk alone will not cause patients to accept these possible side effects. This is especially true if their concerns about side effects either are not factual or can be put in better perspective. In later chapters we will discuss how to address such sustain talk.

Miller and Rollnick's new edition has deemphasized the concept of empathy in favor of the concept of reflection. Similarly, the concept of resistance has been deemphasized in favor of focusing on ambivalence. Finally, rapport is contrasted with discord. Again, for health care situations we find these changes problematic.

Because Miller and Rollnick are heading in a different theoretical direction than we are, we will not discuss their changes in detail. We would, however, like to make clear three major ways in which our approach to MI differs from their current approach.

First, we will draw several major distinctions as alternatives to the foundational distinctions initially offered and frequently modified by Miller and Rollnick. We believe this will allow us to specify how the spirit of MI and the techniques and skills of MI work synergistically to optimize the possibility of constructive health behavior change. We have found that these distinctions make it easier for HCPs to understand on a practical level what options they have in using MI to respond to the concerns expressed by patients. We describe these distinctions in Chapters 4 and 5.

Second, a major difference between our approach and Miller and Rollnick's current approach is the relative prominence given to resistance versus ambivalence. Ambivalence may be the more appropriate concept to stress for clients suffering addictions, marital problems, or anxiety, because these individuals may be well acquainted with the arguments both for and against change. In contrast, patients newly diagnosed with a chronic disease often express strong resistance to treatment regimens prescribed for them. Therefore, it makes sense to us to teach HCPs how to use MI in response to active resistance as well as in response to ambivalence. Instead of allowing resistance to recede into the background, as Miller and Rollnick have done in their third edition, we focus on resistance by distinguishing two major forms of resistance that are dealt with quite differently within MI. We have found that HCPs identify more easily with our emphasis on addressing these two forms of resistance than with Miller and Rollnick's focus on responding to ambivalence. HCPs seem to sense that patient resistance based on misunderstandings has to be addressed. Our theoretical approach allows us to explain how that can be done within the relational dynamics of MI.

Third, we use a range of psychological and communicative theories to explain how MI works to increase the probability of constructive health behavior change. Although Miller and Rollnick have consistently stated that patients must formulate the arguments for changing their behavior, they have not followed the implications of this claim. People make arguments for and against change in the course of making sense of their life and the situation they face. MI works most powerfully when it fully engages the sense-making processes of patients—*both for and against change*. Helping patients to see new reasons for change certainly helps tilt the decisional balance in favor of change. This is what Miller and Rollnick contend in asserting that increased change talk can lead to tilting the balance in favor of change. But if the increased change talk continues to be counterbalanced by extremely weighty doubts and fears on the part of the patient, then increased change talk may never lead to actual change. We contend that it is absolutely essential to address patients' misunderstandings, uncertainties, doubts, and fears about the treatment options open to them. When HCPs use the spirit of MI to address patient sense making both for and against change, MI achieves its optimal impact on the patient. Expressed in Miller and Rollnick's terms, the MI practitioner must establish deep, caring rapport with the patient and then leverage that rapport to both elicit change talk from the patient and address the patient's sustain talk. The decision for or against health behavior change then rests firmly on the patient's shoulders. We believe we have extended MI to include (1) eliciting the patient's sense making and reasoning both for and against change and (2) using the spirit of MI to address the patient's arguments both for and against change. MI achieves its optimal impact only when the spirit of MI is used to address the totality of the patient's sense making and reasoning about the prospect of health behavior change.

## QUESTIONS FOR REFLECTION

1. How is MI different from Rogers's client-centered therapy?
2. Explain why both the spirit of MI and the principles and skills of MI are essential to MI's effectiveness.
3. What is the difference between change talk and sustain talk?
4. Do patients have inside them everything they need to change their behavior? Please explain your answer.
5. Identify the three major ways in which the approach to MI in this book differs from Miller and Rollnick's approach. What are your thoughts about these differences?

## REFERENCES

1. Miller WR, Rollnick S. *Motivational Interviewing: Helping People Change*. 3rd ed. New York: Guilford Press; 2013:xxii.
2. Rogers CR. *On Becoming a Person: A Therapist's View of Psychotherapy*. Boston: Houghton Mifflin; 1961.

3. Rollnick S, Miller WR. What is motivational interviewing? *Behav Cogn Psychother.* 1995;23:325–34. doi: 10.1017/S135246580001643X.

4. Miller WR, Rollnick S. *Motivational Interviewing: Preparing People to Change Addictive Behavior.* New York: Guilford Press; 1991.

5. Miller WR, Rollnick S. *Motivational Interviewing: Preparing People to Change Addictive Behavior.* New York: Guilford Press; 1991:60.

6. Bandura A. Self-efficacy: toward a unifying theory of behavioral change. *Psychol Rev.* 1977; 84:191–215.

7. Bandura A. Self-efficacy mechanism in human agency. *Am Psychol.* 1982;37:122–47.

8. Strecher VJ, DeVellis BM, Becker MH, et al. The role of self-efficacy in achieving health behavior change. *Health Educ Q.* 1986;13:73–91.

9. Miller WR, Rollnick S. *Motivational Interviewing: Preparing People for Change.* 2nd ed. New York: Guilford Press; 2002.

10. Miller WR, Rollnick S. *Motivational Interviewing: Preparing People for Change.* 2nd ed. New York: Guilford Press; 2002:79.

11. Miller WR, Rollnick S. *Motivational Interviewing: Preparing People for Change.* 2nd ed. New York: Guilford Press; 2002:74.

12. Rollnick S, Miller WR, Butler CC. *Motivational Interviewing in Health Care: Helping Patients Change Behavior.* New York: Guilford Press; 2008.

13. Miller WR, Rollnick S. Ten things that motivational interviewing is not. *Behav Cogn Psychother.* 2009;37:129–40.

14. Prochaska JO, DiClemente CC. *The Transtheoretical Approach: Crossing Traditional Boundaries of Therapy.* Homewood, IL: Dow Jones-Irwin; 1984.

15. Butler AC, Chapman JE, Forman EM, et al. The empirical status of cognitive-behavioral therapy: a review of meta-analyses. *Clin Psychol Rev.* 2006;26:17–31.

16. Janis IL, Mann L. *Decision Making: A Psychological Analysis of Conflict, Choice and Commitment.* New York: Free Press; 1977.

17. Miller WR, Rollnick S. *Motivational Interviewing: Helping People Change.* 3rd ed. New York: Guilford Press; 2013:ix.

18. Burke BL, Arkowitz H, Menchola M. The efficacy of motivational interviewing: a meta-analysis of controlled clinical trials. *J Consult Clin Psychol.* 2003;71:843–60.

19. Hettema J, Steele J, Miller WR. Motivational interviewing. *Annu Rev Clin Psychol.* 2005;1:91–111.

20. Lundahl BW, Kunz C, Brownell C, et al. A meta-analysis of motivational interviewing: twenty-five years of empirical studies. *Res Social Work Pract.* 2010;20:137–60.

21. Miller WR, Rose GS. Toward a theory of motivational interviewing. *Am Psychol.* 2009;64:527–537.

# CHAPTER 4

# Toward a New Theory of Motivational Interviewing

I n this chapter we will develop a new theoretical explanation of the nature and power of motivational interviewing (MI). This explanation derives from our research on the types of problems health care professionals (HCPs) have experienced as they attempt to learn and master MI. We are making the assumptions that HCPs wanting to learn MI are genuinely committed to the concept of patient-centered care and that they have a true desire to respect, care for, and collaborate with their patients. We simply do not believe that MI is possible without this. Rollnick and Miller called this orientation "the spirit of MI."[1] This chapter focuses on what is happening in the actual "talk" involved in using MI.

We have spent countless hours viewing, transcribing, and analyzing tape recordings (both video and audio) of HCPs trying to incorporate MI into their interaction with patients (both real and standardized patients). The more we observed and analyzed, the more convinced we became that the efforts of HCPs to use MI with patients were hampered by the following: (1) HCPs talking "on autopilot," unconsciously using taken-for-granted patterns of everyday professional talk and (2) HCPs not listening for and addressing how patients were making sense of their unique situations. We then began to look at communication theory to help orient us to all the ways that MI differs from everyday talk and persuasion.

To our great delight, we soon discovered that our theoretical insights into MI also improved our teaching of MI. When we initially shared what we were noticing about MI, our workshop participants became enthused because these distinctions helped them to understand a major portion of what they were struggling with in learning MI. In other words, these insights made sense to them. Thus we began a constant process of cycling back and forth between (1) analyzing recorded attempts by HCPs and students to use MI with patients and (2) sharing insights with HCPs learning MI in workshops. We experienced the truth of Lewin's assertion that "there is nothing more practical than a good theory."[2] We listened when participants told us that some distinctions and insights didn't help or were too detailed. So we simplified and refined these concepts. We listened when participants seemed to want more insight and detail in other areas. So we extended and elaborated those concepts. Eventually we could see our participants having exciting moments of insight as we explained MI, and we could hear them embracing our concepts as they discussed what had happened during role playing in our workshops. We found additional validation for our theoretical approach to MI as we discovered over the course of two or three years that our workshop participants were making more rapid progress in acquiring greater competence in using MI with patients.

This process no doubt will continue, and our account of MI in health care will continue to evolve. Nevertheless, we feel the need to capture in writing our current account of MI, because it has the potential to spark a new period of growth in the understanding and teaching of MI. We plan to explain in detail our communicative theory of MI for publication in scholarly journals. We are already involved in research that tests the validity of our approach to MI, and later in this chapter we will present some significant results. In this book, however, our intent is to present a practical account of what happens in MI for HCPs who talk every day with their patients about the possibility of voluntary health behavior change. Our hope is that this book will serve as the backbone for training programs that could make MI the acknowledged standard for eliciting behavior change in all health care contexts, including hospitals, clinics, offices, pharmacies, and managed care plans.

## Getting beyond reliance on everyday talk

Human beings have an amazing ability to coordinate with each other through talk. We take talk so much for granted that we often overlook the nature and character of our talk. Scholars refer to talk as a "tacit" behavior, that is, an everyday behavior that we rarely focus on in any conscious way unless something is wrong. A lot of everyday talk is tacit, or taken for granted, in much the same way that windows are taken for granted. We don't usually focus on the qualities of a window unless there is something wrong with the window (e.g., it is cracked or dirty). Similarly, we take all the habits of everyday talk so much for granted that it is difficult to focus on these habits and their effects on our relationships.

One reason why MI is difficult to learn is that it requires us to focus on and then to change tacit patterns of talk that we have practiced most of our lives. Learning MI is made even more difficult by the way that HCPs are often taught in school to talk to patients. We can be initially resistant to training in how to talk to patients more effectively: "Hey, I talk to patients just fine. I do it all the time." The tacit dimension of talk also makes it hard to sense how our interactional assumptions affect the nature of our talk. If we don't focus on how we are affecting patients with our talk, it is easy to blame the patient for not being receptive enough, or for being "difficult." In fact, Bill Miller's recognition that the tacit habits of confrontational counseling led to resistance in patients[3] is the origin of MI. The tacit nature of talk makes it very difficult for us to change our habitual patterns. When we initially venture beyond talking "on autopilot" to try MI, our talk will seem painfully awkward. We are unaccustomed to considering how to treat patients better through our talk. For these reasons, it is most productive to learn MI in a workshop environment where

1. We can be comfortable in looking at what we do when talking with patients,
2. We can see, hear, and feel how MI operates differently than everyday talk,
3. We can first try implementing MI in small steps, and finally
4. We can feel safe enough to try using MI with a role-played patient and understanding, expert facilitators.

Even upon completion of an MI workshop, the tacit nature of talk means that we will need to devote conscious attention to implementing MI with our patients. It will take continued practice and reflection to get to the point where MI itself starts to become tacit and operate on autopilot. Then we can enjoy the smooth, easy flow of MI as we listen to our patients and engage in dialogue with them about their issues and concerns. Patient interaction will seem much more productive and satisfying when we rely on MI instead of relying on the normal patterns of everyday talk.

MI differs significantly from everyday talk in terms of its central purpose and its interactional flow. Everyday talk focuses on getting things done simply and quickly. We share just enough information with other people that we can coordinate with them and get the job done. Because we are usually interested in getting the job done *just well enough for practical purposes*, we tend to scrimp and save on the type and amount of information we put into our messages. We say just enough that the other person should be able to figure out what we really mean—assuming that the other person shares the same knowledge we do and makes sense of the circumstances in the same way we do. These are questionable assumptions, of course. Nevertheless, we tend to move ahead at high speed in everyday talk and assume that the other person understands us and is coordinated with us. Only when problems surface in a fairly extreme way do we slow down and deal explicitly with these problems (or blame the other person for not listening). Even if we do foresee interactional problems, we tend to deal with them by adding supplemental message elements such as qualifiers (e.g., "Your cholesterol is a *little* high at 405.") or disclaimers (e.g., "*I don't want you to be too concerned, but* you have developed diabetes") to ward off misunderstandings. Seldom in everyday talk do we slow down enough to explicitly check the other person's understanding of what we have said, much less to check our own understanding of what the other person has said to us. Thus, everyday talk tends to move ahead at full speed on the assumption that we understand each other well enough for the practical purpose at hand.

When everyday talk is used by HCPs as the basis for their interaction with patients, it can produce unwanted consequences. Significant work has been done to make HCPs aware of some of these consequences. For example, most HCPs are aware that they cannot assume their patients have the same medical literacy as they do, and therefore they must adapt their vocabulary to match the literacy level of their patients.[4] A patient with a grade school education is not likely to understand "myocardial infarction" but is likely to understand some aspects of "heart attack." Most HCPs are willing to slow down enough to educate the patient about significant aspects of the patient's medical situation. However, they still may not assess whether any of new educational material makes sense to the patient or affects the patient's motivation for change.

Unfortunately, the pace of everyday talk is reactive to the perceived job at hand. When an HCP perceives the job to be completion of an office visit, the HCP may produce abbreviated talk designed to get the visit over with. Patients sense this purpose and are likely to go along with it. They may not ask questions they have, because they sense that the HCP is hurried and they don't want to be a bother. As a result, when the visit is over, patients are often left uncertain about what they face and what they are supposed to do. It is quite natural, then, that many of these patients wind up partially or totally noncompliant with the treatment regimen prescribed by the HCP. Why? Because these patients cooperated in the limited act of completing the office visit, not in the act of figuring out what was best for them to do. In addition, the patients were never involved in any negotiations about their treatment plans. The HCP now operates under the illusion that everything is fine and that the patients will be compliant with the treatment plans constructed solely by the HCP.

Even when an HCP focuses on more than completing the office visit, the HCP tends to see the job at hand as one of persuasion—presenting the most forceful case for why patients should change their ways. The HCP will now talk more with patients than if focused on simply getting the visit over with, but the HCP still limits the talk to what is needed to make the case for why the patients should change their ways. The assumption is that the patients should recognize the wisdom of the HCP's recommendations and follow through on them. The operating belief is that the HCP is the sole expert in the room. The patients may end up nodding in agreement, whether or not they agree. Often, such presentation of what the HCP believes is best for the patient is not sufficient to move the patient to make significant changes. In some instances, such everyday persuasive tactics tend to make patients who are ambivalent or resistant even more actively resistant to significant behavior changes.

HCPs need to redefine the nature of the job at hand. Instead of telling patients what the HCP thinks the patient ought to do, the HCP needs to facilitate the sense making and decision making of the patient. The HCP has to help patients think through the risks and consequences they face in their medical situation, their goals for the future, and what they are willing to do and capable of doing to manage their medical situation and achieve their goals. Such facilitation is a complex job, because it requires the HCP to work within the conceptual world of the patient, rather than requiring the patient to work within the conceptual world of the professional. The talk required to achieve such facilitation is more focused on what the patient is thinking than on what the HCP is thinking. The initial flow of such facilitative talk slows down to make certain that the professional is hearing and understanding how patients are making sense of the situation, and that the patients realize the professional understands them without judgment. Although the initial talk may be slower, the overall amount of time spent with the patient may be reduced and the productivity of that time increased by creating an interaction in which the patient has a better understanding of his medical situation and is more ready to engage in constructive health behavior change.

Some HCPs sense the slower initial pace of MI talk when they object that they don't have time for such talk. They are afraid that 7- to 10-minute interactions might grow into 30-minute interactions. Fortunately, our research suggests that using MI might actually save time in patient interaction in addition to improving patient outcomes. At issue is the question of when and how you want to deal with ambivalence or resistance on the part of the patient: "pay now, or pay later."

If your talk with patients relies on the same goals and methods you use in everyday talk, you will move along initially at high speed and assume that everything is fine with the patient. If the patient remains quiet and indicates no problems (because the patient doesn't want to upset you by slowing you down), the visit may seem to end successfully. Patient outcomes may be quite poor, however, because you have "talked at" the patient. Or, if the patient has problems with what you are saying, it may take time for these problems to surface sufficiently to overcome your assumption that everything is fine. Then, you may attempt to argue with the patient to overcome his resistance, which doesn't make sense from your perspective. At this point you will likely get into a wrestling match with the patient and wind up in an extensive "yes, but" interaction that wastes a lot of time and fails to improve any patient outcomes. Either way, the effort you have invested in using everyday talk with the patient will not be particularly fruitful. It may even turn out to be counterproductive by triggering stronger resistance in the patient.

In contrast, if you use MI as the basis for interacting with patients, you will slow down at first to establish a strong interactional foundation that respects and encourages patients' thoughts and feelings and addresses patients' issues and concerns with directly relevant information. Because you have slowed down to establish rapport with patients and to understand the key concerns at the heart of their sense making, patients will realize you are working with them and will learn to trust you. Moreover, rather than doing a generalized "data dump" and hoping you hit on something useful, you will have a much better sense of what information is really needed to address patients' primary concerns. This is the *exchange* of expertise we discussed in Chapter 2. At this point you can speed up as you help patients to think through their situation, assess their options, and finally decide what they want to do.

We have listened to recorded 20–25 minute phone calls made by patient care pharmacists in a major health care organization. What impressed us was how much time was wasted by failing to hear and respond to the patient's primary concerns. We could hear that many patients felt frustrated at the end of the call because their concerns were not addressed. Many of these phone calls could have been handled much more successfully with MI in 7–10 minutes, with far better results and higher patient satisfaction. Our proprietary data very strongly support this contention. We hope you will experience and then learn to trust this dynamic of slowing down at first in order to speed up later.

Another misconception that some HCPs have about MI is that it is a set of new techniques that can be grafted on top of our everyday talk practices to give us more impact on patients. This is not the case. The dynamics and flow of everyday talk are quite different from the dynamics and flow of MI. The truth is that MI requires us to relate differently to our patients, as discussed in Chapter 2. Over time our talk practices will tend to change as we focus on building deeper rapport with our patients and helping them reason their way to constructive health behavior change that will work for them. This change in how we talk with our patients may not happen quickly, but it will happen consistently if we remain committed to becoming more patient centered by using MI. In later chapters we will explore how to build rapport with patients, how to reflect and possibly reframe patients' core concerns and issues, and how to facilitate patients' sense making and practical reasoning about what they need to do to be healthier and achieve their goals in life.

## Two forms of resistance in patients

The next important insight from communication theory is that interpersonal communication has two major dimensions: a content dimension and a relational dimension.[5] The content dimension consists of all the information about the world that we share in symbolic form. The content dimension of messages in a medical setting may express the patient's symptoms ("I've been having to urinate way too frequently"), the type of illness diagnosed ("Your lab tests indicate that you have diabetes"), and the steps in the treatment plan ("There are three options for lowering your blood sugar: taking medication, eating healthier, and increasing your physical activity.")

The relational dimension focuses on expressing the nature of the relationship as seen by the speaker. The relational dimension of any message in face-to-face talk includes indications of how the speaker regards (1) the receiver, (2) the speaker, and (3) the interaction. Whereas the content dimension of communication relies heavily on the content of the words actually spoken, the relational dimension derives from a mix of many different elements. Most of us are sensitive to the nonverbal aspects of how words are said, including the emotional tone of voice, the pattern of intonation and stress, and the accompanying facial expressions and gestures.

Let's look at an example of how the same basic words can carry quite different relational meanings. Suppose that Emily has returned to see her physician after having been diagnosed three months ago with diabetes (A1c = 8.1). Because she dislikes taking any medication, Emily had refused a prescription for oral diabetes medication. Instead she had agreed to try healthy eating and increased physical activity to reduce her A1c below 7.0. Her physician has just informed her that her A1c tested two days ago is 8.0. Suppose that the physician follows up in a calm neutral voice: "Your blood sugar has remained essentially the same. What are your thoughts about this?" The relational meaning implied here is that the physician is not going to shame or blame Emily for not reducing her A1c to below 7.0, but he does want to talk further about how and why her A1c did not go down. Suppose, however, that the physician were to say these same words with a glaring facial expression and a more disparaging tone, as follows: "*Your* blood sugar has remained *essentially* the same! What are *your* thoughts about this?" Now the relational meaning is much more accusatory, implying that Emily is about to be blamed for not reaching the agreed upon goal. Adding a few more words, which don't change the content meaning much, can further intensify the negative relational meaning: "Look, *your* blood sugar has remained *essentially* the same! Well then, what are *your* thoughts about this?" The relational meaning implied by the added words "Look" and "Well then" is that the physician's perspective is the only perspective of value here—even though the physician has asked Emily what her thoughts are about the A1c result. These added words further imply that the physician is about to let her know his negative judgment of the situation. At this point, because Emily senses the heavily negative relational meaning of the physician's comment, she may never open up and share with the physician what happened. Now the physician has no information on which to base his response to Emily, and he will likely reiterate that she needs to get her A1c below 7. He may even prescribe medication, because in his judgment she has failed. She may take the written prescription from him, but it is unlikely that she will fill it.

Extensive interpersonal conflict can be easily explained as the interchange of utterances laced with heavily negative relational meanings. Counselors dealing with couples in marital conflict often have to work through extremely complicated patterns of negative relational meanings. While the content of a couple's conflict may focus on specific issues such as finances or parenting, often the intensity of the conflict derives mostly from the relational messages being exchanged. Successful therapy is often based on teaching couples to talk differently with each other when they experience conflict about an issue. Such talk usually stresses sending positive messages of respect for each other's opinions and working to understand each other fully before starting to discuss options for dealing with the actual disagreements.

The same approach is at the heart of MI. The major difference is that social power, status, and expertise traditionally reside with the HCP and not with the patient. Thus, relational conflict between HCPs and patients is often characterized by the professionals as resistance on the part of the patient. So, HCPs blame "resistant" or "difficult" patients for their "denial" and "noncompliance." It does not occur to the professionals that perhaps *they* are being difficult.

As we looked at videotapes of HCPs counseling patients, we sensed that in addition to ambivalence or resistance expressed by a patient about a health behavior, much patient resistance was relational in nature. Patients expressed resistance as a way of saying that they did not like the way they were being treated by the HCP. When shamed or demeaned by HCPs, patients resisted doing what they perceived the HCPs wanted them to do. Of course, once we could discern relational resistance, we were able then to identify the substantive resistance that was a matter of the issues, doubts, questions, and concerns expressed in the content dimension of the patient's talk. If the patient's issues and concerns about the treatment regimen were not addressed in a way that the patient could hear and accept, the patient would not be likely to institute any positive health behavior changes. Thus, we eventually distinguished between *issue resistance* (not taking the medication, not losing weight, quitting smoking) and *relational resistance* on the part of the patient.

We soon discovered that this distinction between relational resistance and issue resistance allowed us to discern even deeper patterns of interaction between HCPs and patients. For example, it was easy to see how HCPs were triggering relational resistance in their patients. We also saw that if patients were experiencing relational resistance, it was hard for them to hear that the HCP might actually be addressing their issue resistance by answering their questions or addressing their concerns. Next, we realized that relational resistance and issue resistance can vary independently of each other, depending on what the HCP does and says to the patient. It became clear that dealing with relational resistance was different from dealing with issue resistance. In the next two sections we will discuss these two types of resistance.

## Relational resistance and loss of face

One very powerful impulse affecting face-to-face talk is our desire to claim and to defend a positive image of worth and value. Erving Goffman used the concept of "face" from Asian cultures to represent this need to be viewed in a positive light by others. According to Goffman, we all work to avoid loss of face for ourselves and others during interactions.[6,7] Saving face is an inherently social act, because one of the best ways to save face for ourselves is to save face for others. Most of us are acutely aware of the social awkwardness that occurs when we cause someone else to lose face as we talk. For example, we may unintentionally insult someone and then seek to mitigate everyone's embarrassment by using tactics such as apologies, explanations, or reframing. Until we have restored the good face of the other person, it is hard for the social interaction to move forward. As a result, we normally seek to avoid loss of face for those with whom we interact, rather than having to repair it after the fact. Most of the time, we are fairly successful in avoiding major face loss for ourselves and others.

In contrast, minor forms of face loss occur frequently and do not call social interaction to a screeching halt. Instead, minor forms of face loss tend to lead to "sparring matches" in which we trade adversarial responses with each other. The operative dynamic becomes one of implied social disparagement. We may continue talking about the issue at hand, but the relational meaning of our messages implies that we do not like how the other person has caused us to lose face. Then the other person can respond in an equally disparaging way, feeling that we have caused him to lose face. Often the result is unproductive arguing that leads nowhere because both participants are in a defensive mode and neither is listening to the other's perspectives.

For patients, face loss often results from the extent of the expertise claimed by the HCP. Too often, HCPs go beyond being experts about diseases and the associated treatment options to claim expertise about what is best for the patient, what the patient ought to do, and perhaps even what the patient should want to do. Consider the following statement directed to a patient with uncontrolled diabetes: "Look, don't you know that you are going to wind up in extremely bad shape if you continue to allow your blood sugar to remain this high? You've got to start taking your medicine regularly and watching what you eat!" The heavily parental tone of this comment causes the patient to lose face. Consequently, the patient is more likely to respond to the shaming and blaming tone of the message than to the medical issue of what can happen if the patient's blood sugar remains high.

Let's look a little more closely at the relational aspects of this message. Researchers who study face work in communication have identified two major aspects of face: competence face and autonomy face.[8] Here, the HCP's comment causes the patient to lose both competence face and autonomy face.

Competence face consists of the desire to be viewed as a good and capable person. If an HCP implies that the patient isn't capable of making adequate sense of the situation, the patient has lost competence face. We have a simple test for whether a comment causes loss of competence face for a patient. If adding "stupid" to a comment doesn't alter its basic sense, then competence face loss is involved. So, the comment above would start off as "Look, *stupid*, don't you know that you are going to wind up . . . ?" Adding "stupid" to this comment doesn't alter the sense of the comment because there are already two specific features of the comment that cause loss of competence face for the patient. The first is the introductory word "Look" (technically called a discourse particle), which asserts that the patient must give up her own sense making about the situation in favor of adopting the sense making of the HCP. "Look" says to the patient, "What you see in this situation is neither as important nor as valid as what I see." Simply put, "You are wrong and I am right." The second part of the HCP's comment that causes loss of competence face is "don't you know that . . . ?" This grammatical form of asking a question implies that the HCP expects the patient to answer, "No, I don't know that." Put together, these two features cause considerable loss of competence face for the patient. It should come as no surprise, then, that the patient will likely become defensive in response.

Autonomy face consists of the desire to be viewed as an independent person who makes her own decisions. When an HCP tells a patient what to do, the patient can lose autonomy face. When an HCP fails to give a patient any significant choice in deciding the course of therapy, the patient can lose autonomy face and may resist doing what the HCP has ordered. Considerable loss of autonomy face is involved in the HCP's second sentence in the example we've been discussing: "You've got to start taking your medicine regularly and watching what you eat!" This goes considerably beyond prescribing treatment; it becomes an overt command and reprimand. The first part of the sentence has nothing to do with medicine and everything to do with establishing who is in control. Saying "You've got to" specifies that the patient has no say whatsoever in what to do. When patients lose autonomy face, they become defensive and start to find reasons why they cannot do what the HCP has specified. Telling patients that they have to stop their noncompliant behavior only reinforces their face loss and ensures that their "noncompliant behavior" will more than likely continue. Ironically, once patients lose face, they can be told the truth about their condition and their options—and they will *not* be able to hear it because they are focused on their face loss. They may say to themselves, "I'll be darned if I'm going to take that medicine after he talked to me that way!"

The example we have been discussing also illustrates another feature of competence face loss and autonomy face loss: Both forms can be intertwined in the same comment. The two forms of face loss often occur together because there is a conceptual connection between competence face and autonomy face. If I consider that you are incompetent to make good decisions for yourself, I will dismiss your autonomy and assert my need to make decisions for you.

We have seen no evidence thus far that face loss for a patient increases the patient's resistance to health behavior change, but there is evidence that face loss increases resistance to change in other areas of social influence. For example, psychological reactance theory has established that infringement of the patient's autonomy implied in mass media persuasive messages can backfire by increasing the target audience's resistance to the proposed change.[9,10] Similarly, studies of organizational change have documented increased resistance to change when organizational change agents violate the competence face and autonomy face of employees affected by the proposed change.[11]

In summary, one major cause of relational resistance is the HCP's causing patients to lose face. In response, patients will seek to restore their image of competence and autonomy by resisting what they believe the HCP wants them to do. The more HCPs argue for what they want patients to do, the more the patients will resist. Patients can resist passively by saying nothing or by nodding politely. Or patients can resist actively by engaging in a "yes, but" wrestling match with the HCP. No amount of logical argument will overcome relational resistance in a patient, because this form of resistance is about the patient's loss of face. The foundation of MI lies in reducing relational resistance in the patient. One important way to reduce relational resistance is by respecting and maintaining the patient's face. Another important way is by respecting and empathizing with the patient's sense making, which we will discuss later.

# Issue resistance and practical reasoning

Human beings are practical sense makers. We are constantly engaged in sizing up our situation and figuring out what we need to do to achieve our goals. We are capable of impressive chains of "if–then" reasoning that guide our actions. Our lives are governed by practical reasoning that we adjust as we make sense of our changing circumstances.[12,13] "Practical" reasoning does not mean that the reasoning is correct or incorrect; it just means that it makes sense to the patient. What matters is the conclusion the patient draws. If a patient is informed that he has suffered a minor heart attack, he will reason his own way to a conclusion about what he needs (or doesn't need) to do about this heart attack. His sense making may or may not be based on accurate information, and his conclusions may or may not be helpful in avoiding another heart attack. But to him, his sense making and practical reasoning will seem very compelling.

HCPs wishing to constructively influence the sense making of this patient must learn to hear and engage the various lines of reasoning this patient might adopt in making sense of his heart attack. He could say, "Just tell me what to do and I'll do it." Or he could object: "This physician is exaggerating. I've recovered from whatever that episode was and I feel fine now." Or he could probe further, saying, "I need all the information I can get about heart attacks. I want to know exactly what I need to do and why." These three responses are all examples of practical reasoning or sense making that lead to quite different actions on the part of the patient.

Such practical reasoning resides at the heart of what we call issue resistance, which involves all the issues, concerns, worries, and doubts that lead patients to conclude that they

- Don't need to make any health behavior changes in their lives:
  "I don't know what all this fuss is about. I feel just fine."
- Don't want to or aren't sure they should make any health behavior changes in their lives:
  "Smoking is the only pleasure left to me and I just don't want to give up my cigarettes."
  or

> "I heard that this medicine can cause muscle weakness. I'm a truck driver. I don't need that!"

or

> "I like the idea of getting my blood pressure down, but some of my friends have had some male problems from this medicine."

- ■ Cannot succeed at making any health behavior changes in their lives:
  "I've tried to lose weight so many times in the past that I've learned my lesson. I just can't do it."

When patients draw such conclusions based on the information they have at hand, these conclusions seem obvious and straightforward to them. Patients make decisions about what needs to be done based on what is important to *them*, or whether *they* are confident they can do what is being proposed, or both. Patients are strongly motivated not only to defend these conclusions but also to act on the basis of these conclusions. Issue resistance can be extremely strong and must be addressed if HCPs expect to increase the probability of their patients' engaging in significant health behavior change.

The process of reasoning has been examined extensively by classical logicians who have focused on identifying valid forms of argument. They assert that if you are presented with a valid argument supported by true evidence, you *must necessarily accept* the truth of the conclusion. Applying this theory of logic to health care, if HCPs present patients with valid arguments for why they should consider changing their behavior, then patients *must* recognize the truth of the conclusions presented to them. Although this may be true logically, it is far from being true psychologically and interpersonally, because telling patients that they *must* accept the truth of your conclusions about what they need to do causes them to lose both competence face and autonomy face. Instead of reacting positively to the valid argument you have presented, patients may react negatively to the loss of competence face and autonomy face. The more you reiterate your valid argument and its conclusion, the more defensive they will become and the more they will advance reasons for why they cannot possibly do what you have argued that they should do. If you try to force a conclusion on your patients, no matter how valid your reasoning may be, they may resist your conclusion in order to restore face. You will wind up arguing with your patients in the worst sense of the word. As they generate reasons why they cannot accept your conclusions for them, you have prompted them to reinforce their resistance. This is why Miller and Rollnick included "avoid argumentation" as one of their five basic READS principles.[14]

If we are to have any positive influence on patients' sense making and the practical reasoning that underlies their issue resistance, we have to do so in a way that avoids causing patients to lose face. Unfortunately, it is extremely easy to cause loss of face as we attempt to address the patient's issue resistance. Here are some points at which we can cause patients to lose face and shut down any possibility that they will reconsider their issue resistance:

- If we start our interaction with patients by telling them what they need to do, the patients will lose face and will not trust us enough to even share what they are really concerned about.
- If patients do share their concerns and issues with us and we don't give any evidence that we have heard and respected these concerns and issues, the patients will lose face and will shut down further discussion of their issue resistance.
- If we reflect back the issues and concerns that a patient has shared but move on to address other issues and concerns that we consider more important, the patient will lose face and feel manipulated.
- If we reflect back patients' issues and concerns but move on to give patients our standard "data dump" or "lecture" (which in fact may address their issues and concerns), the patients will lose face because we are not treating them as worthwhile individuals deserving an individualized response.
- If we hear their practical reasoning and tell them that they are wrong or off base, patients will lose face and will resist our corrections.
- If we abruptly impose advice on them and suggest that we have solved their problems for them, patients will lose face and will explain how our solution will not work for them.
- If we judge patients' practical reasoning as deficient or illogical and then tell them what they ought to be thinking, patients will lose face and stop listening to us.

Given the numerous ways in which we can cause our patients to lose face as we address their sense making and practical reasoning, how can we have any positive impact on their issue resistance? The answer lies in engaging their practical reasoning by exploring their sense making, respecting their lines of reasoning, and then "throwing a loving wrench into the works" by sharing information or by raising concerns that naturally prompt patients to rethink their conclusions.

This indirect approach to interpersonal influence is known as making a case with an implicit conclusion. In other words, we present the basic information or premises needed to draw a conclusion but refrain from actually stating the conclusion explicitly. So, if we add new information about the risks of their medical situation and then ask patients for their thoughts about this information, we are inviting a conclusion rather than imposing a conclusion. Because the information we have shared is naturally tilted toward drawing a new and more constructive conclusion, we can rely on people's strong inclination to adjust their sense making and practical reasoning in light of new information and new circumstances. We need to help patients indirectly to formulate a new line of reasoning for why they need to change their behavior to better manage their health. When patients figure out for themselves what behavior they need to change, the change is much more likely to be instituted on a long-lasting basis.

The starting ideas in a line of reasoning are called the premises. The conclusion drawn by the line of reasoning is set up, then, by the logical relationship among the premises. By addressing and possibly altering the premises in a patient's line of reasoning, we can predispose the patient to draw a new conclusion.

In MI there are two major types of premises open to being influenced by an HCP. Factual premises focus specifically on medical facts that can be addressed by using our medical expertise in a relationally sensitive manner. Included in such factual premises are statements that describe and explain the patient's disease, the risks faced by the patient, and the treatment options open to the patient. The following statements are examples of factual premises in a patient's line of reasoning that need to be addressed using our medical expertise:

- "If I feel fine, I can't possibly have . . . ."
- "I don't need to reduce my . . . until I start feeling some significant symptoms."
- "Taking medicine should be more than enough to reduce my . . . ."

In contrast, motivational premises are not part of our medical expertise but are part of the patient's expertise. Motivational premises are based on the patient's experience and perspective. They are usually expressed in the form of goals, desires, doubts, or fears that constitute the patient's motivation for health behavior change. As HCPs we can elicit, address, and reinforce these motivational premises by exploring the patient's perspective with regard to the DARN acronym (desires, abilities, reasons, needs) discussed by Rollnick, Miller, and Butler.[15] It is not at all unusual for a patient to fail to see the connection between current health behaviors and personal goals or desires for the future. We can highlight the connection by exploring the patient's goals and then developing a discrepancy between the patient's current behaviors and the patient's goals for the future. As HCPs we have the ability to engage and address both the factual and the motivational premises of the patient's sense making and practical reasoning.

The following dialogue illustrates how the foregoing discussion operates at the heart of MI. A patient whose total cholesterol is over 400 (LDL is over 200 and HDL is less than 40) has been diagnosed with high cholesterol. When the physician tells him she would like to prescribe a statin to help bring his cholesterol levels down, the patient says

Pt: *Don't bother, doc. I feel fine. I'm not even that overweight and I don't eat fried foods.*

HCP: So, because you feel fine, you're not overweight, and you stay away from fried foods, you're wondering, "Why do I really need to start on cholesterol medication?"

Pt: *You got it!*

HCP: You raise a good question. Would you mind if I give you some information, and then you tell me what you think? Ultimately, it is up to you whether you want to take the medication.

Pt: *OK. Go ahead.*

HCP: Unfortunately, high cholesterol may not have any symptoms you might notice. The first symptom may be a stroke or a heart attack. Your total cholesterol is over 400. We know that when total cholesterol drops below 200, the risk of having a stroke or heart attack goes way down. Taking this medicine and making small changes in your eating habits and physical activity can significantly lower your cholesterol and bring it down under 200. I would hate to see you have a stroke or heart attack that's preventable. What are your thoughts now about taking the medication to lower your cholesterol?

Notice that the physician first reflects her understanding of the patient's key motivational issues and lines of reasoning. Letting the patient know that she is really listening to how he is making sense of his situation saves face for the patient and avoids relational resistance. This patient's sense making is that if he feels OK, doesn't eat fried foods, and is not overweight, then there really is no problem. The information the physician provides must address how all of these things can be true and the patient can still be at risk. Next, the physician asks permission to give information for the patient to consider, letting the patient know that ultimately it is his decision. Asking permission to share information and requesting the patient's reaction to the information both save face for the patient and reduce relational resistance. The new information is then presented in a neutral fashion, and the patient is asked how this new information (the "loving wrench in the works") affects his thinking about how to treat his cholesterol. Notice that the physician also saves face for the patient by not drawing conclusions about what he should be doing. Instead she gives information for him to consider, expresses her concerns, and finally asks the patient what he has concluded.

In summary, issue resistance is a matter of all the issues, concerns, questions, and doubts that lead patients to conclude either that they do not need to change their behavior (resistance) or that they are not sure if they should or want to (ambivalence). These issues and concerns are justified by the patient's sense making and practical reasoning, which seem compelling to the patient. We cannot reject outright this sense making and assert our own reasoning, because doing so will cause the patient to lose face. What we can do is

1. Explore the sense making and reasoning that underlie patients' issue resistance,
2. Empathize with patients' sense making and reflect back their reasoning (so that patients know we have heard and respected their perspective),
3. Ask permission to share information relevant to their reasoning,
4. Share that information in a clearly focused and well-adapted fashion, and
5. Then invite patients to tell us their thoughts about this information.

If we have provided information that precisely targets the weak or questionable points in patients' reasoning and have done so without causing them loss of face, patients are likely to reconsider their conclusions. We cannot guarantee that patients will reconsider their conclusions, but we can greatly increase the probability of their doing so.

Let's look at another example of how this approach works, with a 56-year-old man who has very high blood pressure (155/95). The physician has prescribed blood pressure medication, but the patient has not had the prescription filled. The following dialogue occurs during the next visit to the physician's office.

| 1 | HCP: | How are you doing with taking the blood pressure medication that I prescribed for you? |
|---|---|---|
| 2 | Pt: | *Well, to be honest, I never got that prescription filled. I feel fine and just don't see any need for it.* |
| 3 | HCP: | Because you feel fine and haven't personally noticed any symptoms of high blood pressure, you wonder why you need this medication at all. |
| 4 | Pt: | *Exactly.* |
| 5 | HCP: | That's a great question. Would you mind if I share some information with you to help answer your question, and then you can tell me your thoughts? |
| 6 | Pt: | *No, go ahead. That'd be fine.* |
| 7 | HCP: | With high blood pressure, you may not notice any symptoms at all until one day without any warning you suffer a major stroke or heart attack. You may be at work, and then the next thing you know you wake up in the hospital having difficulty moving your left arm and leg. What are your thoughts about this? |
| 8 | Pt: | (two seconds of silence) *Well, I don't want that to happen to me. I have to keep working to support my family. Can taking that pill really prevent that from happening?* |
| 9 | HCP: | Taking your blood pressure medication as prescribed, getting more physical activity, and watching what you eat all help to reduce your blood pressure and thereby reduce your risk of a major stroke or heart |

attack. I'd really like to work with you to help ensure that you don't suffer a major stroke or heart attack that could cripple your ability to support your family. Would it be OK with you if we first talk more about your medication?

10    Pt:    *Yeah, definitely. But I'd really like to know how I could have a sudden stroke or heart attack without any warning at all.*

11    HCP:    It seems really strange that you wouldn't feel any minor symptoms before having a major stroke or heart attack.

12    Pt:    *Yeah, you got it.*

13    HCP:    Would you mind if I use an analogy to help address your concern?

14    Pt:    *Go ahead.*

15    HCP:    When you have high blood pressure over an extended period of time, your blood vessels are like a garden hose that has been left on with very high water pressure in it. Everything seems fine until all of a sudden a weak spot in the wall of the hose ruptures and there's water spurting out all over the place. If that rupture happens with a blood vessel in your brain, you have a major stroke. The way to avoid this is to reduce your blood pressure to a much lower level. How does this strike you?

16    Pt:    *Actually, that happened to a neighbor of mine, and I asked him why he had left the water turned on in his hoses.*

17    HCP:    You made a great point. So it sounds like you want to reduce your blood pressure to a much safer level.

18    Pt:    *Definitely.*

In utterance 1 the physician has asked a neutral, open-ended question to explore how the patient has been taking his medicine. In starting utterance 2 off with "Well, to be honest" the patient acknowledges that this response is not what the physician wants to hear. The patient follows up with the line of reasoning that explains his decision not to take the medicine. At this point the patient has expressed substantive issue resistance. The physician faces a major choice of how to respond. Saying something like "Well, *you really do need* to take this medicine even if you feel fine. Don't you know that your blood pressure is extremely high?" would cause the patient to lose both competence face and autonomy face and would trigger greater defensiveness in the patient. There is great potential for triggering a fruitless series of "yes, but" utterances by both the physician and the patient.

Instead, the physician has chosen in utterance 3 to use MI by rolling with the patient's resistance and by not judging the patient. Even more significantly, the physician reflects back the patient's line of reasoning and poses the essential question the patient is struggling with. The physician has empathized with the patient's lack of understanding about why he needs the medicine. In utterance 4 the patient affirms that the physician has understood. This response helps create mutually acknowledged rapport between the physician and the patient.

Now the physician, in utterance 5, can ask permission to provide information that answers the patient's question. This is considerably different from the physician's dumping information on the patient in an advice-giving mode that causes the patient to lose face. The patient's face is respected through valuing the question that the patient has implied, asking permission to share relevant information, and setting up the chance for the patient to respond with his reactions.

In utterance 7 the physician elaborates on the fact that the patient personally may not sense any symptoms before suffering a major stroke or heart attack. When the patient is asked for his thoughts, he affirms that he doesn't want that stroke or heart attack to happen to him, because he needs to work to support his family. And he quickly progresses to asking whether taking a pill can prevent a stroke or heart attack. At this point it sounds as if the patient has identified personal motivation to avoid a stroke or heart attack and is now focused on how this goal can be accomplished. That's the thrust of the final question in utterance 8. In utterance 9, the physician first addresses the issue of the efficacy of the pill. But in doing so he expands the frame of reference to include increased physical activity and better eating habits. Then the physician reflects and affirms the patient's personal motivation for avoiding a stroke or heart attack. Then he requests permission to talk about the medicine. There is ample evidence to the patient that the physician respects his face, wants to help him provide for his family, and is seeking to address his concerns and questions.

The physician might have been somewhat surprised by the patient's response in 10. After giving permission to discuss the medicine, the patient goes back to the question of how he could have a stroke without any warning symptoms he could personally sense. The physician could have pushed his agenda of getting to the medicine. But that would have damaged rapport with the patient, so in utterance 11 the physician empathizes with the patient's ongoing concern about the lack of warning symptoms. As is indicated in utterance 12, the patient knows the physician is really working with him and wants to clear up any worries he has. The request to share an analogy once again works to preserve autonomy face for the patient. Utterance 15 is an analogy that precisely targets the issue of how something so major could happen so abruptly. The physician hits the jackpot when in utterance 16 the patient identifies with the analogy. At this point the patient has drawn an implicit conclusion about what he needs to do, namely, that he needs to reduce his blood pressure. The physician could follow up with a neutral question about how the patient sees this analogy applying to his situation with high blood pressure, but the physician senses the implicit conclusion and reflects that conclusion for the patient to affirm in utterance 18. Notice that the sequence in utterances 16 through 18 moves at a slightly faster pace because much rapport has already been built and because the physician has caught the point of the patient's utterance 16.

At this point the physician can return to seek permission to discuss the medication. The patient may now be ready to move on with this discussion. The interactional sequence in this example worked well because the physician followed the patient's pace and slowed down to address the issue that continued to bother the patient. If the physician had tried to move ahead with discussing the medication before the patient was ready, he would have lost the rapport that had been built in prior utterances. The other thing this physician did well was to provide targeted information that directly responded to the central concern expressed by the patient. There were no well-rehearsed multipurpose data dumps or lectures delivered by the physician on autopilot. The focused informational responsiveness of the physician created more rapport with the patient and consequently led the patient to pay close attention to the information being provided.

Looking at the flow of this example, it is clear that not only did the physician avoid causing the patient to lose face, but the physician also positively affirmed the patient's face by hearing and reflecting the patient's concerns and directly addressing those concerns with targeted, relevant information. MI achieves its full impact when the HCP creates rapport with the patient by respecting the patient's face and then engages the patient's sense making and practical reasoning by reflecting and empathizing with the patient's issues, sharing targeted information with the patient, and seeking the patient's response.

MI requires close coordination in how the HCP responds to both relational resistance and issue resistance in the patient. An extremely strong synergy occurs in MI when the HCP establishes and maintains rapport with the patient while respond-ing directly to the patient's issues and concerns. Each of these elements—building rapport and addressing the patient's issues—by itself has a positive impact on increas-ing the probability of health behavior change by the patient, but MI achieves a much greater total effect when these two elements are closely coordinated and integrated. Something distinctive happens when rapport with the patient is used to leverage the impact of providing information that directly addresses the patient's issue resistance. Instead of two independent effects operating within MI to increase the likelihood of health behavior change, as in $1 + 1 = 2$, the synergy of MI is much more like $1 + 1 = 6$.

## The synergy of addressing both relational and issue resistance

In Chapter 3 we described the historical development of MI from both a theoretical and a practical point of view. We referred to several systematic reviews of research on the effectiveness of MI in facilitating positive health behavior change. These reviews concluded that although MI is generally more effective than treatment as usual, it is no more effective than other systematic approaches to counseling patients.[16–18] These studies have not documented the effectiveness of MI at the level we would expect based on the theoretical account of MI that we have just presented. We are con-vinced that MI—when fully implemented—achieves a synergy that greatly increases the likelihood of positive health behavior change. The challenge has been to validate the synergy of MI that results from the close coordination of (1) establishing and maintaining rapport with the patient and (2) addressing the patient's sense making and practical reasoning.

Next we will summarize findings of a PhD dissertation by Abhishek Krishna-Pillai at the Harrison School of Pharmacy at Auburn University under the direction of Bill Villaume.[19] Krishna-Pillai was a full member of our research team that exam-ined hours of videotaped HCP–patient role plays to identify the problems HCPs were experiencing in implementing MI. For his master's thesis, Krishna-Pillai had presented a qualitative analysis of the problems in learning MI that revolved around the use of empathy.[20] For his doctoral dissertation he decided to conduct an experimental validation of the two basic dimensions of MI (relational resistance and issue resistance) that we had identified in our team research and the synergy that exists in MI when rapport with the patient is used to leverage positive impact on the patient's sense making and practical reasoning.

Whereas most prior research on MI had taken the form of clinical outcome studies, this dissertation employed a communication research method known as message effects research.[21] Different message strategies were operationalized by videotaped stimulus messages presented to participants who then shared their reactions in the form of quantified judgments. This research method allowed a meticulous examination of the internal structure of MI, because the experimental stimuli were videotaped physician–patient interactions, 75–150 seconds in length, scripted to represent six possible combinations of relational resistance (two levels) and addressing issue resistance (three levels). To increase the validity of the statistical analysis, each of the six cells in the design was represented by two different videotaped interactions. Consequently, participants in the study watched each of 12 videos and provided judgments about the physician and the patient in each video. These judgments were combined to form reliable scores for three dependent variables: the physician's being accepting and respectful of the patient, the physician's medical knowledge, and the patient's likelihood of a behavior change. The statistical analysis tested each of these variables for the effect of reducing relational resistance by itself, the effect of addressing issue resistance by itself, and the synergistic effect of doing both together.

Let's look in more detail at how these videos were experimentally scripted. Relational resistance was scripted as either high or low. In the high relational resistance condition the physician caused the patient's loss of both competence face and autonomy face by acting as the sole expert entitled to judge the patient and tell the patient what to do. In the low relational resistance condition the physician acted as an expert on medical information but also treated the patient as an expert on the patient's situation, needs, goals, and concerns. In this way the physician respected the patient's face by neither judging the patient nor telling the patient what to do. The second independent variable, engaging and addressing the patient's issue resistance, was scripted with three levels of increasing engagement. The first level had the physician ignoring the issue or concern expressed by the patient. The second level had the physician reflecting the patient's issue or concern but failing to provide any information to directly address it. The third level fully engaged the patient's sense making

### TABLE 4-1 Experimental Design

| Condition | High Relational Resistance | Low Relational Resistance |
|---|---|---|
| Ignores patient issue | Cell 1 | Cell 2 |
| Reflects patient issue | Cell 3 | Cell 4 |
| Reflects and addresses patient issue | Cell 5 | Cell 6 |

Source: Reference 19.

by having the physician reflect the patient's issue and then provide information to directly address that issue.

The experimental design of this study is shown in Table 4-1. According to the theoretical account of MI that we have just offered, MI is represented by cell 6, in which the physician respects and maintains the face of the patient and also facilitates the patient's reasoning by reflecting and then addressing the patient's chief issue or concern. Here the patient feels safe talking with the physician because the physician saves face for the patient. When the patient brings up what is bothering him, the physician reflects the issue back so that the patient knows the physician has heard and respected his sense making. The physician responds directly to the patient's issue by providing relevant information and then inviting the patient's thoughts about that information.

Here is an excerpt from a script in cell 6. The physician and patient are discussing the impact of the patient's smoking on his asthma. Note that the patient's first comment discounts any connection between his asthma and his smoking.

> Pt: *Well, I believe that I have asthma mainly because it runs in my family. My grandfather had it, my dad has it, and it's not really surprising that I have it too.*
>
> HCP: So because asthma runs in your family, you feel that smoking doesn't have a lot to do with your asthma, because it's inherited.
>
> Pt: *Yeah.*
>
> HCP: May I share with you a concern that I have?

Pt: *Sure.*

HCP: The asthma you've inherited from your family makes your lungs very sensitive, and it makes them especially sensitive to the impact of smoking. I'm concerned that your smoking will continue to inflame the airways in your lungs and will make your asthma continue to get worse. How do you feel about that?

Because the physician has respected the face of the patient, reflected back the patient's line of reasoning, and directly addressed the patient's issue, the conditions in cell 6 are optimal for the patient to reconsider his conclusion about what he needs to do. Cell 6 provides all the conditions necessary for the synergy of MI to emerge.

In contrast, cell 1 represents a physician who is focused on his own agenda of telling the patient what to do and is not concerned about being patient centered. When the patient expresses the issue or concern that is bothering him, the physician gives no indication of having even heard the patient's concern, much less any indication of responding to that concern. This cell represents a thoroughly provider-centered approach to interacting with a patient. Here's an excerpt from a script in cell 1.

Pt: *Woo. I just can't believe that I have high pressure. You know, I'm only 25 and it's rare for people my age to have high blood pressure. None of my friends have high blood pressure.*

HCP: Well, you do have high blood pressure. There's no doubt about it. And you are going to need to change your diet, and you need to exercise more. And you're also going to need to take your medication on a regular basis in order to reduce your blood pressure.

Note that the physician in this excerpt is not "over the top" in causing face loss for the patient. The face loss comes strictly from the physician's straightforward enactment of the expert role. The conditions in cell 1 are the least favorable for helping a patient reconsider what he needs to do.

From our perspective, cells 2 and 4 are interesting because they represent the behavior of many HCPs as they learn to use MI. It is not too difficult to learn to respect and maintain patients' face—especially if you identify with the paradigm that the patient is an expert on the patient's circumstances, goals, needs, and difficulties.

In reviewing the videotapes of HCPs using MI with standardized patients, we could hear HCPs working at being more accepting and more respectful of the patients. We could hear them rolling with resistance by not judging patients when they expressed resistance. We could hear them trying to support self-efficacy and express empathy with the patients' issues and concerns. And when that was all that they did with the patients, we could sense the lack of any progress in facilitating the patients' reasoning their way to the need for a behavior change.

The following excerpt comes from a script in cell 4 in which the physician and patient are discussing the patient's recently discovered high blood pressure. Here the physician reflects back the patient's issue but fails to address that issue. Instead the physician uses a response that is often appropriate in the face of strongly expressed issue resistance that has been addressed and still remains strong.

> Pt:   *You know, I don't like taking medicines. I'm concerned about their side effects.*
>
> HCP:   OK, so you are concerned about the possible side effects of medication, and right now you feel good about your health, your exercise routine, and your healthy lifestyle and you are not sure you want to make additional changes (*Patient: Yeah*) and if you get to the point where you would like to talk some more about this in terms of managing your blood pressure, I really would like you to come see me. I'd like to talk about it with you further.

In this script the physician gives clear evidence of respecting the patient's thoughts about having high blood pressure but then avoids "throwing a loving wrench into the works." One possibility would have been to formulate a summary of the patient's thoughts in order to create some dissonance between the patient's currently healthy habits and the patient's nevertheless having high blood pressure. Another possibility would have been to explore the patient's concern about side effects of medication. The greatest difficulty in learning MI, from our perspective, is learning how to use rapport with the patient to challenge and influence the patient's sense making and reasoning processes (i.e., learning how to progress from cells 2 and 4 to cell 6).

A few major results of this dissertation study provide initial validation of our theoretical account of MI. Specifics of the experimental procedure and the statistical analysis are available online in the full dissertation itself.[19] Here, we will highlight results that focus on

1. The physician being perceived as accepting and respectful of the patient,
2. The perceived medical expertise of the physician, and
3. The perceived likelihood of behavior change by the patient.

The first set of results focused on the extent to which the participants perceived the physicians as being accepting and respectful of the patient in each videotape. Physicians in the low relational resistance condition were judged to be significantly more accepting and respectful of the patient than physicians in the high relational resistance condition. This difference was highly significant, primarily because relational resistance had been scripted into these videos as a matter of patients' losing face in the high relational resistance ("I am the expert") condition or saving face in the low relational resistance ("We are both experts") condition. In effect, this result was a validity check for the two relational resistance conditions and did not add much new empirical knowledge about the nature of MI.

The effect of addressing issue resistance was also significant for the perception of how accepting and respectful the physicians were of the patients. The physicians who addressed the patients' issues were perceived to be significantly more accepting and respectful of the patients than both the physicians who ignored the patients' issues and the physicians who reflected but did not address the patients' issues. In addition, the physicians who reflected but did not address the patients' issues were not judged to be any more accepting and respectful of the patients than the physicians who totally ignored the patients' issues. This result is quite interesting, because it was expected that the act of reflecting the patient's issue (regardless of whether the physician moved on to address the issue) would be viewed as more accepting and respectful than the act of ignoring the patient's issue. The participants did not perceive this difference, however. This result seems to suggest that participants found the subsequent failure to respond to the patient's issue or concern so disrespectful that it canceled any respect gained by reflecting the patient's issue. Perhaps the participants were thinking, "That physician heard the patient's issue or concern and didn't consider it important enough to even address it." Finally, there was no synergistic interaction effect for cell 6.

In summary, saving face for the patient and addressing the patient's concerns or issues each led independently to the study participants' increased perception of the physician being accepting and respectful of the patient. This effect occurred in a very short interaction, lasting only 90–150 seconds with only one issue expressed by the patient, so you can imagine what the impact might be if such an approach were applied in a 5–10 minute interaction with a patient who expresses several major issues or concerns.

The next set of results examined the perceived medical expertise of the physicians. HCPs often worry that using MI might decrease their expertise in the eyes of their patients. The results indicated much the opposite. Physicians in the low relational resistance condition were judged to have significantly greater medical expertise than physicians in the high relational resistance condition. In other words, if you want your medical expertise to be recognized by a patient, it is best to respect and maintain the patient's face. If you create relational resistance in the patient, it is very easy for the patient to resolve that relational resistance by denying your medical expertise.

Similarly, physicians who reflected and addressed the patient's issues were judged to have greater medical knowledge than physicians who reflected the patient's issue but failed to address the issue. Physicians judged to have the least medical expertise were the physicians who ignored the patient's issue. Clearly, failing to hear and to address patient issues leads patients to discount the medical expertise of an HCP.

Finally, there was a significant synergistic effect for cell 6, representing the full implementation of MI (saving face for the patient coordinated with reflecting and addressing the patient's issues). The physicians who fully implemented MI in cell 6 were judged to have distinctly greater medical expertise than physicians only partially implementing MI or not implementing MI at all.

The most important results were for the perceived likelihood that the patient would make a behavior change. First, the participants perceived the patients in the low relational resistance condition as more likely to consider a behavior change than the patients in the high relational resistance condition. Second, the patients were judged significantly more likely to consider a behavior change when their issues were addressed than when their issues were just reflected or when their issues were ignored by the physician. Finally, there was a significant synergistic effect for cell 6, as expected. Combining low relational resistance with addressing the patient's issues produced a bonus increase in the perceived likelihood of the patient's changing behavior that occurred only for cell 6. In fact, the synergy of this MI cell was estimated to be twice as strong as the summed impact of saving face for the patient and addressing the patient's issues or concerns. Expressed in a simplified mathematical form, the impact of saving face for the patient and addressing the patient's issues—but without any synergy—would be $1 + 1 + 0 = 2$, where 0 represents synergy. With the synergy that occurs between saving face for the patient and addressing the patient's issues, the impact of MI is $1 + 1 + 4 = 6$.

This synergy can be seen clearly in Figure 4-1, which includes a dashed line estimating the likelihood of behavior change if there were no synergy associated with MI. The significant synergistic effect for cell 6 (representing the full implementation of MI) is seen in the increased slope of the line from cell 4 to cell 6. If there were just two significant independent effects (low relational resistance and addressing issue resistance) and no synergy between them, the top and bottom lines would be parallel, as represented by the dashed line from cell 4 to cell 6. Clearly, MI has an extremely large effect on the perceived likelihood of behavior change by the patient—when MI is *fully* implemented.

These results of Krishna-Pillai's dissertation study show that MI facilitates health behavior change in patients when rapport with the patient is used to engage the

FIGURE 4-1 Patient's likelihood of behavior change. (Adapted with permission from reference 19.)

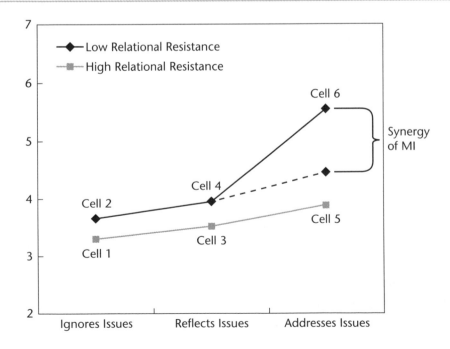

patient's process of sense making and practical reasoning. Furthermore, these results demonstrate the positive response when the patient's doubts and concerns about change are directly addressed—as long as this is done with the spirit of MI. Finally, the strong synergy marking the full implementation of MI may require addressing the major doubts and concerns that weigh against health behavior change in the minds of patients. It is possible that many of the studies that have previously found MI to be no more effective than other systematic counseling approaches may have underestimated the power of MI precisely because these studies were based on an incomplete implementation of MI that stressed eliciting change talk to the exclusion of directly addressing the patient's doubts and concerns.

The strength of Krishna-Pillai's results lies in his use of a message effects method to examine the internal structure of MI interactions by creating experimental messages representing six different combinations of addressing relational and issue resistance. Without this method it would have been extremely difficult to identify the synergy resulting from both creating rapport and addressing the patient's issues or concerns. At the same time, the primary weakness of these results comes from the fact that the perceived judgments used as the dependent variables were all based on the judgments of third-party observers who watched videotaped physician–patient interactions. It is an open question whether the strong synergy resulting from creating rapport with the patient while addressing the patient's sense making would be obtained in actual physician–patient interactions. Is there any evidence that MI can have as strong an impact on facilitating health behavior change in actual patients as it had according to the judgments of the participants in Krishna-Pillai's study?

Fortunately, there is one such clinical trial of MI in health care that supports the claim that the synergy of MI leads to an extremely large effect in facilitating positive change in actual patients. This trial was conducted and reported by Bruce Berger along with Huigang Liang and Karen Suchanek Hudmon in 2005.[22] The study used MI in telephone counseling to reduce the rate at which patients with multiple sclerosis (MS) discontinued their use of Biogen Idec's injectable interferon beta-1a product Avonex. Because the telephone counselors were dealing with one disease and one medication, a software program was created to guide the counselors in the implementation of MI skills and strategies. Instead of implementing the typical MI strategy of seeking to elicit from patients the pros of continuing the injections and avoiding discussion of the cons leading patients to consider discontinuing the injections, the software program was written to guide counselors to elicit from patients what they perceived as the most important benefits and downsides of continuing the injections. The downsides of using the drug were addressed with the spirit of MI. The MI counseling implemented by Berger, Liang, and Hudmon precisely matched the MI counseling strategy used in Krishna-Pillai's cell 6 (i.e., creating rapport with patients while addressing their issues and concerns about continuing or discontinuing use of the drug).

A focus group conducted during a pilot study had identified several issues that the MS patients were struggling with concerning Avonex. The software program was written to guide the counselors in how to address these issues without creating relational resistance. For example, some patients either feared or disliked injections. After empathizing with these patients, the counselors discussed methods for decreasing injection pain and also offered to have a nurse sent to their homes to inject the drug; then they elicited the patients' reactions. Other patients had problems with the flu-like side effects that often occur with the injections for several months until they subside, but they were unaware that these symptoms could be reduced by taking ibuprofen. Still other patients were discouraged after having experienced an exacerbation or flare-up that they were not expecting. They believed that the drug would cure their MS, rather than slow its progression and the rate and strength of the exacerbations. The problem was one of sense making, in that their expectation of experiencing no exacerbations was inaccurate. When they had an exacerbation, they believed that the drug wasn't working anymore. When the counselors first empathized with the patients' fears and concerns and then discussed with the patients how the drug reduced the frequency and severity of the MS exacerbations, the patients often adjusted their perception of the value of continuing with the injections. Thus, the MI counseling followed our concept of MI as using the rapport established with patients to leverage the impact of addressing the sense making of patients. The MI approach used in this study was optimal for producing the synergy that we have been discussing.

The results of this randomized, controlled trial were startling. Whereas 8.7% of the control group discontinued use of the drug during the three-month study, only 1.2% of the patients receiving MI counseling by phone discontinued use. This reduction is impressively larger than the effect of MI in many of the previously reported clinical trials. We believe the large reduction in discontinuation of the drug most likely reflects the synergy achieved by the full implementation of MI in this study.

# Summary

Our theoretical approach stresses that as HCPs we need to create rapport with patients so they feel safe enough with us to share and discuss the issues or concerns that keep them from making health behavior changes. We also need to create rapport to prevent loss of face. Keep in mind that patients are making sense about the relationship, too: Can I trust this HCP? Does she care about me and take my concerns seriously? Once patients have opened up to us about their issues or concerns, we need to address these issues or concerns with directly relevant information that increases the likelihood of patients' reassessing their conclusions about what they need to do. For MI to be fully implemented, rapport with the patient must be leveraged to allow the patient's practical reasoning to be challenged without any loss of face for the patient. When MI is fully implemented in this manner, the full burden of decision making is squarely on the patient's shoulders, with no convenient escape routes such as "Given the lousy way that I've been treated, there's no way that I need to listen to this HCP!" If patients are not ready at that moment to commit to change, there is a strong chance that they will continue to ponder the issues on their own. We've had much feedback from HCPs indicating that patients comment in subsequent interactions, "You know, I've been thinking a lot about what you said last time." In making such a comment, these patients are giving an indirect invitation to discuss what has caused them to think more about the conversation and what changes they think are warranted—because they trust the HCP and recognize that the HCP directly addresses their concerns and issues. They are willing to continue talking because they believe the discussion is productive.

This chapter has presented the heart of our theoretical approach to MI. The synergy of MI that occurs when the HCP creates and maintains rapport with patients while engaging and challenging their sense making and practical reasoning is exciting. In Chapter 5 we will present a broader account of sense making and practical reasoning that explains the powerful synergy occurring within MI.

## QUESTIONS FOR REFLECTION

1. Why did the authors believe that a new theory of MI was needed? What do you think of their reasoning?
2. Why is everyday talk problematic when it comes to talking with patients in health care settings? In what ways can everyday talk actually create

confusion and lack of commitment in your relationships with patients? In addition, how does HCPs' training sometimes create problems in talking with patients?

3. Discuss and distinguish between the two types of resistance you can encounter with a patient. Why is it important to recognize and respond to both kinds of resistance? What does resistance have to do with loss of face?

4. Describe and discuss the importance of practical reasoning and sense making.

5. How does the synergy created by MI come about?

## REFERENCES

1. Rollnick S, Miller WR. What is motivational interviewing? *Behav Cogn Psychother.* 1995;23:325–34. doi: 10.1017/S135246580001643X.

2. Lewin K. *Field Theory in Social Science: Selected Theoretical Papers by Kurt Lewin.* London: Tavistock; 1952:169.

3. Miller WR, Rollnick S. *Motivational Interviewing: Helping People Change.* 3rd ed. New York: Guilford Press; 2013:xxii.

4. Giuse NB, Koonce TY, Storrow AB, et al. Using health literacy and learning style preferences to optimize the delivery of health information. *J Health Commun.* 2012;17(suppl 3):122–40.

5. Watzlawick P, Beavin JH, Jackson DD. *The Pragmatics of Human Communication: A Study of Interactional Patterns, Pathologies, and Paradoxes.* New York: Norton; 1967.

6. Goffman E. *Interaction Ritual: Essays in Face-to-Face Behavior.* Chicago: Aldine; 1967.

7. Domenici K, Littlejohn SW. *Facework: Bridging Theory and Practice.* Thousand Oaks, CA: Sage; 2006.

8. Lim TS, Bowers JW. Facework: solidarity, approbation, and tact. *Hum Commun Res.* 1991;17:415–50.

9. Dillard JP, Shen L. On the nature of reactance and its role in persuasive health communication. *Commun Monogr.* 2005;72:144–68.

10. Rains SA. The nature of psychological reactance revisited: a meta-analytic review. *Hum Commun Res.* 2013;39:47–73.

11. Bisel RS, Barge JK. Discursive positioning and planned change in organizations. *Hum Relat.* 2011;64:257–83.

12. Toulmin SE. *The Uses of Argument.* Cambridge, UK: Cambridge University Press; 1958.

13. Toulmin SE. *Return to Reason.* Cambridge, MA: Harvard University Press; 2001.

14. Miller WR, Rollnick S. *Motivational Interviewing: Preparing People to Change Addictive Behavior.* New York: Guilford Press; 1991:58.

15. Rollnick S, Miller WR, Butler CC. *Motivational Interviewing in Health Care: Helping Patients Change Behavior.* New York: Guilford Press; 2008.

16. Burke BL, Arkowitz H, Menchola M. The efficacy of motivational interviewing: a meta-analysis of controlled clinical trials. *J Consult Clin Psychol.* 2003;71:843–60.

17. Hettema J, Steele J, Miller WR. Motivational interviewing. *Annu Rev Clin Psychol.* 2005;1:91–111.

18. Lundahl BW, Kunz C, Brownell C, et al. A meta-analysis of motivational interviewing: twenty-five years of empirical studies. *Res Social Work Pract*. 2010:20;137–60.

19. Krishna-Pillai A. *An Initial Validation of a Two Dimensional Theory of Motivational Interviewing* [PhD dissertation]. Auburn University, AL: Auburn University; 2012. http://etd.auburn.edu/etd/handle/10415/3057. Accessed February 4, 2013.

20. Krishna-Pillai A. *Use of Empathy by Healthcare Professionals Learning Motivational Interviewing: A Qualitative Analysis* [master's thesis]. Auburn University, AL: Auburn University; 2010. http://hdl.handle.net/10415/2112. Accessed February 4, 2013.

21. Jackson S. *Message Effects Research: Principles of Design and Analysis*. New York: Guilford Press; 1992.

22. Berger BA, Liang H, Hudmon KS. Evaluation of software-based telephone counseling to enhance medication persistency among patients with multiple sclerosis. *J Am Pharm Assoc*. 2005;45:466–72.

# CHAPTER 5

# Understanding Sense Making and Practical Reasoning

I n Chapter 4 we described the journey that led us to our own conceptualization of what happens in motivational interviewing (MI) and why MI is so effective in increasing the likelihood of constructive health behavior change by patients. We stressed two ideas that go beyond the traditional formulation of MI:

1. Health care professionals (HCPs) must use the spirit of MI not only to elicit the benefits of health behavior change from the patient but also to address the doubts, worries, concerns, and issues that arise as the patient attempts to make sense of the need for health behavior change.
2. MI achieves optimal power through a synergy that occurs when rapport with the patient is used to lovingly address the doubts, worries, concerns, and issues arising within the patient.

At the end of Chapter 4, we supported these claims by discussing two of our own studies that document the synergy of MI.

In this chapter we will move beyond our own research to expand the range of support for our approach to MI by reviewing

1. Sense making and practical reasoning,
2. A profound information revolution that is reformulating how information must be expressed and shared to help people achieve their practical goals, and
3. Specific theories that explain important features of our approach to MI (such as the synergy of MI).

Our goal is not to provide an academic review of the literature. Rather, we want to highlight how the central features of our approach to MI are shared across many diverse disciplines. In doing so, we will simplify and homogenize the vocabulary of these disciplines to express the crucial insights shared by these disciplines and to show how these insights affect the practice of MI.

## Sense making and practical reasoning

Our approach to MI stresses the centrality of addressing the sense making of the patient in an appropriate and timely fashion so as to optimize the likelihood that the patient will decide to implement constructive health behavior change. There are two main ways of explaining how this task can be accomplished.

The first employs theories such as balance theory,[1] cognitive consistency theory,[2] and dissonance theory.[3] These theories argue that people, in the course of their sense making, manage complex webs or networks of information, feelings, goals, and behaviors. Furthermore, there is a built-in preference for maintaining harmony, balance, consistency, and order within these webs or networks. The minute that these networks start to exhibit discrepancy, imbalance, or dissonance, people are motivated to restore balance, harmony, and consonance. The experience of discrepancy, imbalance, or dissonance feels bad to people and consequently provides motivation for them to restore the balance, harmony, or consonance that feels good. The problem with such an approach is that there are a number of options for restoring balance, harmony, and consonance, and health behavior change is only one of these options. The other options lead in less constructive directions, such as creating an exception for the present situation or discounting the importance of some elements in the discrepancy.

Thus, patients may find it quite possible to restore consistency and balance to their network of sense making while avoiding the need for health behavior change. If a patient perceives an experience with an HCP as threatening, one way for the patient to restore balance is to simply discredit or blame the HCP: "Why should I listen to that horse's rear end?"

One of the classic READS skills presented by Miller and Rollnick[4] is developing discrepancy. This skill is based on the assumptions of dissonance theory.[3] In the course of exploring the patient's ambivalence or resistance to health behavior change, the MI practitioner needs to listen for aspects of the patient's sense making that are discrepant or contradictory. Sometimes the patient may not be aware of this discrepancy. By formulating the discrepancy as a reflection of what the patient has already expressed, the MI practitioner can help trigger motivating power within the patient to reduce this discrepancy. In MI this is usually formulated as a discrepancy between the patient's current behaviors and the patient's goals for the future. What is notable about this particular goal–behavior discrepancy is that it "tilts" or predisposes patients toward changing current health behaviors to achieve future goals, rather than toward reducing their future goals to allow the continuation of current behaviors. This predisposition toward health behavior change is especially strong if the patient's goals for the future have already been discussed and reinforced in a vividly personal way. Similar practical reasoning is created by a discrepancy drawn between the patient's values and the patient's current behaviors. The patient must figure out what needs to be done to maintain and implement the patient's values.

Let's look at a brief example to review how developing discrepancy works. A patient with high blood pressure has a goal of reducing his blood pressure so that he won't have a stroke or heart attack. Ultimately, the patient wants to see his daughter marry and have children. However, despite this goal, the patient skips doses of his medication and smokes. Consequently, his blood pressure remains very high, putting him at even greater risk for stroke or heart attack. A discrepancy exists between the patient's goal of seeing his daughter marry and have children and his current behavior. A caring MI practitioner would lovingly point out this discrepancy by stating, "On the one hand, you have an important goal of reducing your risk of stroke or heart attack so you can see your daughter get married and have children. I can see your eyes light up when you talk about having grandchildren someday. On the other hand, skipping doses of your medicine and smoking have significantly elevated your blood pressure and put you at much greater risk of stroke or heart attack, which could interfere with your goal. What are your thoughts?" Because the HCP has identified and expressed this discrepancy, the patient must now figure out what he wants to do.

Developing a discrepancy between a patient's goals for the future and the patient's current behaviors can be very motivating for patients who can clearly identify their future goals. It works well because patients are accustomed to figuring out what needs to be done to achieve their goals. The MI skill of developing discrepancy sets up patients to reason their way from their goals to the steps needed to achieve those goals. Thus, developing discrepancy triggers patients' practical reasoning.

The second option for addressing patients' sense-making processes is based on recognizing right from the beginning that sense making occurs in the form of practical reasoning, as discussed in Chapter 4. Patients start with what they know about their disease, its consequences, and its treatment and then combine this knowledge with the limitations, preferences, and values at the heart of their everyday life to conclude what they need to do, are willing to do, are ready to do, and are confident they can do. Miller and Rollnick implicitly recognized that patients are involved in such a process of reasoning when they contended that patients must voice their own reasons for change.[5] At the same time, however, Miller and Rollnick explicated "avoiding argumentation" as another of the basic READS skills.[6] Here, we need to discuss the difference between making an argument and having an argument.[6,7] Making an argument is the process of putting together a line of reasoning that carries a certain logical force in its conclusion. This is the sense in which Miller and Rollnick used the word "argument" when they contended that the patient must formulate the argument for change.[8] It is better for the patient to draw the conclusion that health behavior change is needed than for the HCP to impose the conclusion on the patient and thereby cause the patient to lose both competence face and autonomy face. The patient's loss of face when the HCP makes the argument for why the patient needs to change will cause relational resistance in the patient and will more than likely cause the patient and the HCP to argue with each other. This sense of argument as interpersonal conflict was what Miller and Rollnick meant when they formulated the READS skill of avoiding argumentation. The HCP practicing MI seeks to facilitate the process of patients' formulating arguments for why they need to change, at the same time not arguing with patients. To resolve any ambiguity about the term "argue," we will refer to a logical argument leading to a conclusion as a "line of reasoning" (technically called a "syllogism" in formal logic and argumentation theory). Therefore, using our terminology, MI seeks to avoid imposing our own lines of reasoning on the patient because that leads to arguing with the patient and increasing the patient's resistance. Instead, MI seeks to explore the patient's lines of reasoning and then to address those lines of reasoning with relevant and appropriate information that invites the patient to draw new conclusions.

In Chapter 4 we illustrated this process of addressing the line of reasoning that undergirds the patient's issue resistance. We will elaborate on the specifics of how to address the patient's line of reasoning in a later chapter. Here, though, we would like to make two additional points about the process of practical reasoning. First, patients seldom express their lines of reasoning in a complete and specific form. Rarely will patients say, "If I had a serious illness, I would be experiencing serious symptoms. But I feel fine. Therefore I don't have a serious illness." Instead, they will remark, "Well, you know, I feel just fine." Second, patients often have several related lines of reasoning that jointly lead to the conclusion that health behavior change is not needed. What often happens then is that patients will combine these two lines of reasoning in one utterance that is loaded with sense making and practical reasoning, as in this example:

HCP: How are you doing with taking your cholesterol medication?

Pt: *Well, I forget to take it fairly often. Uh, actually I feel fine. And I'm really worried about its side effects.*

Such an utterance poses a major challenge for the HCP. It is tempting to hear the first issue expressed as the "chief complaint" or core concern. If the HCP focuses on this to the exclusion of the other issues, the HCP may miss the heart of the patient's practical reasoning. Suppose the HCP in this case were to respond,

HCP: Well, let's talk about some ways to remind you to take your medicine.

Such a response forces the patient to talk about the issue chosen by the HCP and ignores the other two issues expressed by the patient. There is not a lot of relational coordination expressed in this response, even though discussing ways to remember to take medication on time may eventually become relevant and informative for the patient. Suppose the HCP were to respond,

HCP: So, it's difficult to take your medicine as prescribed because you forget to take it fairly often, you feel fine, and you're worried about potential side effects. Which of these would you like to talk about first?

This response is a definite improvement, because it reflects back all three lines of reasoning and lets the patient choose which one to discuss first. Such a response gives explicit evidence that the HCP is listening attentively to the patient's sense making and wants to address the patient's concerns. The relational and informational coordination is on a deeper level that the patient can sense and appreciate.

Now suppose the HCP were to respond,

> HCP: So, it's difficult to remember to take your medicine as prescribed because you are really wondering whether you need to take this medication at all, given that you feel just fine. And on top of that you are worried about potential side effects of taking the medication.

This response exhibits even greater relational and informational coordination with the patient, because it not only reflects all three issues but also senses how these issues are related to each other. Even though the patient put forgetting to take the medicine in first place, the HCP caught the implication that it's easier to forget to take the medicine because of the two deeper issues. This is an example of what Miller and Rollnick refer to as reflection that "continues the paragraph."[9] Through such reflection, the HCP gives explicit evidence of deeply understanding and valuing the patient's sense making. The patient is likely to think, "This HCP really gets me!"

Suppose the patient responds in the affirmative: "Yes, you got it." The next response by the HCP can further increase the sense of relational and informational coordination:

> HCP: Would you mind if we first discuss some information relevant to your question of whether you really need this medication, given that you feel fine? It's a great question, and its answer may have an impact on how you feel about the other two issues of side effects and forgetting.

This response is an example of the HCP providing guidance and direction to the patient by responding to the interconnectedness of the patient's sense making and practical reasoning. The ease and appropriateness with which the HCP is handling the relational flow in the interaction predisposes the patient to anticipate the relevance and appropriateness of the information the HCP is about to share.

# The synergy of MI

When the patient discusses the prospect of health behavior change with an HCP, the patient is involved in two interconnected sense-making processes: making sense of the relationship with the HCP, and making sense of the health issues being discussed. In Chapter 4 we described the strong synergy in MI that occurs only when the HCP uses the spirit of MI to create rapport with the patient, which then adds to the impact of addressing the patient's issues. Now, to present our concept of why this synergy appears to be so strong, we will briefly explore three complementary explanations.

The first explanation for the synergy of MI focuses on the sense making of the patient. When the HCP provides information to address the patient's issues and practical reasoning (i.e., the HCP "throws a wrench into the works"), the patient is faced with making sense of "Why did this HCP give me this information at this time?" Attribution theory[10] has established that answering this question is crucial to how the patient will respond to the information provided. Regardless of whether the information directly addresses the patient's issues, the patient will be likely to dismiss or discount it if the patient attributes the provision of information to reasons such as the following:

- "The HCP is just going through the steps."
- "The HCP is giving me the standard lecture."
- "The HCP is running his own agenda."
- "The HCP is putting me down."
- "The HCP is blaming me."

Any negative attribution for what the HCP is really doing by providing the information offers a "back door" or "escape hatch" that allows the patient to avoid having to process the import of the information. The only set of attributions that fully supports the importance of attending to and processing the information is the following:

- "The HCP really cares about me."
- "The HCP really understands the issues and concerns I am struggling with."
- "The HCP has provided information that directly addresses my issues and concerns."

Taken together, these attributions optimize the likelihood that the patient will engage with the information provided and will thereby at least consider the need to draw new conclusions.

This explanation may help to account for why many studies of the effectiveness of MI in health care have found MI to be as effective as but no more effective than other systematic approaches to patient counseling.[11-13] When the HCP seeks to elicit change talk and to avoid sustain talk, the patient is left uncertain about whether the HCP really understands and appreciates the questions, doubts, issues, and concerns that weigh against health behavior change in the patient's mind. Dervin points out that when people are struggling with gaps or uncertainties in their sense making, there is a mandate in that "sense-making instance" for the issues to be addressed in a timely and relevant manner.[14] She further stresses that at such moments people expect information that addresses the gaps in their current sense making. An HCP's failure to provide such information leads patients to wonder how helpful the HCP is trying to be and what the HCP is really doing. Remember that Krishna-Pillai reported in his dissertation[15] that the participants did not seem to attribute any greater likelihood of behavior change to the HCP's reflecting back the patient's issues and concerns without directly addressing those issues than to the HCP's simply ignoring the patient's issues. The data suggested that the participants expected that if HCPs had recognized and reflected back the patient's issues, those issues would be addressed. Thus, MI may not achieve optimal effectiveness if the patient's issues and concerns are not directly addressed, even if the patient realizes that the HCP understands those issues and concerns.

The second explanation for the synergy of MI derives from expectancy violation theory,[16] which asserts that any time another person's behavior departs from or violates your expectation of their behavior, your reaction is amplified because of a state of arousal triggered by the expectancy violation. So, if a patient were expecting an HCP to be impersonal, distant, and controlling, the patient would experience a positive expectancy violation when the HCP exhibited the spirit of MI by being caring, respectful, and responsive. HCPs have shared with us numerous accounts of how patients have responded with looks of surprise when the HCP used MI to empathize with the frustration of the patient and then followed with a question such as "How can I help to make this frustrating situation easier to deal with?" The positive impact of MI is amplified precisely because the spirit of MI contrasts so starkly with the judgmental and parental tone most patients expect.

There is another point at which expectancy violation theory comes into play. Earlier in this chapter we observed how the smoothness and responsiveness of the relational flow between the HCP and the patient may lead the patient to anticipate a similar smoothness and responsiveness in the information flow addressing the patient's issues and concerns. In this sense, there is an expectation, triggered by the use of the MI spirit, that the HCP should address the issues and concerns the HCP has reflected back to the patient. If the HCP does not address these issues and concerns by providing relevant and appropriate information that is helpful to the patient, a negative expectancy violation has occurred. The patient's frustration will be amplified by the arousal involved in the expectancy violation, and any positive impact of reflecting back the patient's issues and concerns will be reduced. Such an expectancy violation through failure to respond directly to the patient's issues and concerns may also help explain why many studies of MI have reported what we consider to be less than optimal impact on health behavior change.

The third and final explanation for the strong synergy of MI derives from the sense of "jointness" or "connectedness" and "wholeness" that marks the smooth implementation of MI. Just as improvisation for jazz musicians is a joint achievement that belongs more to the jam session as a whole than to individual musicians, so too the sense making and decision making that occur within MI are a joint achievement of the patient and the HCP. Even if the patient is not quite ready to implement health behavior change right now, there is a sense that something significant has happened that is bigger than the patient alone. The jointness and the authenticity of the MI experience call patients beyond themselves to take care of their health with the same degree of caring and wisdom they experienced during MI. The patient's calm remembrance of talking with the HCP and feeling accepted and guided is in stark contrast to worried anticipation of being "chewed out" by the HCP during the next appointment. For the patient, this sense of connection makes the difference between wanting to do something that flows out of the sharing that occurred during MI and feeling forced to do something to avoid shame and blame. The contrast is between an experience of change that happens within supportive community and an experience of change that occurs in worried or resentful isolation. Remembering an MI experience calls patients to care for themselves well beyond the end of that particular interaction.

We are proposing that the synergy of MI results from building rapport with patients *and* addressing the issues of the patients in a way that "throws a loving wrench" into their sense making so that they reformulate it. In effect, then, there are three fundamental ways in which the HCP can fall short of achieving the synergy that optimizes the power of MI. Each of the three undermines the possibilities of constructive health behavior change by the patient.

**Building rapport without addressing the issue.** There are two ways that this can be problematic, depending on the nature of the issue involved. If patients have expressed a mistaken or inaccurate belief that may prevent them from achieving their goals or may harm them, it is incumbent upon the HCP to share the correct information with them. Sometimes the HCP can focus so much on building rapport and supporting patients' sense making that the HCP avoids addressing patients' mistaken beliefs. Consider this situation.

> Pt: *Yeah, I plan to quit smoking when I get pregnant. My husband and I are trying to have a baby. We are so excited! When I get pregnant, I will definitely quit.*
>
> HCP: That is exciting news about getting pregnant. I'm glad to hear about your desire to quit once you are pregnant. Sounds like you want to do whatever you can to have a healthy baby.
>
> Pt: *Oh, definitely!*
>
> HCP: Great. Let me know when you get pregnant so we can get you prenatal care.
>
> Pt: *Will do!*

In this example, there is little doubt that the patient will find the HCP to be very supportive initially. The patient has not experienced any face loss or relational resistance. However, the patient's line of reasoning ("I'll quit smoking once I get pregnant") is potentially problematic for her and her unborn child. There are significant risks involved in continuing to smoke until she finds out that she is pregnant. She might not even find out she is pregnant until a month or two after conception. By the time she is able to quit smoking and free her system of nicotine, carbon monoxide, and other toxic substances, the pregnancy may be approaching the second trimester. The baby may have already suffered harm that the patient clearly wants to avoid. Also, the patient seems unaware that it may be more difficult to conceive if she smokes. The

HCP needs to present accurate information for the patient's consideration. It would be unethical not to do so.

Here is a second example of building rapport without addressing the patient's issue. In this case, the patient actually wants the HCP to address her sense making:

> Pt: *I'm taking the medicine the way you prescribed it, every day. I just think I should be doing even more, like exercising or losing weight.*
>
> HCP: You are doing a great job with your diabetes. You are to be commended for that. Now you're thinking that you want to do even more.
>
> Pt: *Thank you. I am really trying. Yes, I do think I should do more than just take the medicine.*
>
> HCP: I know you really are trying. That is obvious. Your blood sugar has come down quite a bit.
>
> Pt: *Right. So, it's come down but it's not all the way there yet.*
>
> HCP: It really has come down thanks to your efforts. I'm confident that it will come down even further. Let's see where it is the next time you come in.
>
> Pt: (reluctantly) *OK, doctor.*

In this example, the HCP was very supportive of the patient's efforts to manage her diabetes by taking her medication. The patient's sense was that she should be doing more, especially since her blood sugar was not yet where she wanted it to be. Although the HCP reflected back the patient's desire to be doing more than just taking medication, the HCP ignored the patient's desire for his input, and she gave up. She left feeling dissatisfied because her primary concern was not addressed. Why the HCP was unwilling to address her desire to do more to manage her diabetes is not clear. One reason might be that although the HCP was being very supportive of her efforts on a personal level, he still may have been running his own agenda based on his experience with similar patients. He may have decided it is unwise to ask patients to do more than take medication until it is quite clear that the medication will not achieve the desired degree of blood sugar reduction. After reflecting back the patient's desire to do more to reduce her blood sugar, MI practitioners would "walk through the open door" to discuss additional steps the patient could take. MI practitioners would put the decision about what needs to be done next in the patient's hands. If the HCP had any concerns about the exercise and weight loss mentioned by the patient, the HCP would express these concerns and ask for the patient's thoughts.

**Addressing the issues or sense making without building rapport.** Rapport gives the HCP the leverage to address the sense making of the patient without causing loss of face. Even if the HCP provides information that directly addresses the sense making issue of the patient, loss of face may cause the patient to discount or ignore that information. Here is an example:

> Pt: *I take the medicine and I've already cut down on carbs. That's more than enough.*

> HCP: Actually, it's not enough, since your blood sugar is still well above 100. You need to bring it down below 100 if you want to lower your risk of serious complications.

> Pt: *Don't count on it.*

In this example the HCP gave accurate and relevant information that directly addressed the patient's issue. However, because there was no attempt to understand or empathize with the patient's position, the message caused the patient to lose face and to dig in even more. This approach has very little chance at achieving the optimal impact of MI, unless the HCP builds rapport with the patient and works to set up a relational basis that allows the patient to hear and accept the personal relevance of this information.

**Failing both to build rapport and to address the issue.** This, of course, is the worst situation in regard to increasing motivation for change. Here is an example:

> Pt: *My cholesterol is not that high. There are plenty of other people whose cholesterol is much higher than mine.*

> HCP: Although I appreciate that, the fact is that you all need to reduce your cholesterol. I'm quite serious about this.

> Pt: *So am I.*

In this example, although the HCP said he appreciated the patient's thought, he did not reflect it enough to address it in any significant way. The HCP simply reiterated his judgment about what needed to be done and attempted to push the patient into taking steps to lower his cholesterol. The patient's concern was still not addressed, and the patient dug in further. Even though the tone of the interaction was polite, there was extensive face loss for the patient. In the end, the relational resistance and the issue resistance were not addressed by the HCP.

## Sense making and the information revolution

We have proposed that HCPs must respect and address the sense making and practical reasoning of the patient if we are to increase the probability that the patient will consider health behavior change. We also propose that the information age we live in has dramatically changed the landscape and the rules of engagement between HCPs and patients. The advent of the digital age profoundly increased the amount of information available to the average person. A simple search of the Internet from a computer, tablet, or smartphone allows most of us to access huge bodies of information about the world. Social media such as blogs, Facebook, and Twitter allow us to join in virtual communities of people making joint sense of this information and sharing perspectives on practical decision making. In effect, the availability of huge amounts of information that may be processed jointly in virtual communities invites people to engage more actively in making sense of their own problems and situations. Information management and dissemination is no longer the sole province of the expert. The digital age has spread expertise beyond the expert.

This digital revolution has had a major impact within health care. No longer are HCPs the sole source of information about diabetes, hypertension, atherosclerosis, and other conditions. Once diagnosed with a disease, many patients will immerse themselves in searching the Internet to make sense of what is happening to them. Some patients will access summary articles from reputable sources such as the National Institutes of Health or the Food and Drug Administration, but patients can just as easily access biased (and perhaps even disreputable) sources designed to sell alternative therapies not prescribed by their physicians. Some may even go to PubMed or Medline for the primary medical literature on their diseases and the therapies prescribed for them. Others may do what people have traditionally done for years, and ask their friends or just make sense of things without any additional insight.

Regardless of their approach, many patients engage in active sense making that is manifested as questions, doubts, concerns, and issues expressed to their HCPs. Unfortunately, it is tempting for HCPs to cling to a "privileged" concept of expertise that discounts and denies the sense-making activities of their patients. In doing so, HCPs cause patients to lose both competence face and autonomy face, thereby triggering relational resistance in the patient. We advocate MI as the exchange of expertise between HCPs and patients. The idea that both HCPs and patients have expertise affirms that both HCPs and patients are involved in sense making. MI achieves its power, then, by focusing the sense making of the HCP on facilitating the patient's sense making.

The essential problem runs deeper than this, however. Many scholars and practitioners have concluded that the nature of informing or information has to be reconceptualized from "the objective expression of static, permanent products such as facts" to "the joint process of making sense of a shared situation." For example, Dervin[17] has developed this idea into a theory, called sense-making methodology, that distinguishes between information as a noun and informing as a verb. This distinction may seem rather abstract, but it turns out to have profound practical consequences for endeavors ranging from making instructional signs[18] to programming computer databases and their associated search engines[14] to assisting library patrons in finding information.[14]

Dervin's work highlights human sense making as a response to perceived gaps or uncertainties in the continuity of personal experience. People engage in sense making to bridge these gaps and thereby maintain continuity and coherence of their experience. For example, gaps or uncertainties are likely in the experience of having a newly diagnosed illness. A patient newly diagnosed with diabetes may struggle with gaps of knowledge ("What the heck is diabetes?") or gaps of expectation ("What's going to happen to me?") or gaps of action ("What do I need to do now?"). Some patients will bridge these gaps with openness to assimilating new information and engaging in new behaviors, while others will work at minimizing or even denying these gaps. All patients engage in sense making, regardless of whether HCPs are aware of these sense-making processes.

According to Dervin, these gaps in the patient's experience cannot be effectively addressed by the simple recitation of medical facts. For example, a standard lecture or "data dump" about diabetes cannot be relied on as a universal response to all questions about diabetes. The facts about diabetes were formulated to answer clinical and scientific questions within medicine and science. A recitation of such facts is appropriate and effective only if the patient has asked clinically and scientifically formulated questions, which is rarely the case. Dervin has expressed it this way:

> To think that effectiveness is embodied in information/knowledge rests on the idea that it can transfer from person to person ... without interrogation and interpretation. But life and work are not like that: there are no old situations: a marketing problem is not the same today; a customer yesterday may well be different today.[14]

Dervin concludes that effective "informing" must be thoroughly immersed in exploring, understanding, and responding to the sense-making gaps foremost in the patient's experience. There must be a joint process of sense making that starts within the patient's experiential world and responds directly to the experiential gaps or issues the patient is dealing with. Information and knowledge must be refocused, modified, and simplified to address the sense-making issues of the patient. Facts merely recited at the patient do not become informative for the patient. Facts become informative only when they are molded to fit patients' issues and are used by the patients to make sense of their situation. Moreover, as discussed previously, the HCP presenting these facts cannot be seen as threatening or adversarial.

Let's consider the case of HCPs who are obese or who smoke or who have chronically elevated blood sugar levels. If medical information were enough, it would be difficult to explain why an HCP would experience any of these problems. HCPs understand the clinical risks of remaining obese, continuing to smoke, and failing to control blood sugar levels. They understand these medical facts. Having another HCP reiterate these medical facts to them does not provide any additional information, and it risks creating relational resistance because of the implied shame involved. These HCPs do not have gaps in their medical knowledge. Their interpretive gaps and uncertainties lie elsewhere in how they are making sense of their lives. For example, they may have short-circuited the impact of what they know medically by avoiding the question of what would happen to their lives and their loved ones if they suffered lung cancer, heart attack, stroke, neuropathy, or renal dysfunction. They may have separated the medical facts from their personal lives. What would be truly informative for them might be helping them probe the risks and consequences on a personal level. Alternatively, they may fully appreciate the importance of reducing the risks and consequences they face, but they may have no confidence that they can accomplish the changes they know are needed. What would be truly informative for them might be sharing a range of strategies that have succeeded for other patients who had stressful and demanding lives and asking which of these strategies they think might work for them. As MI practitioners, we must adapt to how patients are making sense of their lives and to the specific issues with which they are struggling.

This new approach to information is driving the widespread call for reforming a whole host of social systems that are based on sharing information with the end user. Educators have called for learner-centered education.[19] Computer system and web designers have called for user-centered interfaces.[20] Managers and librarians have called for user-centered information systems.[21] We, of course, call for patient-centered health care.

According to Dervin, the process of sense making also involves "sense unmaking."[14] Patients may not be able to make sense of new health situations unless they let go of or reformulate central aspects of their previous sense making. Such sense unmaking is crucial if patients are to engage in steps that are likely to achieve their goals for the future. In essence, we argue for sense unmaking when we advocate that MI practitioners not only elicit positive reasons for health behavior change but also address the negative reasons weighing against change in the patient's mind.

Let's look at a concrete example. During the 1980s and 1990s numerous studies examined the common-sense representations or schemas of illnesses that people construct over time, usually based on their experience with short-term minor illnesses such as colds, sore throat, sinus infections, or skin rashes.[22,23] On the basis of these common-sense conceptions of illness, patients often believe they do not need to take any action until they start to feel some symptoms. And they often assume that the treatment required at that point will be relatively minor and will eliminate or cure the root problem. Such a concept of illness makes little sense when applied to a chronic disease such as hypertension or diabetes. Patients will hint at this sense-making gap by saying, "Gosh, I don't know about all this stuff. I feel fine" or "The doctor told me my blood pressure is down. Why do I need to keep taking the medicine?" Often what they mean is that they have trouble identifying with having a serious illness because they have not experienced any serious symptoms. Consequently, they don't see a need to do anything. For such patients to even consider health behavior change, they must "unmake" their sense that all illnesses have perceivable symptoms that tell the patient it is time to do something about the illness. Helping a patient to accomplish such sense unmaking involves avoiding face loss for the patient, reflecting back the patient's sense-making problem, and finally sharing new information that the patient recognizes as informative. Saying "Well, just because you feel fine doesn't mean you are fine" does not allow the patient to feel the relevance, responsiveness, and appropriateness of this information—even though it directly answers the patient's interpretive problem. Considerable interpersonal work is needed to set up the situation so patients can hear the corrective information as informative to their sense making.

A final aspect of the information revolution that we will discuss involves the integration of sense making and taking action. Previously, sense making and taking action were regarded as entirely separate processes that needed to be explicitly connected at one moment in time by a separate decision-making component. Research from a variety of radically different perspectives has suggested the inadequacy of this approach in accounting for social interaction and even for human–machine interaction. For example, a humanist form of research, known as phenomenology, has demonstrated that it is through the progression of social interaction that sense making and decision making are coordinated and enacted. To illustrate, the ability of jazz musicians to "jam" with each other involves mutual sense making and coordination that leads to improvisation that goes beyond any one individual. The sense making and decision making are more a property of the whole jam session than of separate individuals. Cognitive scientists and computer engineers have found that this perspective solves major problems involved in allowing computers to interact more naturally with human users.[24,25] Essentially, they have realized that the responsiveness of the interaction cannot be separated from the responsiveness of the information provided through that interaction. Computers that force users to conform to rigid predetermined sequences of actions required by the logic of the computing machinery are regarded quite differently by human users than are computers that seem to sense on a move-by-move basis why the user wants certain information and what that information will enable the user to do. The flow of the information is enabled and validated by the flow of the interaction.

So how does this realization apply to MI? Let's go back to the sense making exhibited by the patient with hypertension who says, "Gosh, I don't know about all this stuff. I feel fine." As we have indicated in previous chapters, we would recommend responding as follows:

HCP: You're really wondering just how bad your blood pressure is and whether all these steps are really necessary, because you feel just fine.

Pt:     *Yeah, that's it. I feel fine.*

HCP:   That's a great question. Would you mind if I share some information with you to address your question and then you tell me your thoughts about this information?

Pt:     *Yeah, that would be fine.*

Reflecting back the sense-making issue with appropriate emotion, requesting permission to share relevant information with the patient, and indicating a desire to hear the patient's response create a smooth and responsive interaction that sets up a jointly enacted process of sense making—as long as the information eventually shared with the patient precisely fits the patient's sense-making issue. We will discuss these steps in detail in later chapters. For now, the important point is that the appropriateness and responsiveness of the interaction cannot be separated from the appropriateness and responsiveness of the information. The interaction flow and the information flow are vitally interconnected and mutually reinforcing. When the HCP shares information about asymptomatic illness with the patient in the example above, the patient is likely to find this information to be truly informative because the interaction leading up to this was respectful and compassionate.

Medical information must address the sense-making activities of patients as they attempt to understand and adapt to new health situations. Otherwise, the information HCPs express may fail to appear informative to the patient and will fall short of enabling the patient to make constructive health behavior choices. MI is a prime relational method for offering information that challenges patients to update and improve the way they make sense of their health and the choices they face. The spirit of MI leads the HCP to respect the patient's sense making and to mold information to fit the patient's sense-making issues. MI has optimal impact when patients experience easygoing relational and informational synchrony with the HCP that invites them to reconsider what they need to do.

## Summary

In this chapter we have presented the basis for our theory or conceptualization of how MI achieves its optimal impact. We are sense-making creatures. Our patients make sense of both their health issues *and* how we respond to them about these issues. MI achieves a synergistic effect because the spirit of MI and rapport building inform the patients' sense making that we care about them and take their concerns, issues, and lines of reasoning about their health seriously. This rapport gives us the necessary leverage to use our expertise to address patients' sense making about their health so that they can reconsider their lines of reasoning and formulate new ways to make sense of their health. The synergy created by the use of MI is the result of care and concern for patients, addressing patients' issues in ways that are uniquely meaningful to the patient, and a sense of community and connectedness between two human beings.

## QUESTIONS FOR REFLECTION

1. What is the relationship between sense making and practical reasoning?
2. What is the difference between having an argument and making an argument? How does a line of reasoning fit into making an argument?
3. Patients make sense of both (a) their illness and its treatment and (b) their relationship with their HCP. How are these two kinds of sense making connected to each other? How does one affect the other?
4. At its synergistic best, MI involves building rapport with the patient *and* addressing the patient's issues. Why are both necessary?
5. How has the information revolution affected both the sense making of the patient and the relationship between the patient and the HCP?

## REFERENCES

1. Heider F. *The Psychology of Interpersonal Relations.* New York: John Wiley & Sons; 1958.
2. Markus H, Zajonc RB. The cognitive perspective in social psychology. In: Lindzey G, Aronson E, eds. *Handbook of Social Psychology.* 3rd ed. New York: Random House; 1985:137–230.
3. Festinger L. *A Theory of Cognitive Dissonance.* Stanford, CA: Stanford University Press; 1957.
4. Miller WR, Rollnick S. *Motivational Interviewing: Preparing People to Change Addictive Behavior.* New York: Guilford Press; 1991:56–8.
5. Miller WR, Rollnick S. *Motivational Interviewing: Helping People Change.* 3rd ed. New York: Guilford Press; 2013:8.
6. O'Keefe DJ. Two concepts of argument. *J Am Forensic Assoc.* 1977;13:121–8.
7. Jacobs S, Jackson S. Argument as a natural category: the routine grounds for arguing in conversation. *West J Speech Commun.* 1981;45:118–32.
8. Miller WR, Rollnick S. *Motivational Interviewing: Preparing People to Change Addictive Behavior.* New York: Guilford Press; 1991:58–9.

9. Miller WR, Rollnick S. *Motivational Interviewing: Helping People Change.* 3rd ed. New York: Guilford Press; 2013:54.

10. Jones EE, Kanhouse DE, Kelley HH, et al. *Attribution: Perceiving the Causes of Behavior.* Morristown, NJ: General Learning Press; 1972.

11. Burke BL, Arkowitz H, Menchola M. The efficacy of motivational interviewing: a meta-analysis of controlled clinical trials. *J Consult Clin Psychol.* 2003;71:843–60.

12. Hettema J, Steele J, Miller WR. Motivational interviewing. *Annu Rev Clin Psychol.* 2005;1:91–111.

13. Lundahl BW, Kunz C, Brownell C, et al. A meta-analysis of motivational interviewing: twenty-five years of empirical studies. *Res Social Work Pract.* 2010:20;137–60.

14. Dervin B. Sense-making theory and practice: an overview of user interests in knowledge seeking and use. *J Knowl Manage.* 1998;2:36–46.

15. Krishna-Pillai A. *An Initial Validation of a Two Dimensional Theory of Motivational Interviewing.* [PhD dissertation]. Auburn University, AL: Auburn University; 2012. http://etd.auburn.edu/etd/handle/10415/3057. Accessed February 4, 2013.

16. Burgoon J. Interpersonal expectations, expectancy violations, and emotional communication. *J Lang Soc Psychol.* 1993;12:30–48.

17. Dervin B, Foreman-Wernet L. *Sense-making Methodology Reader: Selected Writings of Brenda Dervin.* Cresskill, NJ: Hampton Press; 2003.

18. Werner CM, Rhodes MU, Partain KK. Designing effective instructional signs with schema theory: case studies of polystyrene recycling. *Environ Behav.* 1998;30:709–35.

19. Norman DA, Spohrer JC. Learner-centered education. *Commun ACM.* 1996;39:24–49.

20. Wood LE. *User Interface Design: Bridging the Gap from User Requirements to Design.* New York: CRC Press, 1998.

21. Dervin B. From the mind's eye of the user: the sense-making qualitative–quantitative methodology. In: Glazier JD, Powell RR, eds. *Qualitative Research in Information Management.* Englewood, CO: Libraries Unlimited; 1992:61–84.

22. Bishop GD, Converse SA. Illness representations: a prototype approach. *Health Psychol.* 1986;9:95–114.

23. Skelton JA, Croyle RJ, eds. *The Mental Representation of Health and Illness: Models and Applications.* New York: Springer-Verlag; 1991.

24. Stewart JR, Gapenne O, Di Paola EA. *Enaction: Toward a New Paradigm for Cognitive Science.* Boston: MIT Press; 2010.

25. Fuchs T, De Jaegher H. Enactive intersubjectivity: participatory sense-making and mutual incorporation. *Phenom Cogn Sci.* 2009;8:465–86. doi 10.1007/s11097-009-9136-4.

# CHAPTER 6

# Developing Rapport

We have learned that for motivation for change to occur, patients must believe the change is important to them and must feel confident they can carry out the change. We have proposed that motivational interviewing (MI) creates a synergistic response by building rapport and addressing the patient's issues in a respectful manner. The following steps are involved:

1. *Develop rapport.* This involves explicitly reflecting your understanding of the patient's understanding and issues in a compassionate and non-judgmental manner and listening for whether there is a lack of motivation due to low importance or lack of confidence or both.

2. *Reframe.* Reframing allows the health care professional (HCP) to clarify an issue or shine a new light on an issue so that the patient may see it differently or make sense of it differently. Much like reframing a painting, using reframing in communicating with a patient may allow a patient to see the painting (the issue) differently, especially when there is resistance to or ambivalence about change. Reframing may allow patients to see aspects of the painting that the previous frame obscured or de-emphasized.

3. *Ask permission to provide information to address the patient's sense making.* Asking permission provides a transition to offering new information to "throw a wrench" into the patient's sense making.

4. *Provide new information.* This information must specifically address patients' current sense making and lead patients to reconsider how they are making sense of the current situation.

5. *Ask patients what they think of the new information.* After providing new information, assess what patients think. Where does the new information leave them now in regard to change? By asking this question, you gain information about what the next steps need to be or what additional information the patient might need to reconsider.

6. *Summarize and discuss next steps.* On the basis of how the patient responds to the new information, summarize your understanding of where things stand so far. If the new information causes patients to change their sense making and be more committed to change, reflect or affirm these changes in sense making and then discuss what the patient would like to do next.

This is all part of the exchange of expertise we have discussed—the dance of MI. Keep in mind that these steps are not a rigid set of rules. They are simply meant to be a guide to the process.

In building rapport, it is important to start by asking patients, especially those with a newly diagnosed condition, what questions or concerns they have about the illness and its treatment. Chapter 2 addressed this, but it bears repeating here. It is important to ask the following questions:

1. In patients' own words, how are they making sense of the illness? What does it mean to them?

2. What do they think of the treatment? Do they believe it will work? Do they believe it is necessary?

3. What is their understanding of what can happen if they don't treat the illness?

4. If they are committed to treating the illness, especially a chronic illness, what will keep them on track and what might get in the way over the long term?

Asking these questions will give you a much better idea of what education and information may be needed to fill in gaps, what doubts patients may be having about treating the illness (this allows you to ask what would make treating the illness important to them), and finally, how to plan for change. Without knowing these things, you may provide information that does not address the patient's unique needs and concerns. It may be important to use some of these same questions to reassess patients who are not newly diagnosed. The questions may reveal sources of nonpersistence in treating the illness. And it is feasible that these questions were never asked in the first place and that patients went along even though their commitment was weak because of ambivalence or resistance.

The focus of this chapter is building rapport with the patient so that the issues of importance and confidence revealed in answer to the four questions above can be explored and addressed effectively. In later chapters we will discuss additional ways to influence importance and confidence. We know that simply telling a patient why something important is not sufficient, especially when the new information conflicts with or challenges the patient's beliefs or sense making in a confrontational manner. For example, a patient says, "I don't see the point in taking medicine every day for my blood pressure when I feel just fine!" The physician responds, "Well, you're not fine. You have high blood pressure, and high blood pressure doesn't have symptoms. You don't want to have a stroke or heart attack, do you? You need to take the medicine to get your blood pressure down. We've talked about this before." This response does explain why the patient can feel OK and still be at risk, but it does so in a way that shames the patient or puts him in his place. It does convey the importance of taking the medicine, but it does not honor and respect the patient's perspective. In addition to the issue resistance about taking the medication, we now have relational resistance caused by loss of face. When this happens, patients have a relational justification to not listen to the information and to disregard what was said. A better approach would have started with "Because you feel OK, you're wondering if it is really necessary to take the medicine for your blood pressure." This response respects the patient's concern or perspective (sense making) and lets the patient know that he has been listened to without judgment. After the patient affirmed this response, the HCP would continue, "That's a great question. Would it be OK if I give you some information to address your question and you let me know what you think?" The HCP would then explain how the patient can feel OK and still be at risk. These responses respect the patient and allow the patient to draw his own conclusions, without chastising him.

When rapport is built *first*, the patient can hear the importance of the information provided by the HCP without feeling threatened.

What we have come to understand is that rapport building is crucial to influencing a patient's sense making in a positive way. Rapport is the leverage that HCPs need so that the information or exploration they provide in response to the patient is seen as an extension of caring rather than a way of putting patients in their place. Patients are not only trying to make sense of what is happening to them regarding their illness and treatment (how important it is, whether they can do what is necessary), they are also making sense of how HCPs are talking to them. As discussed in Chapter 4, there is synergy when a patient expresses concern, resistance, or ambivalence and the HCP responds in such a way that the patient feels understood, valued, respected, and safe. Then, the HCP can safely address the concern of the patient in a way that does not feel threatening or cause loss of face. This is when MI is operating at the highest level of increasing the chance for change.

Developing rapport involves creating and maintaining a patient's trust. Generally speaking, we trust HCPs until they give us a reason not to. Patients are making sense of how they are being treated by the HCPs. Are HCPs treating them in a way that leaves them feeling respected, cared for, and safe? Patients are making sense of the relationship and drawing conclusions about it as well. Patients are observing and listening to determine "Can I can trust this person? Does she have my best interest at heart?" When this trust is violated and rapport is severely compromised, the patient does not view information and education provided by the HCP as helpful. Often, the information is viewed as threatening, and as a result it is ignored or discounted. Therefore, it is crucial that we do not violate this trust. A patient's trust can be violated by an HCP in several ways:

1. *The HCP does not pay attention to or listen to the patient.* If the HCP is, for example, entering data into a computer, taking notes, interrupting the patient, or being interrupted by others, this conveys to patients that they are not of utmost importance. It is especially important early in the process of developing a therapeutic and trusting relationship for HCPs to give their full and undivided attention to their patients. We have to slow down in the beginning of the relationship to develop rapport so that we can speed up later.

2. *The HCP consistently discounts or judges what is important or meaningful to the patient.* Any discounting or judging of patients' thoughts, feelings,

actions, or ideas will create distrust. How patients make sense of what is happening to them may not always be accurate or factual, but it is important to them. Correcting patients before acknowledging their thoughts and feelings creates distrust and hurts rapport. For example, a patient may say, "I just don't think my diabetes is that serious. I feel fine." Responding, "Just because you feel fine does not mean you are fine. Your blood sugar is elevated and you need to bring it down. You don't want to go blind or have kidney failure, do you?" causes a patient to feel that his thoughts are being attacked and not respected. The patient is treated like a child and is likely to become defensive and not listen to the new information. While the information provided may be accurate, it is provided in a way that challenges or attacks the patient and causes loss of competence face. Then, it is very easy for the patient to ignore or discount the information. A more appropriate response would have been "Because you feel fine, you're really wondering if your diabetes is all that serious and whether you really need to do anything about it." This response honors and respects how the patient is making sense of his diabetes and the fact that he feels fine. The patient is likely to be far more open to new information, especially if the HCP asks permission to provide information answering the patient's question. For example, "That's a great question you ask. Would it be OK if I give you some information to answer your question and you let me know what you think?" Notice that the response of ". . . you're wondering . . ." sets up the patient's concerns in the form of a question. Questions beg for answers. Next, the HCP praises the patient ("That's a great question . . ."), which encourages future questions and openness. Then the HCP asks permission to give information to answer the question. Finally, the HCP states, ". . . and you let me know what you think." This says to the patient that the patient ultimately decides and that the HCP sees this relationship as a collaboration in which the patient's thoughts and input are vital. Under this rapport-building condition it is much more likely that information provided to address how the patient can feel fine but still be at risk of serious complications will be viewed as helpful and not threatening. Rapport provides leverage for information to be seen as supportive, as an extension of caring, and as nonthreatening. When there is deep rapport and the patient feels respected and safe, the HCP and the information provided by the HCP are not threatening to the patient.

3. *The HCP scolds or chastises a patient for "noncompliance."* When patients don't take their medications as prescribed, lose weight, or make other positive changes, they are often scolded or blamed in some way by the HCP. This approach is not only demeaning; it fails to uncover the source of the problem. What has made it difficult for the patient to carry out the health behavior? Why doesn't the patient want to quit smoking? Keep in mind that noncompliance is a practitioner-centered concept. The patient is being labeled as noncompliant because he did not follow instructions set out by the HCP. This in itself is problematic. The patient may have agreed to the directions simply to appease the HCP in the first place. This is why negotiating goals for behavior change is crucial. It requires collaboration by the HCP and the patient.

4. *The HCP is consistently inaccurate in reflecting the patient's thoughts and feelings.* We believe that on balance, it is far more important to patients that you make an honest and sincere effort to understand them than it is for you to always be 100% accurate in reflecting back their ideas and feelings. However, it is important to be as accurate as possible; otherwise, it may seem that you are not really listening. It is important to match the words you use to the emotional level of the patient. You can do this only by listening to the patient.

5. *The HCP consistently imposes her ideas and goals on the patient without the patient's input.* When patients are not involved in the process of discussing and determining treatment options, there is less likelihood that change will occur or be sustained. Furthermore, in imposing the HCP's ideas and goals, the HCP is assuming that the patient believes treating a problem is important. Before moving to treatment options, it is critical to explore the patient's understanding of the importance of treating the illness. If the patient does not believe treating the illness is important or the patient is not confident in his ability to do so, then discussing treatment options really is not appropriate at this juncture. Priority should be given to exploring what would make treating the illness more important to the patient or what would make the patient feel more confident in treating the illness.

In effectively building rapport, the HCP does not impose conclusions on or draw conclusions for the patient. The HCP allows the patient to draw his own conclusions. Here is a dialogue illustrating this point:

Pt: *You said my A1c has come down from over 9 to 8.5. That's good, isn't it?*

HCP: It really is quite an improvement. Way to go. What have you been doing that caused it to come down?

Pt: *Well, I take my medicine pretty regularly, and I've been trying to cut down on sugar and carbs.*

HCP: That's great. It seems to be paying off. When you say you take your medicine pretty regularly, how are you taking it?

Pt: *I take it nearly every day. I miss maybe a couple days a week.*

HCP: What might cause you to miss a few days a week?

Pt: *I feel pretty good. Plus, finding out my A1c has come down says that what I'm doing is working.*

HCP: So because you feel good and your A1c has come down to 8.5, you're wondering, "If isn't broke, why fix it?"

Pt: *Exactly.*

HCP: You make some very good points. Would you mind if I share some additional information with you and you let me know what you think?

Pt: *Sure. Go ahead.*

HCP: You really have made a lot of progress in bringing your blood sugar down. Unfortunately, you can feel fine even though damage to your organs is slowly taking place, and you don't feel it until major complications occur. We know that when A1c drops below 7, your risk of serious complications such as kidney failure, blindness, and circulation problems that could result in amputation goes down dramatically. Your A1c is at 8.5, which is still quite a bit higher than 7, putting you at high risk of serious complications. Where does this leave you now in regard to taking your medication every day and perhaps thinking about other changes to decrease your A1c?

Pt: *I had no idea. So even though I am doing better, my A1c is still too high.*

HCP:   As I said, we know that risks go down with an A1c below 7. How
       important is it to you to reduce your risks?

Pt:    *Very important. Besides taking my medicine every day, what else
       can I do?*

Notice that in this dialogue the HCP first builds rapport by supporting the
efforts the patient has made in bringing down his blood sugar. The HCP does
not immediately jump to telling the patient that 8.5 is still not good enough. The
patient's sense making is that he feels good and things are moving in the right direction, and therefore there is no problem. The HCP reflects this back to let the patient
know he has listened and understands the patient's perspective. This is done before
any additional information is provided. Keep in mind that any new information
provided by the HCP must address the issues of how the patient can feel fine and
still be at risk and why an A1c of 8.5, while an improvement, is still potentially
problematic. Notice that after this new information is provided the HCP does not
say, "Therefore you need to take your medicine every day." Instead, the HCP says,
"Where does this leave you now?" The decision is the patient's to make. One last
point: The patient is not told, "Your goal is to get your A1c down below 7." This
would be imposing a goal on the patient, and it is not the patient's goal. Instead,
the HCP gives the patient good information about what happens when A1c drops
below 7 and about where the patient is now and then allows the patient to draw
his own conclusions. The rapport building throughout allows the patient to see the
HCP as nonjudgmental and caring, and as a result the new information is seen as
an extension of that caring.

We have found that the information we provide to patients must affect their
reasoning processes. It cannot simply answer a question; it must guide them to
rethink their line of reasoning or their sense making. When a patient with high blood
pressure says, "I don't know why I need this medicine. I feel fine," the patient's way of
making sense is "If I feel fine, I am fine." Unless the information we provide causes the
patient to rethink this and conclude, "I can feel OK and still be at risk," change will not
take place. This is a critical point. The HCP needs to lovingly "throw a wrench" into
the patient's sense making so the patient will reconsider. The mistake made by many
HCPs is correcting the patient's sense making without letting the patient know that
they respect and follow the patient's reasoning (rapport building).

The following dialogue is another example of correcting the patient without rapport building and the problem that results:

Pt: *Taking the medicine should be enough. I really don't like to exercise and I don't want to change my eating habits.*

HCP: It's not enough. Your blood sugar is still elevated and it needs to come down. You need to do more. You don't want to have kidney failure and serious circulation problems, do you?

Pt: *I'm not stupid. Of course I don't want to have that happen to me.*

Notice that the HCP provides accurate information but does so in a condescending and paternalistic manner that shames the patient and treats him like a child. The patient then pushes back with his response. What is especially problematic is that often patients may not even verbalize their dislike of how they were treated and may discount the information without saying anything. Because the patient feels threatened by *how* this information is presented, the patient may discard the information and be nonadherent to the medication regimen.

The following is a response that builds rapport:

Pt: *Taking the medicine should be enough. I really don't like to exercise and I don't want to change my eating habits.*

HCP: You have been prescribed medicine for your diabetes and you feel like that should do the trick. Plus, exercising and changing your eating habits don't sound at all appealing.

Pt: *Exactly. If I don't have to do those things, I would rather not.*

HCP: You raise some legitimate concerns. Would you mind if I give you some information to address them and you let me know what you think?

Pt: *Sure. But don't expect me to change anything.*

In this dialogue, the HCP legitimizes and respects the concerns of the patient and encourages the patient to ask questions in the future. In addition, the HCP asks permission to give some additional information to address the patient's concern. Finally, the HCP invites the patient to let him know what the patient thinks of this new information. This does two things: First it tells the patient that this is a collaborative relationship and that the HCP is interested in how the patient thinks, and second it provides feedback to the HCP about whether any new information alters the patient's sense making. In a later chapter we will discuss the content of this new information and how to present it in a patient-centered way. Because rapport has been built in this dialogue, the new information is seen as an extension of the HCP's caring.

To have rapport with another human being means to be "on the same page," to be in harmony or in synch with that person. To have rapport in a patient-centered relationship means patients sense that they are genuinely understood and they are not being judged or criticized. Having rapport with a patient means that we listen to the patient without judgment and reflect our understanding in a way that says, "I fully hear your concerns or beliefs, I sense how important they are to you, I respect them, and I want to help." We do all that we can to acknowledge the patient's concerns without causing defensiveness or loss of face. In this conception of rapport, the HCP gives a response that is empathic or reflective of the patient's concerns and feelings. The HCP acknowledges and respects the concerns or beliefs (sense making), regardless of whether they are, in fact, true. To establish deep rapport with the patient, the HCP must not judge or argue the validity of the patient's perspective.

Our research has shown that this kind of rapport is critical to facilitating motivation for change. MI is an *exchange* of expertise and information. When patients tell us how they think or feel (make sense) about their health or illnesses, it is critical for them to be listened to carefully, without judgment. When this happens, they feel understood, cared for, and safe. This response begins the process of developing rapport. Remember, rapport is the leverage HCPs need so that the information or exploration they provide in response to the patient is seen as an extension of caring rather than a way of putting patients in their place. MI uses rapport to address the concerns and sense making of the patient. It addresses how patients are making sense out of what is happening to them and the resultant decisions. Without rapport, new information can be perceived as threatening. It is unfortunate that HCPs often skip rapport building in favor of correcting the patient's sense making or giving the patient information. That correction or new information may feel threatening to the patient, and the result may be loss of face. Then, the patient will not hear the information, even though it may be vital to the patient's understanding and decision making. Patients may even fight the information. The spirit of MI provides the basis for developing rapport. With rapport, change is possible; without it, change is dubious at best.

So far in this chapter, we have taken a close look at the importance of developing rapport with the patient. Now we will discuss examples that illustrate what rapport building is not. Next, we will highlight the importance of listening, reflecting, and empathic responding in building rapport so that ultimately we may help the patient consider beneficial health behavior changes. Finally, we will examine specific kinds of responses that build rapport.

## What is not rapport?

Let's look at some examples of responses that lack rapport at some level:

> Pt: *I hate that he has added another medicine. He says I need it to control my blood pressure. I just don't like it.*
>
> HCP: Well, at least there are medicines that can help you.
>
> Pt: *That doesn't make me feel any better. It seems that as I get older, I just have to take more and more medicine.*
>
> HCP: That happens to a lot of patients. You're not alone.
>
> Pt: (dejected) *Thanks. I'm sure they don't like it either.*
>
> HCP: Some don't mind. Some are glad there is something they can take.

In this exchange, the HCP does not listen to the patient's concerns. If he did, it was not evident in his response to the patient. The HCP's own anxiety causes him to want to fix the situation or make it better for the patient. This is called the *righting reflex*. The HCP's anxiety about the patient's comments causes him to want to make this right. He tries to make the patient feel better by asking the patient to consider that at least there is medicine available to help her. She is not ready to be "cheered up" by this news, because she has not had her feelings and concerns acknowledged and addressed. The HCP is essentially putting the patient in her place, telling her, "You should be glad there are medicines that can treat this." The message is that the patient should be grateful, not upset. As a result, the patient is unwilling to discuss this any further, and the reason for her resistance is never explored.

How is the patient making sense of this situation? We don't know what the patient doesn't like about the addition of a new medicine. Is it cost? Side effects? Fear that her condition is getting worse? We simply don't know, because this was not explored. The patient lets the HCP know that she wasn't comforted by his response. Further, she tells the HCP that as she has grown older it seems she has had to take more medicine. She implies that this is distressing to her and has been hard to accept. The HCP now compares her situation to other patients' and, once again, this is not comforting to her. The comparison invalidates the patient's unique perspective. The HCP doesn't know how to respond to the way the patient is making sense in this situation. He ends up using "yes, but" communication with the patient: "yes, but at least there are medications that can help you" and "yes, but that happens to a lot of patients." The message to the patient is "Your thinking or concerns or feelings are not what is most important here. Here is what is more important to consider." These statements discount the patient's meaning and concerns, and the patient pushes back and withdraws. It is unfortunate that this HCP is losing his ability to influence the patient in a positive way because he does not empathize with her distress. The conversation gets stuck and the patient does not feel understood. Consequently, we never find out how any of this affects the patient's decision to take these medications. Did the physician and the patient discuss these concerns and any other ways to reduce her blood pressure without an additional medicine? Is this even a possibility? We don't know the answers to these questions because there was no attempt to build rapport with the patient first.

Here is a second example of a problematic response:

> Pt: *I hate that he has added another medicine. He says I need it to control my blood pressure. I just don't like it.*
>
> HCP: Did you discuss this with the doctor?
>
> Pt: *Yes, but he said I need the extra medicine.*
>
> HCP: Did he tell you why?
>
> Pt: *Yes, he said my blood pressure is still up and then he scolded me and said if I lost about 30 pounds I might not need the extra medicine.*
>
> HCP: Well, there you go! Are you going to lose the weight?

Pt:    *You sound just like my doctor. You all make it sound so easy to just lose 30 pounds.*

HCP:    Do you want to lose the weight or take the medicine?

Pt:    *Thanks* (sarcastically). *Just fill my prescription.*

In this encounter, the HCP uses a cross-examination style of communication. It is characterized by closed-ended questions and feels like "cross-examining the witness." At no point does the HCP acknowledge the patient's distress. Consequently, the patient becomes defensive and withdraws from the conversation.

In both of these examples, the patient's concerns are neither acknowledged nor explored, and the patient does not feel understood.

Here is an example of *appropriate* rapport building:

Pt:    *I hate that he has added another medicine. He says I need it to control my blood pressure. I just don't like it.*

HCP:    It seems like the doctor just keeps adding medicine to control your blood pressure, and that worries you.

Pt:    *Exactly.*

HCP:    Tell me more about what you don't like about adding another medicine.

Pt:    *It seems that as I get older I have to take more and more medicine.*

HCP:    Growing older and having to take more medicine has been difficult to accept. Perhaps you're even wondering if more medicine is really necessary.

Pt:    *Yes. Exactly! And, does this mean my blood pressure is getting worse?*

HCP:    So, it's both wondering if you need all of this medicine and wondering if are you getting worse. Both of these have you feeling pretty anxious.

Pt:    *Right.*

HCP:    What have you discussed with the doctor regarding these concerns?

Pt: *He said if I would lose 30 pounds I might not have to take so much medicine—like it's so easy to lose 30 pounds.*

HCP: Losing weight, especially 30 pounds, seems like a lot of work and quite difficult even though it might result in less medicine.

Pt: *You got it! Either lose more weight or take more medicine.*

HCP: Neither seems very attractive right now.

Pt: *No.*

HCP: It sounds like you aren't questioning whether your blood pressure has gone up. You just don't like either solution for bringing it down.

Pt: *Right. I don't want to have a stroke or heart attack. I just wish I didn't need more medicine or have to lose weight.*

HCP: If you could snap your fingers and be at the weight you would like to be, what would you like about it? In addition to lowering your blood pressure and reducing your risk of stroke and heart attack, what else would you like about losing 30 pounds?

This HCP is doing a great job of reflecting the patient's concerns in a nonjudgmental way. In addition, the HCP explores the patient's concerns about taking more medication and aging. The patient offers additional information because she feels safe and understood. MI takes this to the next level and begins to explore the patient's decisions about lowering her blood pressure. In addition, the last question by the HCP engages the patient in change talk. It will now be the patient who talks about the benefits of losing weight.

Here is an another example of building rapport using MI; it contains all the elements necessary to positively influence change:

Pt: *I hate that he has added another medicine. He says I need it to control my blood pressure. I just don't like it.*

HCP: The doctor keeps adding medicine to control your blood pressure, and you just wish more medicine wasn't necessary.

Pt: *Yes, I know I need to get my blood pressure down. I just don't like that it means more medicine.*

HCP: It's important to you to control your blood pressure. What have you discussed with the doctor?

Pt: *He said if I lost 30 pounds I might not need more medicine—like it's so easy to lose 30 pounds.*

HCP: So, you want to control your blood pressure to reduce your risks of stroke and heart attack. Right now it sounds like the doctor has told you that you can do that either by adding another medicine or by losing some weight. Which of these choices seems to fit you and what you can do right now?

Pt: *Well, I just can't lose 30 pounds all at once.*

HCP: Losing 30 pounds all at once is a daunting task. It sounds like you would be more comfortable with taking the medicine and losing the weight gradually.

Pt: *Yeah, and then maybe I can get off one of the medicines.*

HCP: That sounds like a great plan. What are your thoughts about how you might lose weight?

In this conversation, the HCP accurately reflects the patient's concerns and thoughts and then asks the patient to talk about what choices she can make. He also suggests that the weight can be lost gradually, and he nonjudgmentally corrects the patient's sense making that she most lose the weight very quickly. For the patient, this begins the process of making a commitment to change.

## Listening and empathic responding

Listening and empathic responding are foundational to MI. They are fundamental to creating rapport and letting patients know that you have listened, understood, and respected what they are feeling and thinking, and that you have not passed judgment. Empathy requires what Rogers called unconditional positive regard.[1] This means that no matter whether patients quit smoking, take the medicine, lose weight, or make some other change, we will still care about *them*, even though we may be concerned about their decisions. Our desire to provide care does not wane when patients do not do what we would like them to do. This is consistent with agape and the spirit of MI.

Probably no other skills are more valuable in developing trust than listening and empathic responding. Trust is essential in developing rapport. Trust results when the HCP consistently listens to the patient and accurately reflects the patient's concerns or sense making without judgment.

## The listening process

As an HCP, what should you be listening for from the patient? What do you need to understand? Is it the progression of the disease? Is it the presentation of symptoms? These things are vital, but far too often this is the only information the HCP listens to or gathers. What is also needed is an understanding of how illnesses uniquely affect people. How are patients making sense of what is happening to them, and what are the feelings associated with their sense making? For example, one patient with high cholesterol says, "I will do whatever you tell me to treat it. I don't want to have a stroke or heart attack." Another patient says, "Hey, I know that I need to get my cholesterol down, but I'm a truck driver and need to do heavy lifting. I heard this medicine can cause muscle weakness. I don't need that!" Yet another patient says, "Look, everyone in my family has high cholesterol. They eat what they want and no one has died from it." Each of these responses requires understanding and caring from us. In addition, the information we provide to each patient to affect that patient's sense making will need to be very different if motivation for change is to occur and endure. In the first case, the patient understands the importance of treating his cholesterol, so we simply need to support his readiness, present things he can do to lower his cholesterol, and then ask which of these things he wants to work on. In the second case, the patient's sense making is that muscle weakness will interfere with his job. We need to acknowledge the fear associated with this, provide information to put the side effect in perspective, and discuss how to prevent it from becoming a serious problem. In the last case, the patient's sense making is that high cholesterol has not affected the rest of the family and it will not affect him. Our response needs to acknowledge this ("Sounds like you have some good genes, and I hope you live a long life too") and then present information asking the patient to consider how he *might* be different from the rest of his family (just as there are people in the same family with different heights and eye colors), and letting him decide how important it is for him to reduce his risks just in case he is different.

Basically, we need a shift from treating the disease to treating people who are ill. Even our language in health care reduces people to their illnesses. We call patients diabetics, arthritics, hypertensives, and so on. In actuality, diabetes is only part of who the individual is. Our lives are far more complex than our illnesses. If we are to be effective in helping to treat a patient's illness, we need to start understanding more about the individual. How does this patient interpret or make sense of the illness and the treatment? How is the patient making sense of what is happening to her? Does the patient believe it is important to treat the illness? Does she have confidence that she can treat the illness? For example, does the patient understand what diabetes is? Does she understand the treatment plan? Are there any perceived barriers to carrying out the treatment plan? Is the patient frightened? Overwhelmed? This kind of information needs to be gathered, understood, and responded to in a way that conveys caring. How do we do this?

To get clarification and accurately see the world as the patient sees it, listening is absolutely necessary. Without listening, an accurate empathic response is not possible. Listening is hard work. It takes effort. Listening is an active process, whereas hearing is passive.

The process starts with an act of will. We must will ourselves to listen; we must consciously say, "I am going to listen." Next, we must give someone our complete and undivided attention. Often, people do not pay attention for long enough to be good listeners. Attention is an essential element of listening. Attention must be given; therefore, it is a gift. Giving patients your attention is one powerful way to let them know they are valuable. Everyone needs this. To give someone your attention takes will and conscious effort. Giving attention requires that you not be distracted or interrupted, not hurriedly saying to the other, "Go ahead, I'm listening. You just said. . . ." Listening is not simply repeating back the words. Attention means that you focus your energy on the needs of this person. Multitasking, note taking, and interruptions distract from listening. They often convey a message to patients that they are not what is of utmost importance.

Probably the greatest barrier to true listening is our tendency to judge or evaluate the communication, problem, or feelings of the other. Understanding is different from evaluation of rightness or wrongness, goodness or badness. To truly listen, we must temporarily give up our need to judge—give up the perspective that our frame of reference is the correct one. It is very difficult to do. To do this we must actively become a clean slate, *tabula rasa*, and remind ourselves that any preconceived notions about how a patient thinks or feels will only get in the way of seeing what is unique and important to this patient. Listening without judging means not comparing this patient's experience or situation to that of any other patient or to our own experience. For example, a woman tells her physician that she worries about her arthritis getting worse and about not being able to take care of her husband. The physician thinks this premature worry is typical of the way many women respond, and he says, "Let's not jump the gun. I am quite certain your husband can take care of himself if need be." Because of the judgment he has made, he is not listening. By lumping her with all women, he fails to see how she uniquely has been affected by her experience, regardless of whether she is a woman. As a result, he fails to truly listen and be empathic.

HCPs often hear patients convey information or sense making that is faulty and think they need to correct it right away. In a previous example, a patient with high blood pressure stated, "I feel fine. I just don't know why I need the medicine." Too often the HCP's response is "Just because you feel fine does not mean you are fine. Your blood pressure is elevated, and you can't feel that. You need to take the medicine." The patient loses face and stops listening. In addition to the patient's questioning the need for the medicine, we now have a conflict in the relationship. The patient does not feel understood. A rapport-building response that does not threaten the patient's face would be "So because you feel OK, you're wondering if this medicine is really necessary." This response is nonjudgmental and respects the patient's perspective.

Only through listening can a person be empathic. The focus of true listening is not on the correctness of an idea that is expressed. The idea itself is often subjective; it is not an absolute. With listening, the focus shifts from the idea to the feelings used to express the idea—the commitment to the idea. True listening is about understanding and feeling the idea from the other's perspective, then feeding that back. Through one person's empathic response, the other person begins to feel understood. The consistency of empathic responses over time produces trust. Listening takes great courage, because in the process of truly listening to someone else's ideas or feelings without judgment, you run the risk of being changed by the ideas—of questioning your own ideas.

A common way of responding that gets in the way of listening is trying to fix a problem the other person is describing. When people present us with a problem, are resistant or ambivalent about change, or are having a difficult time emotionally, we often become anxious. We believe we must *do* something immediately. We want to quickly fix or minimize whatever is wrong in order to reduce our own anxiety. Usually the problem does not get solved this way, and the patient ends up feeling even less understood. Becoming aware of our own anxiety can be a stimulus to listen rather than to fix. For example, a patient with an A1c over 9 says, "I'll take the medicine, but don't count on me exercising or changing my eating habits." When the HCP gets anxious, the response might be "That's not enough to get your A1c down. You need to exercise and eat a healthy diet or the medicine can't do its job." Although this statement is factually correct, it will probably cause loss of face and more defensiveness. This statement comes from the HCP's anxiety and need to fix things. It does not demonstrate listening and understanding. A better response might be "You are committed to taking the medicine. That's a very important step in getting your diabetes under control. I also hear your reluctance to make changes in your eating and exercise habits. Tell me more about this decision." Notice that this response does several things: (1) it acknowledges that the patient is willing to take the medicine; (2) it constructively dissipates the anxiety by exploring the patient's resistance about changing her eating and exercise habits; and (3) it respects the patient's autonomy by letting the patient know that it really is her decision. Eventually, as practitioners get more and more comfortable with MI and with truly accepting that the patient is in charge, fixing and anxiety are used less often than listening and empathic responding.

One of the primary reasons for listening and empathic responding is to help the patient feel less alone or isolated. As Rogers stated,

> For the moment, at least, the recipient finds himself or herself a connected part of the human race. . . . If someone else knows what I am talking about, what I mean, then to this degree I am not so strange, or alien, or set apart. I make sense to another human being. So I am in touch with, even in relationship with, others. I am no longer an isolate.[1]

Put another way, when we feel alone in a problem, hopelessness often goes with that. If no one else understands, the problem seems unsolvable. If someone can express understanding at an emotional level, then the person is not alone. If someone else can understand, then the problem may be solvable. At least, so it seems. Therefore, listening and empathic responding offer hope. Moreover, listening and empathic responding are the only way we can let the patient know that her feelings and thoughts are understood. The next time a patient presents a problem and you feel anxious, use that anxiety as a trigger to demonstrate your understanding, rather than trying to escape your anxiety by minimizing or correcting the problem or the information.

Empathic responding is crucial in building an effective therapeutic relationship. The word empathy is derived from the German word *Einfühlung.* This word means that we can actually share the emotional experience of another. It is different from sympathy. Sympathy is feeling sorry for another. Empathy is feeling or experiencing *affectively* with another. It is a neutral process; there is no judgment or evaluation of the person or the feelings involved. Sympathy, in contrast, is not neutral. Empathy has been defined as an objective identification with the affective state of an individual.[2] This means we do not pass judgment. We do not evaluate whether the feelings expressed are appropriate. We objectively accept that these are the unique feelings and response of this patient, and it does not matter whether any other patient would feel the same way. It also does not matter whether we would feel that way. Squier[3] discussed the importance of practitioner empathy in predicting treatment adherence, noting the following:

1. Patient adherence is higher when physicians allow patients to express and dissipate their tensions and anxiety about their illness and when physicians take the time to carefully answer the patient's questions;
2. Practitioners who demonstrate responsiveness to patients' feelings have patients with higher adherence rates and better satisfaction with the relationship;
3. Patients who perceive their physicians as understanding and caring are more likely to carry out the treatment plan and ask for further help or advice when they need it; and
4. HCPs who encourage patients' expressions of feelings and participation in the treatment plan have patients with higher rates of adherence.

These findings have important implications for health care. Again, feeling understood strengthens the bond between the patient and the professional. This, in turn, improves treatment adherence.

Several concepts are key to understanding empathy: identification, imitation, and affective communication. Before an empathic response can be made, one must experience the affective state of the other. Empathy involves identification with the affective or emotional experience of the other. It does not involve identifying with the other person in total, nor does it mean sharing the same experience in actuality. For example, it is not necessary to have high blood pressure to understand and empathize with the surprise, fear, or worry patients experience when they receive the diagnosis. Too often people believe that one must have had the same experience to be empathic. However, thinking about how you might respond (or did respond) in the same situation can simply get in the way. Doing this may actually interfere with your capacity to identify with how this patient uniquely responds. Empathy takes courage, because it means you must be open to the affective experience of another. Often this experience can be painful or uncomfortable for both the patient and HCP. (Of course, we should also be empathic with the joy and happiness of others.) We have a tendency to avoid the experience of discomfort and to not bear the patient's emotional response rather than to be with the emotional experience and be truly useful and available to the other. Feeling discomfort often leads to the righting reflex on the part of the HCP. We try to fix the patient's situation to escape our own discomfort. Here is an example:

Pt: *The doctor was very disrespectful to me. I'm in a lot of pain, and he just dismissed it like it's in my head. It's not in my head.*

HCP: He was probably busy and just didn't have time to respond. Their offices are really packed these days.

Pt: *That's no excuse! I am in pain. Then he reluctantly gave me this prescription to shut me up rather than listening to what I was saying.*

HCP: Well, see, he gave you a prescription for an anti-inflammatory drug, so he must have listened.

Pt: *Just give me that! I'll fill it elsewhere!*

What happened here? The patient's sense was that the physician did not take her pain seriously and that he wrote the prescription not because he believed her but as a way of dismissing her. Whether any of this is true really does not matter. The patient was upset, and this is how she sensed what happened. This HCP does not acknowledge any of the patient's concerns and simply provides a perspective (twice) that the patient is not ready to hear because she does not feel understood. The patient is upset and agitated and wants to feel respected and understood. This HCP's anxiety in response to the patient's apparent conflict with the physician and her resultant emotional state causes him to try to "fix" or "right" the situation and the patient, because he simply cannot bear the conflict. Paradoxically, all his response does is cause further upset and agitation, to the point that the patient decides to leave. The patient's health issue is not even addressed.

Let's look at how this might have been handled without the righting reflex:

Pt: *The doctor was very disrespectful to me. I'm in a lot of pain and he just dismissed it like it's in my head. It's not in my head.*

HCP: You're worried about your pain and what's causing it, and you don't feel that the doctor took you seriously.

Pt: *Exactly! It was horrible. Then he reluctantly gave me this prescription to shut me up rather than listening to what I was saying.*

HCP: When he gave you the prescription for the anti-inflammatory medicine, that felt like he was dismissing you, and you're still left wondering what's causing your pain.

Pt: *Yes. He did say it felt like I'd pulled a muscle in my back that this medication would help, and that I needed to rest it, maybe put some ice on it. But he barely even touched where it hurt.*

HCP: When he spent so little time examining the area the pain was coming from, that made you feel like he was not taking you seriously.

Pt: *I suppose so. So, this medicine is for inflammation?*

HCP: Yes, it's very effective, especially if you have a pulled muscle and some inflammation.

Pt: *I guess I'll try it and see if it helps. It's been a rough day.*

HCP: Sounds very stressful. Make sure you take the medication with food, and let me know if you don't get any relief in the next few days.

Pt: *Thanks.*

This HCP really listens to the concerns of the patient. He does not take sides; he simply reflects back his understanding of how the patient is feeling. Consequently, something very interesting and important occurs. The patient feels safe enough and respected enough to consider the possibility that the physician did listen to her, even if he did seem rushed. As a result, she decides to take the medication. Things may not always go this way. However, because she felt understood, her anger dissipated and she was able to consider another possibility that did not even surface in the dialogue with the righting reflex.

Imitation is also part of the empathic process.[2] Often, without realizing it, we imitate or mimic the facial expressions or body posture of the other, or the tone of voice, particularly when a painful experience is being recounted. This is a form of identification with the affective state, and it signals empathic understanding. This is affective communication. It cannot be accomplished if one is distracted or interrupted—a key reason why giving total attention is important. In addition, empathic responding involves both a verbal and a nonverbal component. Simply repeating a patient's words without appropriate nonverbal cues to express the emotion will not be experienced as empathic by the patient. Empathy is not a technique, something formulaic or mechanical. Being empathic is a way of being with the patient, a way of expressing genuine care and concern.

The empathic process always results in the acquisition of knowledge by both parties—the patient and the HCP—in coming to know one another. By being open and nonjudgmental, the HCP learns about the patient's experience of illness or change and how it uniquely affects that patient. Through an empathic response by the HCP, the patient learns that the HCP can be trusted. This is a neutral process; it does not involve like or dislike, good or bad. Behavior is not prescribed, and the other's feelings are not evaluated. One person simply comes to know more fully how the other person relates to a problem or a situation.

Reflecting this understanding back to the other can be transforming or growth producing. A few cautions are in order, however. First, although empathic understanding is always transforming, it is not always comfortable. Consider the following dialogue:

> Pt:   *I am scared to death. Both of my parents died from high cholesterol and heart disease. I don't want that to happen to me.*

HCP:    You think about what happened to your parents and how they suffered, and you don't want that to happen to you. You don't want to see your life cut short.

Pt:     (Tears up) *Yes. I miss them and I don't want to do that to my children.*

HCP:    It was a huge loss, and you don't want your children to suffer the way you did at your parents' premature deaths.

Pt:     *No, I don't. I want to do everything I can to prevent that.*

HCP:    I'd like to work with you to support you in preventing your children from suffering in the way you did.

In this exchange, the HCP's empathy, while fully supportive, also brought up old feelings of loss and fear on the part of the patient. Despite the fact that these memories were painful, the patient was now willing to discuss her fear of causing her children the same kind of suffering. Her tears were about not only the loss of her parents but also her desire to prevent her children from suffering—which becomes part of her motivation to reduce her cholesterol and prevent serious heart problems. The HCP then expresses his desire to help her prevent her children from suffering the way she did; this is critical to deepening the rapport between the HCP and the patient. It is an affirmation of something the patient holds dear. The process of affirmation is critical to rapport building.

This particular exchange raises concerns that many HCPs have expressed about the use of empathy:

1. I am not a therapist. Am I getting in over my head?
2. I don't have an hour, as most therapists do, to deal with all of a patient's problems (nor am I qualified).
3. Can't empathy make the relationship *too* personal?

You don't have to be a therapist to be sensitive to your patients. Ignoring a patient's strong display of emotion would really interfere with the therapeutic relationship. Sadly, many physicians and other HCPs are taught to be clinically detached, which can only leave the patient feeling more isolated and not understood. It does not build rapport, and therefore it decreases your ability to help the patient make constructive decisions about health behavior change.

In regard to the issues of time limitation and getting in over your head, we are not advocating that HCPs become psychotherapists. Unless you are a mental health professional, your focus must be on the health issue at hand (e.g., high blood pressure, smoking). This being the case, not all emotional displays are germane or need to be explored. A patient may be angry because the traffic was horrible on the way to the HCP's office, but delving into the patient's anger is not appropriate or relevant, unless the way the patient deals with stress is affecting his blood pressure, for example. Even then, referral to another professional may be in order. What we are asking HCPs to do is become attuned to and sensitive to verbal and nonverbal responses by the patient that are germane to the health problem. For example, if you are talking to a patient about the use of medication to lower blood pressure and the patient rolls his eyes and sighs deeply, that response needs to be explored. If you say to another patient that this medication is an anti-hypertensive and the patient looks confused or quizzical, this response should be explored. One patient may have no idea what you mean by anti-hypertensive. Another patient might say, "But, I am not tense. I thought I had high blood pressure." In any case, the exploration allows you to know what the emotional display was about so you can address it in a way that it is meaningful to the patient. Both individuals in the encounter learn something useful to the clinical situation at hand.

When the HCP is concerned that being empathic will make the relationship with the patient too personal, the HCP's solution often is to remain aloof or emotionally distant. According to Gadow,[4] "A solution to the personal/professional dichotomy can be proposed in the following way. Professional involvement is not an *alternative* to other kinds of involvement, such as emotional, esthetic, physical, or intellectual. It is a deliberate synthesis of all of these, a participation of the *entire* self, using every dimension of the person as a resource in the professional relation." Anything less than this reduces the patient to an illness or a condition, an object not a person. As stated by Rogers,[5] "To withhold one's self as a person and to deal with the other person as an object does not have a high probability of being helpful." What Rogers and Gadow are saying is that professional involvement should respond to objective data (e.g., clinical observations, lab results) *and* personal data (emotional displays and communication).

Moreover, an important question to consider is why an HCP worries about making the relationship too personal. We suspect it is because of a sense of responsibility for the patient that really is not appropriate. Recall the example of the patient who started to cry because her parents had died prematurely from heart disease and she did not want her children to go through the same suffering. As in this example, the HCP's responsibility is not to cure or relieve the patient's suffering. The HCP's responsibility is (1) to understand how her suffering affects her decisions about her present health and (2) to let her know that you care about what has happened to her. It is not the HCP's responsibility to solve these problems, nor is it the HCP's responsibility to make the patient do anything. However, empathic responding increases the probability that patients will consider new information and make appropriate changes to improve their health.

This leads to another caution about empathy. Empathy does not mean giving in or giving up. Empathy relates to a person's affective state or situation, not the person's ideas. For example, if a patient says, "I am not ready to quit smoking. I have too much stress in my life. I'll take my chances on how it affects my asthma," an appropriate response would be "Because of the amount of stress in your life, it's hard to imagine quitting smoking. It really is your decision. I'm worried about the long-term impact of smoking on your asthma. It can do permanent damage that cannot be reversed. I would hate to see that happen when it can be prevented. If you get to the point where you would like to quit or cut back, I'd like to help." This response involves empathy, yet it also lets the patient know about the risks involved in his decision. This may not be comfortable for the patient or the HCP, but it seems necessary both ethically and from a caring perspective. The empathic opening allows the concern expressed by the HCP to be seen as caring and not lecturing.

One last example will help to bring all of these ideas together. Byron Smith, age 62, says to the pharmacist, "I really don't give a damn what you and my doctor say. I'll use aspirin with my warfarin if I want to. It's the only thing that gives me relief from my arthritis. Besides, the only reason he wants to do blood work all the time is so he can make extra fees." If you are offended by the patient's initial accusatory response, you might become angry, feeling that he has no right to talk to you that way. Furthermore, if you are thinking that it is dangerous to use aspirin with warfarin without regular monitoring, you might be tempted to say, "Well, you need to see the doctor and get monitored. Taking aspirin with warfarin is dangerous, and you don't need to do that." No matter how nicely you say this, it is likely to produce defensiveness and loss of face. Even though you would be telling the truth, you would not be addressing and recognizing the patient's core concern ("I get relief from my aspirin, and I don't want anyone telling me I have to stop getting relief") and line of reasoning ("This is not that big a deal, and my doctor just wants to make more money off monitoring"). It is unlikely that the patient would listen.

This patient is feeling angry. Anger is born from powerlessness, helplessness, or a sense of injustice. It is useful to think about what is making the patient feel powerless. It seems reasonable to believe he feels powerless because he thinks someone is going to take away his arthritis relief by discontinuing the aspirin. Understanding the patient's core concern allows the HCP to make a more effective empathic response. It is also crucial to stay separate but present and to not take the patient's response personally.

Here is a dialogue that incorporates all of these elements:

HCP:   Mr. Smith, it sounds like you have gotten a great deal of relief for your arthritis by using aspirin and you don't want anyone telling you that you can't use it. Plus, you're wondering if the doctor just wants to do blood work to make more money.

Pt:   *Damn right!*

HCP:   I don't want to stop you from getting relief. I want you to feel better. Would you mind if I give you some information and then you tell me what you think about it? Ultimately, this is your decision.

Pt:   *OK, I suppose so.*

HCP:   Thank you. As you know, warfarin thins your blood so it doesn't clot as easily, and this reduces the risk of another stroke. Aspirin can make the levels of warfarin in your blood go up, and if it is not monitored, your blood can become so thin that you could spontaneously hemorrhage and even bleed to death. In fact, if your aspirin use varies, so do your warfarin levels. A lot of aspirin could lead to bleeding. Also, stomach irritation from aspirin can become dangerous while using warfarin. I don't want that to happen to you. If your doctor monitors the warfarin level in your blood, you can use aspirin to relieve your arthritis pain as long as you take the aspirin on a consistent basis. That allows your doctor to adjust your warfarin dose to fit your aspirin dose so nothing dangerous happens. Where does this leave you now in regard to being monitored by your doctor?

The HCP's responses recognize the core concern of the patient and correct the sense making of the patient without causing loss of face and defensiveness. This can happen only when the HCP stays separate and does not take the patient's anger personally. How can the HCP do this? One way is to continually ask, "What is the patient's central concern?" In this case, the HCP is able to hear that the patient is angry because he feels threatened by the loss of his aspirin. When the HCP recognizes this concern immediately and responds empathically to the patient, the patient feels understood and is willing to listen to what the HCP has to say.

The second utterance by the HCP is "I don't want to stop you from getting relief. I want you to feel better. Would you mind if I give you some information and then you tell me what you think about it? Ultimately, this is your decision." This lets the patient know that (1) the HCP supports the patient's desire to get relief, (2) the patient's input is wanted, and (3) the decision ultimately is the patient's. The last statement by the HCP is "Where does this leave you now in regard to being monitored by your doctor?" This shows that the HCP wants to know how the new information affects the patient's sense making. The HCP does not assume that the patient accepts the new information; instead, he asks for the patient's input. The HCP does not draw conclusions for the patient by saying, "Therefore you need to get the blood work done." Drawing conclusions for the patient would cause loss of competence face and autonomy face. Instead, information is provided and the patient is allowed to draw his own conclusions.

After his last question, the HCP would listen carefully. If the patient said, "I didn't know taking aspirin could hurt me if I wasn't monitored. I will see the doctor," that would be ideal. In the worst case, the patient would say, "I'll take my chances." Then, the HCP could say, "It really is your decision. I want you to know that I am concerned enough about the risks involved if you are not monitored that if you don't see the doctor and get blood work done, I will call his office and let him know you won't be coming in for the blood work." This response fulfills the HCP's ethical obligation, and it also shows care, concern, and respect for the patient. The HCP is forthrightly sharing his concerns with the patient face-to-face. Calling the physician behind the patient's back would have disrespected and manipulated the patient. Although the patient might not like the response the HCP has given, we believe he would sense that he is being treated as a full person.

## Things to avoid in empathic responses

It is important to realize that everyday conversation is not the same as conversations we have with patients. Everyday conversation is far less formal. Saying, "I hear ya" may work just fine with a longtime friend. It can create problems with a patient, especially one that does not know you very well. "I hear ya" doesn't tell the patient what you heard or tell him that you heard him accurately.

More examples of empathic responding are presented throughout this book. Now, though, we would like to make several important points about appropriate empathy.

**Don't presume understanding.** People often say, "I understand how you feel" or "I understand that you're frustrated" or "I hear ya." All of these responses presume understanding. It is not up to us to decide whether we understand. The *patient* decides whether we understand. When we preempt the patient's judgment, we are causing loss of face. Our job is to state, with care and compassion, what we think the patient is saying and then let the patient tell us whether it is accurate. For example, a patient says, "The doctor didn't take me seriously. I am in a lot of pain." The HCP responds, "You're angry because the doctor discounted the severity of your pain." The patient responds, "I'm not angry. I'm frustrated and hurt." Since the patient is saying that the HCP's understanding wasn't quite accurate, the HCP would now say, "So, you don't feel that the doctor understood how much pain you are in, and when he discounted that it was frustrating and hurtful to you." Patients are more concerned about our intention to care and understand than about whether we get it right 100% of the time. Our working to get it correct is impressive to the patient.

We have found that many HCPs like to use the response, "I hear you saying that. . . ." Although the HCP may be accurately reflecting the patient's feelings, the response "I hear you saying that you are frightened at finding out you have high blood pressure" may sound clichéd to the patient. (We call such a response "TV psychology.") Removing "I hear you saying that" and simply stating, "You are frightened at finding out you have high blood pressure" works just fine and avoids sounding clichéd. "I hear you saying that" adds nothing to the meaning reflected by the HCP.

**Be explicit in your empathy.** A full empathic response contains three elements: feelings, content, and reasons. Here is an example: "You're very frustrated (feeling) because you don't feel that the doctor took you seriously (reason) when you told him how much your back hurts (content)." Too often, we cut our responses short and say things like "You're frustrated" or "You don't think he took you seriously." Both of these responses leave the patient to wonder whether you fully understood.

There is another danger in cutting empathic responses short. Too often the patient may misinterpret what you mean because it is not explicit. This can cause a serious breach of trust or problems with rapport. The following story will illustrate this point.

At one of our workshops a participant took issue with the idea of being explicit. She was a social worker in an HIV clinic. She told a story about a young man in his twenties who came to see her and said, "I just saw Dr. Smith. He said I'm HIV positive. I just can't believe it. If that wasn't bad enough, he scolded me and said that's what happens when you don't have safe sex." The social worker had responded to this patient by saying, "Oh my." She said she had then paused to see how the patient would respond; she claimed that her abbreviated response would serve as a stimulus for his response. The workshop facilitator listened carefully to her story and her point. Then he said to her, "Oh my" and asked what she thought his "Oh my" meant. She said, "I'm not sure." The facilitator said, "And that's the problem. It leaves open to interpretation what is meant. When the young man heard your response, he might have thought that you meant, 'Oh my, you're HIV positive' or 'Oh my, you didn't have safe sex?' and that would have felt as uncaring and judgmental as the physician's response. Is either of these what you meant by 'Oh my' "? The social worker said she had wanted to convey that she could hear how shocked the young man had been at finding out that he was HIV positive and then on top of that feeling shamed and embarrassed by the physician's remark about safe sex. The facilitator then asked, "What do you think you could have said to make sure that is what you conveyed?" She replied, "I could have said, 'On top of receiving the devastating news that you are HIV positive, rather than providing any comfort the physician shamed you about safe sex and that felt just awful.' " The facilitator agreed that this statement would have conveyed to the patient her true understanding and that it would not have been misinterpreted.

It is especially critical early in the relationship to be explicit so that the patient knows exactly what you mean and what you understand. Explicit responses give clear evidence that you listened to the patient's issues. This is vital to building rapport.

**Avoid semantic reductions.** Empathy and reflections should be as accurate as possible. Being explicit and accurate in your reflection of feelings is important in order to avoid reducing a feeling like frustration, anger, fear, or shock to "You're concerned . . ."—a response that minimizes the importance of the feeling to the patient. For example, a woman says, "I just found out I have herpes. I am so ashamed and embarrassed. I don't want my roommates to find out." A response of "You're concerned about having herpes and your roommates finding out" diminishes the emotional meaning of the patient's statement, and the patient may not feel understood.

A more appropriate response would be "It has been embarrassing and very distressing to find out you have herpes. It would be even more embarrassing if your roommates found out."

**Avoid generalized references.** Patients often say things like "I'm really shocked that my A1c is still above 8. I've worked so hard to bring it down." In response, an HCP may say, "That would be disturbing" rather than "You've worked so hard to get your A1c down and you're really shocked that it's still so high." Again, avoid responses that result in information and understanding being lost.

**Empathy in the form of a question.** Empathy should be framed in the form of a statement, not a question. It takes courage to be empathic. An important part of building rapport and using empathy is taking the risk of saying to the patient, "Here is what I am hearing." If you are not accurate, the patient will let you know. Asking a question like "Are you upset?" may cause a patient to think, "Why don't you get this? How could you ask such a question?" It is a response that hedges your bet and keeps you from truly being emotionally invested in the patient.

**Comparison to others.** Empathy is not expressed in the form of a comparison. Comparisons are often motivated by an attempt to care and help, but they run the risk of minimizing the uniqueness of the problem to the patient. Here is an example:

Pt:   *I just can't believe I have high blood pressure. I had no idea. I felt fine.*

HCP:   Mr. Jones, millions of people have high blood pressure, and we can work together to get it down.

Pt:   *What do you mean? I'm going to get it down. I'm not stupid. I know I need to get it down. I just didn't expect to find out I have it.*

Because of the comparison, three things happen: (1) the patient feels minimized by having his problem compared to someone else's; (2) the HCP loses information because he doesn't explore what the patient's shock is about and whether he might have any difficulty treating his high blood pressure; and (3) there is loss of autonomy face from the implicit imposition of a goal (get it down) on the patient. As a result, rapport is hindered. A better response would have been "You just didn't expect to find out you had high blood pressure, especially since you felt fine. It really came as a shock." The patient probably would have said, "Right," and then the HCP could have said, "What are your thoughts about treating your blood pressure at this point?"

A few other points should be made about comparisons. One might ask, is there ever an appropriate time to make a comparison? The answer is, only if the patient asks for one. If the patient asks, "Have other people felt that way?" it is certainly appropriate to answer, saying "Yes, being surprised to find out you have high blood pressure is a common response" to comfort the patient.

We are asked how to respond when patients say things like "Do you smoke?" Whether you smoke is irrelevant. Your experience with smoking may give you some compassion, but responding to the question runs the risk of missing what is unique about the patient's experience with smoking and her attempts to quit. An appropriate response would be "I would really like to know more about your thoughts and desires about quitting. How important is this to you?" If the patient says, "How can you talk to me about quitting if you've never smoked?" she is really asking, "How can you help when you've never smoked?" An appropriate response would be "You're wondering if I can really understand your struggles to quit if I've never been through that." The patient would probably say "Right," and then we would respond, "That's where I need your help. I really want to understand your thoughts about quitting so I can best help. Would that be OK?"

If the patient suspected that you did smoke and said, "How can you talk to me about quitting (or being overweight) when you are a smoker (overweight)?" she would now be saying you are a hypocrite. The best response would be to simply acknowledge the patient's concern directly and say, "It seems hypocritical that I smoke (I'm overweight) and I am now talking to you about quitting (losing weight). I know that quitting isn't easy. I've struggled with it myself, and I know that the effects on my health are not good. So, I really would like to help, if that would be OK."

**Talking about yourself.** Often, out of a desire to help, HCPs who share a condition or situation with the patient will say, "I struggled with weight loss too, so I know what you're going through" or "I was shocked too when I found out I had diabetes." Although the patient may perceive this to be helpful, it can backfire. The patient might respond, "We're not talking about you. We're talking about me." The HCP's statement shifts the focus from the patient to the HCP. Also, the HCP's experience with the illness or condition may prevent the HCP from objectively seeing how the patient is uniquely affected. Talking about the HCP's experience shifts the frame of reference from the patient to the HCP and can imply that the solution that worked for the HCP should be adopted by the patient. The patient can lose face as a result. When tempted to share your own experience with the issue facing a patient, remember that empathy is the opposite of egocentricity. Instead of sharing your experience, stay focused on empathizing with the patient's issue: "You are really shocked and surprised to find out you have diabetes. What surprises you the most?"

Thus far we have explored building rapport and its importance in therapeutic relationships. Listening and empathic responding were examined and discussed as foundations for building rapport. Rapport is crucial for allowing information provided by the HCP to be accepted as an extension of caring. This can happen only when the perspective of the patient is acknowledged and respected without judgment.

The following are some additional examples of using empathy. In subsequent chapters we discuss the transition from being empathic to influencing the patient's sense making or line of reasoning in order to increase the probability of change.

# Ways of being empathic

## Simple empathic reflection

*Example 1*

> Pt:     *All of those years of smoking and now I am told I have lung disease.*
>
> HCP:   You regret that your decision to smoke may have contributed to your current lung problems.
>
> Pt:     *Yes.*

The patient's sense is that her smoking is now responsible for her lung disease, and she feels regret. That is what is reflected in the HCP's response. In this situation we would not attempt to change the patient's thinking about smoking and lung disease. We would want to explore her commitment to quit and treat her current problems.

*Example 2*

> Pt:     *I was really shocked to find out I have high blood pressure. I felt OK.*
>
> HCP:   Because you felt fine, it startled you to find out you have high blood pressure.

The patient's sense is that she did not have any idea she had high blood pressure, because she felt fine and did not have any symptoms. Any information the HCP provides, after empathizing, would address how the patient could feel fine and still be at risk.

*Example 3*

> Pt: *What a relief. I thought something horrible was wrong with me. Turns out that water pill was making my potassium too low and that's why I felt so sluggish and weak and queasy all the time. I didn't know that pill could do that and that low potassium could make you feel so bad. All I have to do is eat a banana each day or drink a glass of OJ.*
>
> HCP: Sounds like you had quite a scare about how bad you were feeling. What a relief to know what was causing it and to find out that drinking orange juice or eating a banana each day will do the trick!

Empathy is also important when positive things happen. This patient was relieved and glad to know that a simple solution would solve his problem. This needs to be supported.

## Angry or challenging patient

*Example 1*

> Pt: *I am so sick and tired of all of this medicine! They just keep adding more medicine.*
>
> HCP: It is frustrating that they seem to keep adding more and more medicine and you're not even sure why.
>
> Pt: *No, I know why. They said my blood pressure is not under control and they need more medicine to bring it down.*
>
> HCP: And perhaps you wonder why one medicine is not enough to do the job.
>
> Pt: *Exactly!*

The patient's sense is that one medicine should be enough to take care of his high blood pressure, and he is angry, frustrated, or perhaps even worried about needing additional medication. Empathy is important to allow the patient to feel safe in venting. Remember, anger is born of powerlessness or a sense of injustice. This patient is feeling powerless about what is happening to his blood pressure. After empathizing, the HCP should provide information addressing the need or rationale for the additional medicine and should try to reassure the patient of the need to continue to take it with his other medication to reduce his risk of stroke or heart attack.

*Example 2*

> Pt: *You people kill me. All you're interested in doing is making money off us patients. It stinks! (The physician has prescribed a new medication with a high co-pay.)*
>
> HCP: (calmly) It feels like no one really cares about you—that we only care about getting your money.
>
> Pt: *Damn right!*
>
> HCP: (calmly) It would be awful to feel like you are just some illness for us to exploit for our benefit.
>
> Pt: *Well, if the shoe fits . . .*
>
> HCP: (calmly) This medication is relatively new for treating diabetes. It is very effective, but because it is new the co-pay is higher than you are used to paying. I feel confident that this medication can help. I really would like to work with you to get your diabetes under control. What would you like to do next?

This is a good example of an HCP who stayed separate yet fully available to the patient. The patient is angry about the increase in his cost for a new medication, and he levels an accusation at all HCPs. The pharmacist, in this case, is able to not take the attack personally. She reflects her understanding of the patient's frustration and then supports the decision of the physician and indicates her desire to work with the patient.

*Example 3*

> HCP: Mrs. Jones, I've noticed that you were supposed to get a refill on your 90-day supply of blood pressure medicine about 30 days ago. Are you having any difficulty taking the medicine?
>
> Pt: *I don't need you telling me what I should be doing! How dare you imply that I'm not taking my medicine! I take it every day just like I'm supposed to take it!*
>
> HCP: Mrs. Jones, I sure didn't mean any of this to sound like an accusation. The most important thing to me is that you are taking your medicine every day. I worry about some of my patients with high blood pressure who don't take their medicines every day because they feel fine and don't realize their blood pressure is still high. It would be very sad if any of them had a stroke or heart attack they could have prevented. So, I'm relieved that you're taking your medicine every day. Is this a good time for a refill?

This patient became defensive when she was asked about being late on her refill. It is likely that she was not taking the medicine as prescribed and felt "caught" by the pharmacist's inquiry. The pharmacist could have responded like a prosecuting attorney, proving the witness is lying. However, this would have created more relational resistance and loss of face. Instead, the pharmacist stayed in the spirit, saw that this was a sensitive subject to the patient, and decided to talk about other patients so the patient could hear the information he believed was important for a possible behavior change. The pharmacist had to stay focused on the reason for his concern, rather than on a need to be right or to win.

## Reflecting misinformation or lack of education

*Example 1*

> Pt: *I haven't gotten AIDS after taking all this medicine for three years after being diagnosed as HIV positive. Maybe I don't need all of it.*

HCP: You have really been committed to taking all of your medication, and now you're wondering whether it's necessary to keep doing so since your HIV hasn't become AIDS.

Pt: *Exactly.*

HCP: You raise a great question. May I share some information with you, and then you can tell me what you think about it?

Pt: *Sure.*

This patient's sense is that if he hasn't gotten AIDS after three years of taking his medication, maybe he doesn't need to keep taking it. The temptation is to immediately correct the patient and explain that it is his taking the medication that has prevented his HIV from becoming AIDS. Although that may be true, this approach could cause face loss and defensiveness. By first acknowledging the patient's sense making, we let the patient know that we have listened, and we also let him know that he is raising a good question. Then, after asking permission, we can let him know that his conscientious effort in taking the medication is probably why he has not gotten AIDS.

*Example 2*

Pt: *You worry too much. I know Evan is overweight, but he'll grow out of it. He's only 6 years old. It's just baby fat.*

HCP: Because Evan is still so young, you're not worried about his carrying extra weight right now and you think he will lose it as he grows up.

This parent's sense is that her child will eventually grow out of being overweight. As an HCP you may know that childhood obesity greatly increases the probability of type 2 diabetes, but providing this information without acknowledging how the parent is making sense of the situation would most likely cause loss of face. This parent may already feel a bit defensive that her child is overweight, so information needs to be provided in a way that does not cause further defensiveness or face loss. Any information that is eventually provided has to address the parent's sense that Evan will grow out of it, explaining that we grow fat cells primarily early in life and that although they can shrink, they don't go away. Only changing one's eating habits and physical activity can keep fat cells from growing or forming.

## Final considerations in rapport building

Several times in this chapter we have mentioned the HCP's anxiety, the righting reflex, and the ability of the HCP to stay separate yet fully available to the patient. Earlier in the book we mentioned the importance of introspection—becoming more aware of yourself in relationship to your patients and reflecting on that awareness. There are three major areas in which introspection and reflection are very important:

**Anxiety in response to the patient.** HCPs find themselves becoming anxious with patients if they are uncomfortable with the patients' emotional displays (e.g., crying or being upset, hurt, or frightened) or uncomfortable with conflict (this includes the patient's reported conflict with another person or HCP as well as conflict directly with the patient). The HCP's anxiety often leads to the righting reflex or to dismissing, discounting, or judging the feelings of the patient. None of these responses are supportive of building rapport. In fact, they undermine rapport building.

Part of your work toward becoming competent in the use of MI is to become increasingly aware of how your own anxiety undermines your relationship with the patient. Even more fundamentally, why does the anxiety come up in the first place? There may be numerous answers to this question, but one reason for this anxiety is that the HCP feels a need to have all the answers or solve all the problems encountered. This is certainly unrealistic and not consistent with MI. You cannot fix the patient or the patient's problems. You can care and provide good, balanced information. Ultimately the patient must decide. We ask that you try to become more aware of your own anxiety and reflect on what kind of MI responses would be most useful to your patients.

**Frustration or anger toward the patient.** It is not unusual to hear HCPs express frustration or even anger toward their patients for one of two fundamental reasons, both of which revolve around issues of control or the illusion of control. In the first case, the HCP relates that the patient has been told many times why she needs to quit smoking, take her medication, or lose weight and still has not done so. Rather than exploring the patient's reluctance to engage in the behavior, the HCP presses on even harder with persuasion, blaming, shaming, or scolding. Of course, these don't work. Not only do they add to issue resistance, they create loss of face and relational resistance. The HCP's behavior and frustration are driven by the illusion that the HCP is in control, is the expert, and therefore patients should listen to the HCP and do what they are told. This doesn't work, because it is actually the patient who decides, and patients are also experts. There are many reasons HCPs experience this need for control. One reason is their training. Regardless, it is an area for introspection and awareness. It interferes with rapport.

Another source of HCPs' frustration or anger involves situations in which patients say they will take their medications as prescribed, or lose weight, or quit smoking, and then don't, repeatedly. The HCP gets frustrated. When we ask HCPs why they get frustrated, we find that they think the problem is actually the patient. They say things like "Well, why did they say they were going to do something if they weren't going to do it?" The simple answer may be that the patient was never really committed to doing it (remember, patients have to believe that the behavior is important to them and be confident they can do it) and went along with the HCP to avoid being chastised or judged. The more important question to HCPs is why they are so frustrated. It is easy and not particularly honest to blame their frustration on patients' not keeping their word. Here is a more honest explanation. HCPs as a group are "doers." They are people who get things done. It is part of their identity. There are personal and professional rewards associated with getting things done. When patients are not ready to get things done (as defined by the HCP), HCPs must either suspend their rewards or find a new way to feel rewarded by being a caring resource for the patient and consistently staying in the spirit of MI. If this is not done, HCPs become frustrated, angry (remember, anger is born of powerlessness), or anxious. If they do not reflect on these feelings, they are likely to engage in scolding, judging, and fixing— none of which builds rapport.

**Staying separate yet fully available.** Earlier in the chapter we presented the case of a patient who wanted to take aspirin with his warfarin and said, "I really don't give a damn what you and my doctor say. I'll use aspirin with my warfarin if I want to. It's the only thing that gives me relief from my arthritis. Besides, the only reason he wants to do blood work all the time is so he can make extra fees." When patients express anger or frustration toward us or objectify us ("You people kill me"), there is a tendency to become defensive and either defend ourselves by explaining or become angry or frustrated in return. Again, none of these responses builds rapport. It is important to stay separate and not take the patient's responses personally, so that you can give a genuinely empathic response. Reflection and introspection are needed to begin exploring why you are taking these responses personally. We are not saying this is easy, and abusive language should not be tolerated. Responding to patients' anger and frustration is a necessary part of being in a caring profession. You are there to care for the patient, not the reverse.

## QUESTIONS FOR REFLECTION

1. How does rapport leverage the expertise of the HCP?
2. In what ways does developing rapport affect the patient's sense making?
3. Explain how the HCP's own anxiety or need to fix can get in the way of developing rapport.

## REFERENCES

1. Rogers CR. *A Way of Being*. Boston: Houghton Mifflin; 1980.
2. Basch MF. Empathic understanding: a review of the concept and some theoretical considerations. *J Am Psychoanal Assoc*. 1983;31:101–26.
3. Squier RW. A model of empathic understanding and adherence to treatment regimens in practitioner–patient relationships. *Soc Sci Med*. 1990;30: 325–39.
4. Gadow S. Existential advocacy: philosophical foundation of nursing. In: Spicker SF, Gadow S, eds. *Nursing: Images and Ideals*. New York: Springer; 1990:79–101.
5. Rogers CR. *On Becoming a Person*. Boston: Houghton Mifflin; 1961:47.

# CHAPTER 7

# Reframing the Issue

I n Chapter 6 we discussed the importance of building rapport, noting that patients are making sense of the relationship as well as of their illness and treatment. Developing rapport is critical in helping patients see that you are compassionate, caring, understanding, and respectful of how they are making sense of their health issues. As we develop rapport, we listen carefully to whether the patient is having difficulty making a change because of importance issues, confidence issues, or both.

Now we will discuss the next step in assisting the patient in the process of change: reframing.[1] We have found over years of teaching motivational interviewing (MI) that health care professionals (HCPs) do a very good job of learning empathic responding and reflection. They learn to slow down and listen for how patients are making sense of their illness and the prescribed health behavior changes. They learn how to reflect back and empathize with the patient's lines of reasoning in order to establish rapport. However, HCPs often get stuck with what to say or do next.

They are able to identify what information they want patients to consider as they invite the patients to reassess their sense making. But they simply do not know how to make a comfortable transition from expressing empathy and building rapport to addressing the patient's issue by sharing their expertise. If the HCP abruptly shares unsolicited information with the patient, with no prior preparation, the patient is likely to suffer loss of competence face and autonomy face. Here is an example: "Well, you know, high blood pressure is an asymptomatic illness. There are no symptoms you can sense that would tell you that you have high blood pressure." This unsolicited information causes the patient to lose face because it strongly implies that the HCP's perspective on the patient's situation is more valuable than the patient's perspective. To avoid this loss of face, it is helpful to formulate the provision of medical expertise as a response to some aspect of the patient's sense making. In addition to responding empathically and exploring resistance, another prominent way of accomplishing this is by *reframing the patient's issues.* This is extremely effective in helping the patient accept the medical information provided by the HCP as responsive to the patient's concerns and therefore truly informative to the patient.

If you've ever had a painting framed professionally, you have experienced the tremendous impact of framing. With a black frame around the painting, certain features in the painting may jump out at you. With a gold frame, entirely different features may grab your attention. The frame provides a context that causes certain features to become more or less prominent. Similarly, in communicative reframing we provide a new context for the patient's issues that causes different aspects of the patient's perspective to become more prominent. By reframing, we can make the provision of medical expertise an entirely natural response to the patient's issues—one that poses no risk of face loss while inviting patients to reconsider their sense making. Reframing can help patients see the issues differently, especially when there is resistance or ambivalence to change. In the following paragraphs we will discuss how reframing can be used to address four common issues or concerns that patients express.

**"I don't understand why I need to . . . ."** One major way to reframe an issue is called "You're wondering . . .". It is used when a patient makes a resistant statement that can be reframed as a question. For example, when a patient with high blood pressure says, "I just don't understand why I need this medicine. I feel fine" or another patient says, "No one in my family has died from high cholesterol. I don't see the point in treating it" or a third says, "My blood sugar isn't that high and I take my medicine. That should be enough" they are also saying, "Why do I need this medicine if I feel fine?" or "Why should I do anything about my cholesterol when no one else in my family treated it and it didn't hurt them?" or "Why do I need to do anything else if my blood sugar isn't very high and I take my medicine?" We developed this maneuver to take advantage of the shared social expectation that questions deserve answers. The question–answer sequence is technically a strong form of an adjacency pair, in which the first utterance (the question) sets up a social expectation for the performance of the second utterance (the answer). In other words, there is a very strong shared expectation that the HCP is under a social obligation to provide an answer to a question asked by the patient.

If we can reframe a patient's objection as really expressing an underlying question, then we have a natural reason to provide information in response to that question. Here is how "You're wondering . . ." works:

Pt: *I just don't understand why I need to take this medicine. I feel fine.*

HCP: Because you feel ok, you're wondering why you would need to take this medicine. (reflection; reframing as "You're wondering")

Pt: *Exactly.*

HCP: You raise a good question. (affirmation) Would it be OK if I give you some information to address your question and then you let me know what you think? (request to share information)

Pt: *Sure.*

HCP: Unfortunately, high blood pressure is a condition that does not have any symptoms until something serious happens. Usually the first symptom is a stroke or heart attack. We know that when blood pressure drops below 140/90 your risk of having a stroke or heart attack goes down substantially, even if you have no symptoms. Your blood pressure is 155/100. That puts you at a much higher risk of stroke or heart attack. I would hate to see that happen, especially when it is preventable. Where does that leave you now in wanting to lower your blood pressure?

In this dialogue, the patient's sense is that if she feels OK, she is OK. The HCP acknowledges the patient's sense making by saying, "Because you feel OK, you're wondering, 'Why would I need to take this medicine?'" This statement does two things: It builds rapport by reflecting back the patient's concern without judgment, and it poses the patient's concern in the form of a question, which now requires an answer. The HCP then tells the patient, "You raise a good question. Would it be OK if I give you some information to address your question and then you let me know what you think?" The HCP praises the patient for raising the question. This encourages the patient to ask questions in the future or to push back if the patient doesn't understand or doesn't like something, which will give the HCP an opportunity to address it. The exchange between the patient and the HCP sets up a question–answer sequence, because questions, especially good ones, require answers. When the HCP asks if he can now provide some information to address the patient's question, it would be difficult for the patient to say no. This allows the transition from reflecting and empathy to providing information.

In addition, the HCP says, "and then you let me know what you think." This indicates that this is a discussion and collaboration (not a parent talking to a child) and that the decision ultimately is the patient's. Information is then provided that explains how the patient can feel OK and still be at risk of stroke or heart attack, and the patient is asked how this new information affects her decision to lower her blood pressure. Without asking, "Where does this leave you now?" the HCP cannot know how this new information has affected the patient's decision making. Remember, MI is an exchange of expertise. The patient tells us how she is making sense of things—the patient's expertise. The HCP acknowledges and respects that and then asks permission to provide new information—the HCP's expertise. Then the HCP asks what the patient thinks of this new information.

**"I'm worried about side effects."** Many patients worry about the side effects of medications. Often they state that they cannot or will not take the medication because of a potential side effect. If the HCP counters that the patient needs to take the medication in spite of the side effect, the patient is likely to produce a "yes, but" response that can lead to unproductive arguing and increased relational resistance. Reframing avoids this problem by reformulating the patient's initial expression of resistance as a conditional commitment to change. So if the patient objects, "I can't take this medication because I heard that it can cause insomnia," the HCP can reframe this objection as a positive statement of commitment to take the medication *if* this particular side effect can be managed, reduced, or eliminated: "It sounds like you would be quite willing to take this medication if the insomnia can be eliminated or greatly reduced." Of course, this type of reframing is particularly effective when you already know that you can share information with the patient to alleviate the patient's concern. The effectiveness of reframing lies in the fact that you get a commitment from the patient before sharing the information. Then, when you have provided information that meets the patient's condition of eliminating or reducing the side effect, the patient feels the need to commit to trying the medication.

Here is an example of how to use reframing to respond to a patient's reluctance to take a medication because of a side effect.

> Pt: *I've heard that this medicine can cause some side effects. I don't know if I want to take it if that's the case.*
>
> HCP: You sound worried about side effects. (empathy) Tell me more about what you've heard. (exploring the issue)
>
> Pt: *My biggest concern is that I've read it can cause stomach upset. I can't handle that.*
>
> HCP: It sounds like if we were to either reduce or eliminate the chance of stomach upset with this medicine, you would be more willing to take it. (reframing)
>
> Pt: *Can you do that?*
>
> HCP: I believe so. Most of the stomach upset comes from taking this medicine on an empty stomach. If you take it with a meal, that eliminates the problem for most people.
>
> Pt: *But some still get an upset stomach?*
>
> HCP: A very small percentage. Would you like to try taking it for a few days and see if you can tolerate it with food?
>
> Pt: *Isn't there anything else I can take?*
>
> HCP: There are some alternatives that aren't as effective, but some of them can also cause stomach upset. I would be happy to discuss this with your doctor. What would you like to do?

Notice that this patient starts off not wanting to take the medication. The HCP first empathizes with the patient's worry and then explores what the patient has heard so that they can focus on the specific problem. Once the patient has identified stomach upset as the side effect that worries her, the HCP knows that reframing is a viable next step since taking this medication with food alleviates most patients' stomach upset. After the HCP has reframed the issue, the patient begins to explore taking the medication. The HCP listens to how the patient is making sense of the situation; the patient seems to be saying that the side effects are getting in the way of taking the medication, making it less important to do so. Through reframing, we find out whether that is the case or if other factors are involved. It's possible that the patient is unsure that she really needs the medication, so she mentions the side effects as a way to avoid taking it. By reframing, the HCP can find out how important the issue of side effects is and what, in particular, is troubling the patient. In this case, the main focus is stomach upset, and the pharmacist addresses that concern. The patient still has some doubts, and the pharmacist offers to allow her to try taking the medication for a few days. The patient then asks if there are any medications she could take that would not have this problem, and the pharmacist explores alternatives and asks the patient what she would like to do next.

**"I've tried that before."** Patients are often asked to consider losing weight or quitting smoking for better health in general or to help manage a chronic illness (e.g., diabetes, high blood pressure). Many times, patients are discouraged about the prospects of making the change because they have tried before and failed. Reframing can often help with this issue, as shown in the following dialogue:

Pt:    *I've tried losing weight before. Every time I do, it seems I gain it back. I once lost 30 pounds, but I eventually gained it all back. What's the point?*

HCP:    It's discouraging when you work so hard to lose weight and then you gain it all back. (empathy)

Pt:    *Yes, it is. I just don't want to go through all that again.*

HCP:    From what you're telling me, it sounds like you *have* been successful in losing weight. What has been very difficult is keeping it off. (reframing)

Pt:    *I suppose so. I haven't thought of it that way, but what difference does it make, if I gain it back?*

HCP:    You ask a good question. (affirmation) Would you mind if I ask you a few questions that might help answer your question? (request to elicit information)

Pt:    *OK.*

HCP:   When you have lost weight, what kinds of things were you doing that allowed you to lose the weight?

In this interaction the HCP started by empathizing with how discouraged the patient is about the cycle of losing weight and gaining it back. The same could have been done with a patient who stopped smoking and then began to smoke again. It is important to start the process of developing rapport by letting patients know that you see their perspectives. Here, the patient is saying he is discouraged by the fact that he loses the weight and then gains it back. He feels defeated, so he doesn't want to go through that again. His sense is that the same thing will happen if he tries again. In fact, if he tries again in the way he has tried in the past, he is probably correct.

By reframing, the HCP helps the patient see that he has been successful at losing weight. That may provide some encouragement. The real problem is sustaining the weight loss. In the process of rapport building and reframing, an open dialogue is started. The HCP inquires about how the patient was successful in losing weight, and she will listen carefully to what the patient tells her. Next, she will ask the patient what happens to undermine his ability to sustain the steps he took to lose weight. What often comes out in this line of inquiry—and it is different for each patient—are factors that make sustaining the weight loss problematic. These could involve diets and exercise routines that are overzealous and almost impossible to maintain, the need for an exercise partner or other diversion (e.g., television) if the patient finds exercise boring, weight loss goals that are unrealistic, or difficulty with healthy eating in restaurants. Through reframing and then exploring, factors such as these can emerge, enabling the HCP to work with the patient on a weight loss plan that more closely fits what is doable for that patient. The same strategy can be used for patients who have tried to stop smoking and relapsed. It is important to recognize that the patient has been successful at stopping and that the problem is sustaining smoking cessation. In all cases, it is important to understand whether the patient's problems involve importance or confidence. With patients who have tried losing weight or quitting smoking numerous times, it is likely that they understand the importance of the change but are not confident that they can successfully sustain the weight loss or smoking cessation. With patients who are not sure they want to quit smoking or lose weight, importance tends to be the dominant issue, although confidence in being able to make the change also comes into play.

**"It doesn't apply to me."** When HCPs suggest to patients that they consider making a change, such as quitting smoking or losing weight, to manage a chronic illness or improve their general health, patients often respond that these conditions or issues don't apply to them. Patients may contend that because they are only "social smokers" who have a few cigarettes now and then, their smoking is really not a problem. The temptation is for the HCP is to say something like "Well (or 'yes, but'), any amount of smoking is bad for you, even a few cigarettes." This, of course, is argumentative and runs the risk of creating loss of face and defensiveness on the part of the patient. Here is a dialogue that uses reframing to respond to "It doesn't apply to me."

> Pt: *Look, everyone in my family has high cholesterol. They have always eaten whatever they want to eat, and none of them died prematurely. They all lived well into their 70s and 80s, and they didn't take anything for their cholesterol.*

> HCP: It sounds like you have great genes in your family (reflection), and I certainly hope you live a long and healthy life, too. (affirmation of patient's goal)

> Pt: *Right. It's not a problem.*

> HCP: And I sure hope that is true for you, too. Would you mind if I ask you to consider something and you tell me what you think?

> Pt: *Sure, but don't expect me to make any changes.*

> HCP: (calmly) OK. It really is up to you. Here are my thoughts. It sounds like people in your family, despite having high cholesterol, have not died prematurely from strokes or heart attacks caused by high cholesterol. In all families, there is always some individual variation—for example, some family members are taller, some have different colors of hair or eyes—even though they are all from the same family. (reframing) There is a good chance that your high cholesterol won't affect you any differently than it has the rest of your family. But it might, because of variation even within your family. Taking cholesterol medicine or losing weight or eating less cholesterol-containing food is like taking out an insurance policy against the chance that

the way cholesterol affects you may be slightly different. You have to decide: Do you want to take some steps to reduce possible risks for you, or do you want to bet on the idea that you're just like the rest of your family and your high cholesterol will not cause any problems? It really is up to you, and I would be happy to help you with steps to reduce your cholesterol if that's what you would like to do. What are your thoughts?

Pt:   *You make some good points. Can't I just wait and see if I have any problems?*

HCP:   That's really a good question. My concern with a wait and see approach is that by the time you notice any symptoms, the underlying problem can be major and may not be reversible. In fact, sometimes the first warning is a stroke or a heart attack or a blockage in the heart or brain that can cause paralysis or serious circulation problems.

Pt:   *That sounds dangerous.*

HCP:   It is.

Pt:   *Well, you've given me some things to think about.*

HCP:   Give it some thought. If you decide you want to work on lowering your cholesterol, let me know how I can help. Whatever you decide, I promise I won't bother you about it.

Pt:   *Thanks. I appreciate that.*

This patient's sense is that because many family members have high cholesterol, eat whatever they want, have not treated their high cholesterol, and have not suffered any serious consequences, he doesn't need to do anything either. After all, he is from the same gene pool. Again, the temptation is to say, "Yes, but that doesn't mean that is the case for you," and then explain about individual variation. If no attempt is made to reflect understanding of the patient's perspective (and he may be right that it won't affect him), this kind of response can cause loss of face and is likely to be discounted.

In this dialogue, the HCP first acknowledges the patient's perspective (sense making) and expresses that she hopes the patient will not be negatively affected by high cholesterol. This affirmation supports the patient's implicit goal of living a long life. The patient then knows that the HCP has listened without judgment, and the patient confirms this by saying, "Right. It's not a problem." The HCP reiterates that she hopes this is the case for the patient, too. Notice that the HCP consistently expresses care and concern and support of the patient even though she is aware that the patient is not planning to treat his cholesterol right now. She stays in the spirit of MI. She doesn't allow any anxiety she may have about the patient's sense making to keep her from supporting the patient. This does not mean that she agrees or disagrees with his thinking. She simply wants him to know that she, too, wants him to be healthy.

Next, the HCP asks the patient to consider some information and let her know what he thinks. The patient agrees, but he reinforces that he is not going to make any changes. The HCP lets the patient know that it is his decision, and by doing so she lets the patient know she is not trying to impose her will on him. Next, the HCP reframes the issue as one of variation within the family, by shining a light on how even family members vary in many different ways. She then asks the patient to consider lowering his cholesterol as "taking out an insurance policy" just in case he is somewhat different from his family. She does not draw any conclusions for the patient; she simply frames his choices and then asks what his thoughts are. Not surprisingly, the patient acknowledges the new information in a positive way ("You make some good points"). He is not defensive, because he feels understood and there is no loss of face. He is still not quite ready to take action, but this new information and the way it is presented cause him to reconsider his sense making. The chances are good that this patient will continue to think about his high cholesterol, because the HCP has reframed the situation as a matter of variation within the family. This is very powerful in regard to motivation for change.

For patients who say, "I don't smoke that much" or "I really don't need to lose weight," the same approach is recommended. First, acknowledge the patient's sense making ("Since you don't smoke that much, you don't really see that it's a problem" or "Your weight is not a problem for you at this point"). Next, ask if you may provide some information and have the patient tell you what he thinks. Then (reframe) give the new information in a "more" or "less" format instead of an "all or nothing" context ("Any weight you could lose will help put less strain on your heart, reduce your blood pressure, and decrease your risk of a stroke or heart attack. It's really a matter of how much risk you are willing to assume. What are your thoughts about this?"), and listen carefully to the patient's response to see if there has been any change in his sense making.

**"This (medicine, procedure, physical therapy) is too expensive."** Patients will often state that they can't afford the co-pay or deductible for some pre- scribed therapy (e.g., medicine, diagnostic procedure, physical therapy). It is very important for the HCP to respectfully sort through this issue. There certainly are patients who cannot afford the prescribed service or product. Every effort should be made to explore options such as assistance programs and generic drugs.

On the other hand, some patients may complain about the amount of a co-pay even though they can afford to pay it. They simply think it's a lot of money. We know a patient who was prescribed a nonsteroidal anti-inflammatory drug (NSAID) for chronic arthritis pain. His co-pay was $50 because this drug was brand name only and had not gone off patent. No generic equivalent was available yet. The patient got a lot of relief from this particular NSAID and was not interested in any other medication. He was very compliant; he just wished the co-pay were not so high.

Finally, some patients can afford the co-pay for their chronic medication but are noncompliant and constantly complain about the high co-pay. Their complaints suggest that they don't understand the need for or the importance of the medication because they feel just fine. Such patients are saying that they prefer to spend their hard-earned money for other things that seem more important to them.

Talking empathically with patients who say the cost of their therapies is an issue, and reframing their issues, will enable you to distinguish among the three types of patients just described. Here is an example:

Pt:   (handing over a prescription) *How much is this going to set me back?*

HCP:   The co-pay on this medication is $50.

Pt:   *Fifty dollars? Wow. That's expensive.*

HCP:   It is a high co-pay. (reflection) Will that cause you any problems in being able to take the medication? (elicit information) I would hate to see you go without it. (affirmation)

Pt:   *I can't see paying that much money when I'm not even sure I need this.*

HCP:   You're having some doubts about whether you need this medicine. (empathy)

Pt:   *Yes, I am. I feel fine. Seems like doctors these days want to zap you with medicine, and sometimes I wonder if you even need it.*

HCP: So, given that you feel pretty good and so much medicine gets prescribed, you wonder if this medicine is really necessary, especially since it's so expensive. (reframing)

Pt: *Exactly.*

HCP: What did the doctor tell you about why he was prescribing this medicine?

Pt: *He says I have diabetes, but I just don't know.*

HCP: Mostly because you feel fine.

Pt: *That, and no one in my family has ever had diabetes.*

HCP: So you're having some doubts about the diagnosis, too.

Pt: *I suppose.*

HCP: What would make you feel more confident in the diagnosis at this point?

Pt: *I guess I just didn't expect it.*

HCP: Diabetes can surprise you because, early on, patients often don't have symptoms. If it's left untreated, serious problems like circulation problems, blindness, and kidney failure can occur.

Pt: *That's what he said.*

HCP: So, right now, it sounds like all of this has hit you quite unexpectedly.

This dialogue could have gone in any number of directions. At the beginning, the HCP set the tone by exploring whether the amount of the co-pay would make it difficult for the patient to take the medication. Through empathy, exploration, and reframing, the HCP learned a great deal about a patient who on the surface seemed to simply be complaining about the amount of the co-pay.

**"I am just not ready to quit smoking (or exercise, lose weight, take the medicine)."** In some cases, patients may not be ready to consider change. Reframing can help them become ready. Here is a dialogue that uses a type of reframing called "a look over the fence."[2]

Pt:     *I know smoking is bad for me. I know I should quit.*

HCP:   So on the one hand, you know that smoking can cause serious health problems that affect your heart, lungs, and circulation, while on the other hand it's been hard to make the decision to quit. (reflection)

Pt:     *Right. I don't want to have cancer or emphysema, but my life has so much stress right now that I don't think I could quit.*

HCP:   If you were to wake up tomorrow morning, and you were no longer a smoker, what would you like about it? (a look over the fence)

Pt:     *Gosh, I wouldn't be so out of breath, and my clothes wouldn't smell. It's expensive, so I would have money to do other things that are better for me. I might not get cancer or emphysema. A lot of things would be better.*

HCP:   You see a great many benefits to no longer being a smoker—benefits to both your health and your finances. You are already getting winded, so that makes you wonder what problems may be occurring with your lungs. (reflection)

Pt:     *Absolutely. That worries me. But, I would still be stressed.*

HCP:   It sounds like if we were to find ways to help you manage your stress that didn't involve smoking, you might consider quitting or cutting back. (reframing for a conditional commitment)

Pt:     *I would definitely at least consider cutting back.*

In this dialogue, the patient understood the importance of quitting in general terms, but he was ambivalent about quitting because smoking relieved some of his stress. At this point his decisional balance was between the generally understood reasons for quitting smoking and his personal need for stress relief. Using a look over the fence, the patient lists benefits of quitting that are vivid and personally important to him. This shift to a personal level can strengthen the patient's commitment to change. Often the HCP will ask permission to name additional benefits that other patients have elaborated on and will then ask the patient if any of these apply to him. All of this can be important in tilting the decisional balance in favor of change. Notice that this patient still came back to stress, and the HCP reframed again for a conditional commitment. As a result of both types of reframing, the patient is now considering change.

**"It's not that bad."** When patients consider the consequences of, for example, allowing their blood sugar or blood pressure to remain high, they often do so in general terms rather than in very personal terms. Consequently, it's relatively easy for patients to discount the seriousness of their situation. Reframing can be used to shift the patient's attention from the consequences in general to the specific personal consequences for the patient's everyday life. Here is an example:

Pt:     *OK, the doctor said my blood pressure is up. He hassled me about my smoking and the fact that I don't take all of my medicine. I only miss a few doses a week. Look, other than the smoking, I am in really good shape.*

HCP:   You felt pressured by the doctor to quit smoking and take your medicine every day as prescribed. You didn't appreciate that. In addition, you are in good shape, so you wonder if there really is a big problem. (empathy; reframing as "So you're wondering . . .")

Pt:     *Right. I think he's making a mountain out of a molehill.*

HCP:   Things don't seem as bad as he's making them. (reflection)

Pt:     *Exactly!*

HCP:   What would have to change for you to consider taking your medication as prescribed and quitting smoking? (exploring)

Pt:     *I don't know. I guess if I had symptoms of problems or something like that.*

HCP:   If you woke up tomorrow and found yourself in a hospital bed because you'd had a stroke, and you were partially paralyzed and had difficulty speaking because of the stroke, what would that be like for you? (reframing as "What would happen if . . .")

Pt:     *That would be terrible. I am a trial lawyer. That would be devastating to what I do. Come on now, I haven't even had any symptoms.*

HCP:   Having no symptoms makes this hard to imagine. (reflection)

Pt:     *Yes.*

HCP: Would you mind if I share some information with you and then you tell me what you think? (asking permission)

Pt: *OK.*

In this situation the patient wasn't ready to quit smoking or take medication every day for his high blood pressure. Because he had not had any symptoms and he believed he was in good shape physically, it just didn't seem important to him. After the HCP's reflecting, empathizing, and exploring, and then reframing by asking the patient to consider "What would happen if," the patient was willing to receive additional information addressing how the first symptom he might ever notice could be a devastating stroke or heart attack.

**Conclusion.** We have explored the use of reframing to help patients re-examine their sense making. By honoring the patient's expertise and reflecting it back, HCPs can effectively use reframing to ask the patient to see a problem or concern about a health behavior in a new light.

## QUESTIONS FOR REFLECTION

1. How is reframing different from simply exploring a patient's resistance or ambivalence?
2. Which form of reframing do you think might be helpful to you in interacting with patients? Why?
3. Discuss the appropriate use of "You're wondering . . .". What are the advantages of using it? When might it not be appropriate to use "You're wondering . . ."?

### REFERENCES

1. Miller WR, Rollnick S. *Motivational Interviewing: Preparing People to Change Addictive Behavior.* New York: Guilford Press; 1991: 107–9.
2. Rollnick S, Mason P, Butler C. *Health Behavior Change.* London: Churchill Livingstone; 1999.

# CHAPTER 8

# Next Steps

In the previous two chapters, we've discussed the first two steps in motivational interviewing (MI): developing rapport, and reframing patients' issues as a way of making the transition to information giving. In this chapter, we discuss the remaining steps in the exchange of expertise that we call MI:

3. *Ask permission to provide information to address the patient's sense making.* Asking permission provides a transition to offering new information to "throw a wrench" into the patient's sense making.

4. *Provide new information.* This information must specifically address patients' current sense making and lead patients to reconsider how they are making sense of the current situation.

5. *Ask patients what they think of the new information.* After providing new information, assess what patients think. Where does the new information leave them now in regard to change? By asking this question, you gain information about what the next steps need to be or what additional information the patient might need to consider.

6. *Summarize and discuss next steps.* On the basis of how the patient responds to the new information, summarize your understanding of where things

stand so far. If the new information causes patients to change their sense making and be more committed to change, reflect or affirm these changes in sense making and then discuss what the patient would like to do next.

# Ask permission

Step 3 is "Ask permission to provide information to address the patient's sense making." After accurately reflecting the patient's concerns and sense making, it is respectful to ask the patient's permission to provide new information. We have suggested saying something like the following: "Would you mind if I give you some additional information and you tell me what you think?" or "Can I tell you some things that are on my mind and you tell me what you think?" or "May I share some information with you that is relevant to your concern (or question) and then you tell me how well this information fits your situation?" Asking permission respects the patient's autonomy, avoiding loss of face and letting patients know that the patient is the one who decides. It treats the patient as a partner in the relationship. Adding ". . . and you tell me what you think" lets the patient know that you are interested in how the patient thinks about the new information and that you understand that, ultimately, the patient decides.

We have developed a way of asking permission that we call "the insurance card." Sometimes patients' resistance to change is based on erroneous information or beliefs (or sense making) that can actually be harmful. For example, many illnesses are asymptomatic, and patients may decide not to treat such an illness because they believe they are not at risk. They may say, "My diabetes is not that bad" or "My blood pressure is not that high" or "I really don't need that medicine" or "I am not that overweight" or "I don't smoke that much. . . . It's not an issue" when in actuality, all of these things pose serious risks. The temptation, especially if we become anxious when we hear such comments from the patient, is to correct the patient without asking permission and to thereby create face loss and defensiveness. Using the insurance card helps health care professionals (HCPs) avoid having our anxiety predispose us to "fix" or "save" the patient. The insurance card is simply "May I tell you what concerns me?" Practitioners can use their anxiety as a stimulus to use the insurance card instead of fixing or correcting the patient. As HCPs become more comfortable with MI and more comfortable with empathizing and asking permission to provide new information, they will have less need to use the insurance card. Until then, it is a tool to help

HCPs overcome their anxiety when patients make statements about their health that HCPs perceive as potentially harmful.

We have discussed reasons for asking permission to give information or express a concern, but there is one scenario in which asking permission can be counterproductive: when you strongly sense that if you ask permission the patient will say no, yet you know that not providing new information for the patient to consider would be an ethical breach. An example is the scenario in Chapter 6 with the patient who was taking the blood thinner warfarin, insisted on using aspirin for his arthritis, and did not want to be monitored by his physician. The patient's decision to continue taking aspirin and not be monitored was potentially dangerous, since taking aspirin along with warfarin can cause serious or fatal hemorrhaging. In that dialogue (page 133), the HCP reflected his understanding and then asked permission to give information, and the patient reluctantly agreed. If the HCP in that scenario believed the patient would refuse the information, it would be prudent for the HCP to calmly state the serious concern about hemorrhaging and how that could happen and then to ask the patient where that left him regarding being monitored. Failing to provide this information would be both dangerous to the patient and unethical.

If you ask permission and the patient says no, we recommend one of two responses, depending on the possible risk to the patient. If not giving the information poses a serious risk to the patient, as in the aspirin–warfarin example, the HCP can say, "I want you to know that ultimately this is your decision. I am very concerned about your taking the aspirin without being monitored. You could bleed to death. I feel so strongly about this that I am going to let the doctor's office know you are continuing to use aspirin with your warfarin and will not be coming in for monitoring. It would be truly tragic if you were injured or died when this is preventable. I don't want that to happen to you." The patient may not like the fact that you asked permission and then gave the information anyway. However, this information could save the patient's life. This option must be used in the spirit of care and concern.

On the other hand, if the patient's resistance may not pose an immediate risk but may pose a long-term risk, the following approach can be used:

Pt: *I'll take the medicine, but don't expect me to do anything else. I don't exercise, and I like what I eat. The medicine should take care of my sugar.*

HCP: I'm glad to hear that you are committed to taking the medicine. That's an important step in getting your diabetes under control.

(affirmation) What's your understanding of how more physical activity and healthier eating habits can help lower your blood sugar to avoid serious complications like kidney disease or heart and circulation problems? (exploring)

Pt:     *I don't care. The medicine should be enough.*

HCP:    So you're wondering why you should do anything else when the medicine should take care of it. (reframing as "So you're wondering . . .")

Pt:     *That's correct.*

HCP:    That's a great question. Would you mind if I share some information with you to answer your question and you tell me what you think? (request to share information)

Pt:     *No. I am not doing anything else. I'll take the medicine.*

HCP:    OK. I really am glad to hear that you are committed to taking the medicine. Please keep an eye on how your blood sugar is doing. I would hate to see you have any serious complications that you could avoid.

Pt:     *Fine.*

In this situation, it would not be prudent to disregard the patient's "No" by sharing the information anyway, since relational resistance and loss of face would probably occur. What would be appropriate is to simply and sincerely support the patient's commitment to take the medicine and then to express concern about the possibility of complications that could be avoided.

In both of these situations, it would be important to put a note in the patient record about the interaction and your attempt to advise the patient. Note that in both situations the patient was willing to take the medication prescribed. This should not be ignored. It is important to *support self-efficacy* about health behaviors even when other behaviors or the lack of them may be detrimental. It is also important to support self-efficacy regarding thoughts, not just behaviors. For example, a patient might say, "I've been thinking more about losing some weight to get my blood pressure down." The temptation might be to say, "Great, how much weight are you going to lose?" or

"When are you going to start?" The patient is considering losing weight, but this does not mean he is ready to do something. It would be important to notice his statement and explore it: "I'm glad to hear that you're thinking of losing weight to bring your blood pressure down. What's got you thinking more about it at this point?" We would then listen carefully to what the patient said and reflect that back.

## Provide new information

This is Step 4. We recommend that new information provided to challenge the patient's sense making meet three criteria: It must address the patient's sense making, it must make sense to the patient, and it must be expressed in a neutral form. The following paragraphs discuss these criteria.

The patient's sense making and the information used to address it can be pictured as a lock and key. The patient's sense of the illness or treatment has the patient "locked into" keeping things as they are. Our information must be the key that can open the lock to allow the possibility of change. The information must fit the lock. For example, a patient may say, "I am not overweight. Why do I need to exercise to get my blood pressure down if I'm not overweight? I hate exercise." After rapport has been developed, any information provided must address why an increase in physical activity can help reduce the patient's blood pressure even though she is not overweight. General information about high blood pressure, strokes, and heart attacks, although accurate, would not address this patient's question. An appropriate response would be "You ask a really good question. Physical activity, like walking, even in small amounts, can raise your heart rate and strengthen your heart muscle. A stronger heart can pump your blood with less effort, and this actually lowers your blood's pressure against your arteries. This lowers your risk of stroke and heart attack. What are your thoughts about adding some physical activity, like walking, now that you've heard this?" Such a response encourages the patient to ask questions in the future, directly addresses the patient's sense making, and then asks how this new information affects the patient's decision about adding physical activity.

If this patient really was overweight and said, "I'm not overweight. Do you think I'm overweight?" the HCP could say, "Any weight that you can lose will help put less stress on your heart, lower your blood pressure, and decrease your chance of stroke or heart attack. What are your thoughts?" This focuses the discussion on the reason for losing weight, not on the patient's actual weight.

Since the information you provide must make sense to the patient, it is important to avoid the use of jargon whenever possible. Sometimes HCPs use terms such as hypertension, hyperlipidemia, and proton pump inhibitor when using high blood pressure, high cholesterol, and heartburn medication would be perfectly appropriate and would make sense to the patient. To avoid losing face, patients may not let the HCP know that they don't understand medical jargon. It is best to also connect the new information to old information that the patient already knows and considers important. Otherwise, the new information may not have an impact on the patient's sense making.

The information must be expressed in a neutral form. Typically, when HCPs provide information about medical conditions it is expressed in a prescriptive format that states or implies what conclusions the patient should draw from the information. Such "shoulds" cause patients to become defensive and resistant. For medical information to have maximum impact, it must be expressed neutrally, as a simple statement of fact. If the information precisely addresses the patient's issue and is expressed clearly and simply enough for the patient to understand, the patient should naturally feel the impulse to re-evaluate her conclusion. If the patient doesn't feel this impulse, the next step will be to ask the patient for her thoughts about the information. The following are two examples of "shoulds" that have been layered over simple information and need to be eliminated.

**"You have to understand that . . . ," "Don't you realize that . . . ?" "You need to know that . . . ."** Prefacing the expression of relevant medical information with such phrases strongly implies that you are the best judge of what the patient should be thinking. It further implies that if the patient really understood this information, she would be drawing the same conclusion you are drawing. The solution to this problem is sharing the information as a simple statement, without such prescriptive prefacing. Thus, "You need to understand that you are at high risk of suffering a major stroke or heart attack because of your high blood pressure" would be rephrased as "Your high blood pressure places you at high risk for a major stroke or heart attack."

**"Your goal is to get your . . . below . . ." or "You need to get your . . . below . . . ."** This phrasing often reflects important treatment guidelines, such as national guidelines on the treatment of high blood pressure and diabetes that explicitly refer to therapeutic goals (e.g., reducing blood pressure below 140/90, reducing A1c below 7.0). It is very easy for HCPs to refer to such goals when talking with patients. The problem is that such wording preempts decision making by the patient and thereby causes defensiveness and loss of face. Therapeutic goals have to be rephrased as thresholds below which the risks of complications significantly decrease. "Your goal is to get your LDL level below 100" should be rephrased as "When LDL is below 100, your risk of a stroke or heart attack goes down significantly. Your LDL is 150, which is quite a bit higher and increases your risk of stroke or heart attack. Where does this leave you now in regard to lowering your LDL?"

## Use analogies

Using analogies is a powerful method for communicating new concepts and information to patients in a way that makes sense. Analogies can help patients make sense of what may seem like an abstract idea concerning their illness, its treatment, or some health behavior change. When used properly, analogies can stimulate thinking (cognition) and help clear up confusion or misunderstandings patients may have, so that they can draw new conclusions or make better sense of what is being proposed. To be effective, an analogy must do the following:

- The analogy must connect a new idea or concept (that is abstract or confusing to the patient) to a concept that is already part of the patient's understanding or knowledge. This connection must be congruent with the patient's experience and educational level so that the patient can identify with the analogy as sensible, realistic, and relevant.
- The main point of the analogy must directly address the particular issue the patient is struggling with and help the patient to vividly sense the problem being faced.
- The comparison or parallelism at the heart of the analogy must be clear, consistent, and logical. The characteristics of the new concept must match up with the characteristics of the already known concept. If the patient is confused about the logic of the comparison, the force of the analogy will be lost on the patient.

The following dialogue shows the effective use of an analogy. Bill Reynolds is a 51-year-old patient who jogs two or three miles a day, is very fit, does not smoke, follows a low-salt diet, and has less than 15% body fat. His physician has taken his blood pressure several times on two different visits, and it remains elevated. The physician has prescribed a mild diuretic to treat the elevated blood pressure. The patient presents the new prescription to his pharmacist.

Pt: *The doctor said my blood pressure is 145/95. He told me that my goal is under 140/90 and that 130/80 would be even better. I am not that far off. Do I really need this medicine?*

Ph: If I remember correctly, Mr. Reynolds, you're a runner and have a healthy lifestyle. Since your blood pressure is not that far above 140/90, you're wondering if it's really necessary to start taking medication to bring it down.

Pt: *Right. I'm in pretty good shape. I watch the salt in my diet. I'm not that far off.*

Ph: You raise a good question. Would it be OK if I give you some information to address your question and you let me know what you think?

Pt: *Sure. Absolutely.*

Ph: Great. If I could draw an analogy, I think it might help. If your blood pressure is the fuse, the explosion is a stroke or heart attack. Lowering your blood pressure below 140/90 reduces your risk of having a stroke or heart attack. Here's the problem. Even though your blood pressure is not far from 140/90, we simply don't know how long your fuse is. Because of genetics, family history, and other factors, people can have long or short fuses. Someone whose blood pressure is quite a bit higher than yours might have a really long fuse. You might have a really long fuse. There is just no way to know for certain. By lowering your blood pressure below 140/90, this medicine can help protect the integrity of your fuse, regardless of its length, so it won't burn down. This reduces the chance of the explosion—the stroke or heart attack. You have to decide how important it is to you to lower your risk of having an explosion by taking the medicine. I would hate to see you have a stroke or heart attack when you could prevent it. Where does this leave you now in regard to taking the medication?

Pt:    *I had no idea. No one ever explained it to me that way. I sure don't want my fuse to burn down.*

Ph:    I don't either.

Pt:    *Well then, let's go ahead and fill my prescription. And thanks. That helps.*

Several things in this dialogue should be pointed out. Before using the analogy, the pharmacist develops rapport by acknowledging the patient's question ("Since your blood pressure is not that far above 140/90, you're wondering . . .") and the legitimacy of the question ("You raise a good question"). This encourages the patient to ask questions in the future and makes it feel safe to do so. The pharmacist also uses previous knowledge about the patient ("you're a runner and have a healthy lifestyle") to establish rapport and personalize the discussion. This information is also important to the discussion in that more running and lifestyle changes probably are not going to bring this patient's blood pressure down. Since the patient's main concern is already expressed in the form of a question, it is appropriate for the pharmacist to provide new information in the form of an analogy to answer the patient's question and thereby to address the patient's sense making. In this example, the patient is essentially saying, "If my blood pressure is not that far off, is it really necessary to take the new medication? Am I really at risk?" Any new information must address this question, or the patient may decide not to take the medication. Simply responding, "Yes, you need to take the medicine" or "Yes, any blood pressure that is elevated is potentially dangerous" does not fully answer "Why?" Notice also that after presenting the analogy and the problem ("we simply don't know how long your fuse is"), the pharmacist frames the risk issue and allows the patient to draw his own conclusions ("You have to decide how important it is to you to lower your risk of having an explosion by taking the medicine. I would hate to see you have a stroke or heart attack when you could prevent it. Where does this leave you now in regard to taking the medication?")

The fuse and explosion analogy meets the three criteria for an effective analogy. A fuse and explosion are knowable and understandable to the patient. The patient can vividly sense a fuse burning down and the explosion taking place. Not knowing how long the patient's fuse is directly addresses how a patient whose blood pressure is "not that high" can still be at risk. The comparison between the fuse and explosion and the patients' blood pressure and stroke or heart attack is logically consistent throughout.

This analogy explains the problem in a very honest way; HCPs really don't know how long someone's fuse is, and this explains why a patient may be at risk.

Using the same patient scenario, here is an example of an analogy that does not work:

Pt: *The doctor said my blood pressure is 145/95. He told me that my goal is under 140/90 and that 130/80 would be even better. I am not that far off. Do I really need this medicine?*

Ph: If I remember correctly, Mr. Reynolds, you're a runner and have a healthy lifestyle. Since your blood pressure is not that far above 140/90, you're wondering if it's really necessary to have to start taking medication to bring it down.

Pt: *Right. I'm in pretty good shape. I watch the salt in my diet. I'm not that far off.*

Ph: You raise a good question. Would it be OK if I give you some information to address your question and you let me know what you think?

Pt: *Sure. Absolutely.*

Ph: Great. If I could draw an analogy, I think it might help. If you think of your car as your heart, it's important to change the oil frequently enough so that it doesn't get too low or sludgy. Then the pistons don't work right and the engine can break down.

Pt: *I'm not sure I see how my blood pressure being slightly up is like changing the oil.*

Ph: Well, even if the oil gets slightly low, your car can have serious problems.

Pt: *Sorry, I'm just not following you. My blood pressure is high, not low.*

This analogy violates two of the three criteria for effectiveness. Although the patient does know what a car is, the analogy does not help him visualize the problem. Moreover, the patient cannot sense the direct comparison between damage from low oil and the risk of slightly elevated blood pressure. The problem is that this analogy does not pose a clear comparison that helps the patient grasp the significance and seriousness of his problem. This patient wound up frustrated trying to follow the analogy. He expressed his confusion about the point of the analogy, but many patients would not do so because they don't want to cause themselves, the HCP, or both to lose competence face. We recommend that you pilot test prospective analogies on colleagues and friends to see if they are clear and sensible. Then try the analogies out with patients and assess their responses. You may need to refine and reformulate an analogy until it works effectively.

Here is another example of the effective use of an analogy. Tanya Smith is a 43-year-old cook in a fraternity house. Her A1c has dropped from 9.0 to 8.6. She has made some lifestyle changes but is not interested in doing anything more. She does not exercise, and she eats a lot of bread and pasta. She takes her medication as prescribed.

Pt: *Look, my sugar has come down some and I feel just fine. I'm happy with my life, and I am not interested in making any more changes.*

HCP: First, you are to be congratulated on the changes you've made that have helped your blood sugar come down.

Pt: *Thank you.*

HCP: It often takes a lot of changes in lifestyle to make significant changes in blood sugar.

Pt: *That's right. I've made enough. Like I said, I feel fine.*

HCP: Because you've made a lot of changes and you feel good, it's hard to imagine making any more changes at this point.

Pt: *You got it!*

HCP: Ms. Smith, it really is your decision. Would you mind if I give you a little more information and you tell me what you think?

Pt: *Go ahead, but I'm not making more changes.*

HCP: Fair enough. Your blood sugar has come down. We know that when A1c (your blood sugar) goes below 7.0, your risks of kidney failure, eye disease, circulation problems, and stroke and heart attack go down a great deal. Your A1c is 8.6. That's still quite a bit higher, and it increases your risks of those serious complications. Here is the problem: Our body can use only so much sugar. After that the sugar remains in the blood, and it accumulates over time. After a while it's as if your blood vessels, heart, kidneys, eyes, nerves, and the like are soaking in more and more syrup. At first, you don't feel like anything is wrong. Then, once serious damage occurs, you have symptoms and it's too late. If you've ever watched a pancake sit and soak in syrup, it starts to fall apart after a while. That's what is happening to your tissues when your blood sugar builds up. It's very dangerous, even though you feel OK right now. What are your thoughts now about trying to bring your blood sugar down even more? I would be glad to help.

Pt: *I never thought about it that way. I can feel OK, yet this is going on in my body?*

HCP: Unfortunately, yes. Anything you can do to bring your blood sugar down under 7.0 will really decrease your risks of these serious complications.

Pt: *I just don't know if I can do any more.*

HCP: Doing more seems overwhelming.

Pt: *Yes.*

HCP: I sure don't want you to do anything that's unnecessary or overwhelming. Would you mind if I suggest a few small steps that can have a significant impact on your blood sugar and you tell me what you think?

Pt: OK.

This patient is now ready to consider additional lifestyle changes to lower her blood sugar. How did this happen? First, the pharmacist acknowledged her efforts in lowering her blood sugar. Even though it is still high, the pharmacist avoided the temptation to say, "Yes, but it's still too high." Instead the pharmacist began building rapport by recognizing the patient's efforts. Next, the pharmacist acknowledged that lowering blood sugar is not easy and summarized the patient's concerns: She feels fine, and she's made enough changes already. The pharmacist then asks permission to give some additional information for the patient to consider. The patient reluctantly agrees, and the pharmacist summarizes the current situation. The pharmacist provides guideposts for the patient and her A1c. She tells the patient that the risks fall substantially when A1c drops below 7.0. Two things should be noted: (1) the pharmacist names the risks or complications so they are not vague ("complications" is too vague) and (2) the pharmacist does not impose a goal (e.g., "Your goal is to get your A1c down below 7"). Instead, the pharmacist simply states what is true objectively. Next, the pharmacist uses the analogy to answer the patient's unstated question, "How can I be at risk when my blood sugar has come down and I feel fine?" The syrup analogy works because the patient can both understand and visualize how syrup will cause a pancake to degrade. Finally, the analogy explains how the patient can feel fine at first but still be at risk of serious health consequences. Although the patient still expresses concern about being able to do anything more, she is now interested and understands that there are health consequences. Notice that, originally, the patient's sense making focused mostly on issues of importance. She did not believe any more steps were needed beyond taking her medication, because she felt fine and her blood sugar had come down some. Now the issue is entirely one of confidence in her own ability to do anything more to bring her blood sugar down. The pharmacist recognizes this implicit change in her perspective ("I sure don't want you to do anything that's unnecessary or overwhelming. Would you mind if I suggest a few small steps that can have a significant impact on your blood sugar and you tell me what you think?") Such an approach reassures, respects, and engages the patient. All choices are left to the patient.

Now let's suppose that the patient is Jeff Smith, a 43-year-old electrician whose A1c has dropped from 9.0 to 8.6. He has made some lifestyle changes but is not interested in doing anything more. He gets no vigorous exercise, and he eats a lot of bread and pasta. He takes his medication as prescribed. With Jeff, the pharmacist might consider using an analogy that is more congruent with his background as an electrician and that explains in more detail the harm caused by excessive blood sugar. This analogy creates a parallel between power lines and nerve cells to explain glycosylation, the process of excess sugar molecules bonding to proteins in various organs of the body. Just as tree branches that make contact with power lines hurt the transmission of electricity in those lines, excess sugar molecules that bind with the proteins in nerve cells damage the transmission of nerve impulses. The only difference is that while utility companies can trim away the tree branches to restore the efficiency of the power lines, the sugar molecules cannot be stripped away from the nerve cells once they have bonded. The damage to the nerve cells is permanent. Similar damage occurs elsewhere in the body as sugar bonds to cells in the heart, blood vessels, eyes, and kidneys. The patient's only option is to reduce blood sugar to more normal levels so there is no excess sugar to bond to these cells. If Jeff has suffered no noticeable symptoms from his excess blood sugar, and if in the future he keeps his A1c below 7.0, he may avoid having symptoms that hurt his quality of life. Although the syrup analogy might raise concern for Jeff, this analogy may be more powerful in creating ongoing commitment to keep his blood sugar level close to normal.

The following are a few other analogies that HCPs have used successfully.

**Exquisitely sensitive.** A mother could not understand why her son's asthma made him so sensitive to so many things in his environment—dust, smoke, pollen— especially if he didn't use the chronic inhaler each day. The following analogy was used to help her understand. "If you were at a party and someone brushed up against your arm because it was crowded, you would not think anything of it. However, if you'd had the skin burned off your arm the day before and someone brushed up against you accidentally, you would say, 'Hey, watch it!' because your skin would be exquisitely sensitive. Your son's lungs are somewhat inflamed already because of his asthma. The chronic inhaler reduces his lungs' inflammation and protects them. When he does not use the chronic inhaler every day, his lungs become inflamed even more and are exquisitely sensitive to even small amounts of irritants such as dust, pollen, and smoke, much in the same way your arm was exquisitely sensitive without the protection of your skin."

**Grapes and watermelons are both fruits.** A man had an allergic reaction that produced a rash on his arm. He was prescribed a topical cream for the rash. When he looked up the name of the drug, he saw the word "steroid" and became concerned that the topical cream had an anabolic steroid in it. That frightened him. When he asked the pharmacist about it, the pharmacist used the following analogy after empathizing with the patient's concern about the medicine being an anabolic steroid: "This medication for your rash is a corticosteroid, and it's in the same broad family of medications as the anabolic steroids that you are worried about. If I can draw an analogy for you, I think it will allay your fears. Grapes and watermelons are both in the family of fruit, yet they are very different. If you ate one grape, it wouldn't bother you at all. If you ate an entire watermelon it would probably make you sick. Plus, the two fruits look and taste very different. This medicine, while it is in the same broad family, is not an anabolic steroid, and since it is used externally, very little gets absorbed. Also, it is for inflammation and does not have any of the masculinizing or hormonal effects of anabolic steroids."

**Pac-Man or cops and robbers.** A patient with high cholesterol was confused by the difference between "HDLs" and "LDLs"—which were the "good cholesterol" and which were the "bad cholesterol," and why were the bad ones harmful? His HCP had two different analogies, depending on whether a patient was familiar with the game Pac-Man. If the patient was familiar with Pac-Man, the HCP said, "The bad cholesterol or LDLs can get together in your blood and stick to the blood vessel walls or form a clot that can break loose and either get stuck in your heart and cause a heart attack or get stuck in your brain and cause a stroke. The HDLs are like Pac-Man. The HDLs travel around in your blood and gobble up the LDLs so they can't stick around or form a clot. The more HDLs, the better. The fewer LDLs, the better. So, anything you can do to increase your HDLs and lower your LDLs is a good thing." If the patient was not familiar with Pac-Man, the HCP used the analogy of cops and robbers, where the LDLs were the robbers and the HDLs were the cops who patrolled the streets (blood vessels) to prevent the robbers from congregating or breaking loose somewhere and stealing something. The cops escorted the robbers away so they wouldn't cause trouble. Using either of the above analogies, the HCP went on to explain what patients could do to raise their HDLs and lower their LDLs.

Every now and then, an analogy just doesn't work with a particular patient. What do you do then? The most important thing is to be sensitive and observant, and save face for the patient. If you observe and listen to the patient and you can tell that the patient is not tracking, simply take responsibility (after all, it is your analogy) and say something like "I can see that I'm not helping very much. Would you mind if I start over? I'm not being very clear." At this point, try another way to answer the patient's question. Responding in this way saves face for the patient; it says that the problem is that you've been unclear in your analogy and that the patient is not the problem. This builds rapport and keeps communication more open.

# Ask patients what they think

After providing new information, ask what the patient thinks of this new information. Where does it leave her now in regard to change? By asking this question, you gain information about what the next steps need to be or what additional information the patient might need to consider. By asking either "Where does this leave you now?" or "What are your thoughts?" you not only engage the patient, you let the patient know you are interested in how she thinks about the new information. This is the only way you can know the impact of your new information. Did the new information cause the patient to reconsider her sense making? If you don't ask, the patient may nod her head while you are talking, out of deference, and you may believe she agrees when in reality she may not agree. Because MI is an exchange, we need to know how the patient is thinking after we provide new information.

After the HCP provides information and asks, "Where does this leave you now?" or "What are your thoughts?" the patient may say one of several things, as discussed in the following paragraphs.

**"I really need to change my behavior."** This is what we would hope the patient would say. If this happens, we simply need to move on to Step 6, summarize and discuss next steps (or plan for change).

**"I didn't realize that before."** The ideal reaction would be for the patient to realize the need for behavior change, but the more frequently encountered reaction is an intermediate-level change in a thought or belief that serves as a premise in the patient's line of reasoning. The patient has yet to think through the full impact of this new realization and therefore has yet to adjust the conclusion of her line of reasoning. *But there has been a change in how the patient thinks and feels!* The crucial thing here is to reflect back this change and reinforce it. Any positive change in thought, feeling, or perspective needs to be reflected and affirmed so that the change becomes part of the social reality shared by you and the patient. Letting an implied change go unreflected and unaffirmed creates the possibility that the impact of the patient's realization will be fleeting. Once the patient knows you have heard the change implied in her "realization," the realization becomes a landmark in your interaction. You can refer back to this realization at later points in your interaction. It has a much more permanent nature now.

When reflecting back and affirming a new realization, try to match the degree of certainty and clarity in the patient's utterance. Reflect the change in thought or feeling as strongly as possible without taking the risk that the patient will reject your reflection. If the patient has said, tentatively, "I didn't see the connection between high blood pressure and the risk of stroke," an appropriate reflection would be "You understand now that your risk of suffering a stroke goes up as your blood pressure remains high over time. Where does this leave you in terms of your thoughts about reducing your blood pressure?" But suppose the patient has said, emphatically, "Gosh, I don't want a major stroke. That would be horrible." In this case a stronger reflection would be warranted: "You sound like you want to do everything you can to reduce your blood pressure and avoid the possibility of a major stroke disrupting your life. There are three ways to reduce your blood pressure: taking medication, increasing your physical activity, and eating a healthier diet. Which of these would you like to talk about first?"

Once a patient has acknowledged a change in her thinking or feeling, it is often wise at a later point in your interaction to incorporate this change in an intermediate summary of the patient's current decisional balance. Such a summary provides a second reinforcement of the change and can prompt the patient to consider its impact on the ultimate decision about health behavior change. Since the patient is still engaged in the interaction, you can move on to address other concerns or issues the patient has previously expressed.

Even though you have addressed the patient's major issues and concerns (or the first major issue presented by the patient), the patient may still lack sufficient motivation to decide for health behavior change. You should not assume that when the issue has been addressed to the satisfaction of the patient, the patient is now ready to engage in change. The reasons against health behavior change may not seem as strong or as important as before, but the decisional balance may still be tilted against change because the patient has yet to identify strong reasons for change or because other issues may emerge. This may be especially true if rapport has been established and the patient now feels safe enough to bring up other concerns. Here, one strategy is to follow your affirmation of the patient's new realization with an open-ended question that probes what other positive reasons are needed for the patient to decide in favor of health behavior change: "Controlling your blood pressure seems more important to you now, because you understand the connection between high blood pressure and the increased risk of a major stroke. What would make taking steps to control your blood pressure more important to you at this point?"

Another, more comprehensive strategy is to explore and then summarize the patient's current sense making and reasoning. Listen for important gaps in the overall distribution of reasons in the patient's current perspective. For example, consider a patient with newly diagnosed high cholesterol who was initially very resistant to the thought of using a statin. The patient had strong fears about "serious muscle weakness" as a potential side effect, because that is what his friend had experienced with a statin. In addition, the physician had created significant relational resistance by telling the patient, "Don't worry about it. Just take the medicine." Now, after you have created rapport with the patient, empathized with his fear about muscle weakness, and provided information about this side effect, the patient has relaxed his fear of taking a statin. Still, he feels no strong need to take the statin. One possible reason is that as long as he was gripped by his fear of the side effect, he wasn't listening to any other information about high cholesterol and its treatment. It is also possible that he feels OK and really wonders if he needs the medication. Now that you've resolved his relational resistance and addressed his issue resistance, he's open to learning more about the benefits of lowering his cholesterol. It's extremely important at this point to explore (1) his understanding of the risks posed by high cholesterol: "Tell me in your own words your understanding of the risks of not treating your high cholesterol" or "Tell me in your own words your understanding of the benefits of treating your high cholesterol," (2) his personal goals for the future: "What things do you still want to accomplish that would make treating your cholesterol important to you?" and (3) his understanding of the treatment options open to him: "What is your understanding of the ways you can lower your cholesterol and reduce your risks?" When appropriate, request permission to share relevant information to help fill in his understanding, and then ask his thoughts about how this information applies to him.

**"I need some time to think about all of this."** It is not uncommon for a patient to need some time to absorb new information and weigh its importance. A reasonable response by the HCP would be "Let me know if can answer any other questions for you. If you decide you would like to . . . , I would like to help." During subsequent interactions it is important to listen for and reflect any implied changes in the patient's thoughts or feelings. If the patient says, "I've been thinking some about what you said last time," it is important to reflect back and then explore what the patient has been thinking. Some options are "Tell me more about what you've been thinking" and "What's got you thinking more about this?"

**"I'm not sure I buy all of this."** This statement can appear in many forms, but basically the patient is saying she is skeptical about the new information and whether it applies to her. An appropriate response would be to reflect and explore this concern: "You're still having some doubts about whether all of this is true (for you). What would you need to know to decide that you really do need to lower your blood pressure? What would make it more important to you?"

**"I don't care. I am not going to . . . ."** This patient is simply not ready to change. At this point an appropriate and caring response would be "It really is your decision. If you get to the point where you would like to . . . , I would really like to help." If you have any serious concerns about the patient delaying any change, express them: "I really am concerned about your elevated blood pressure. I would hate to see you have a stroke or a heart attack when you could prevent it, but I respect that it really is your decision."

## Summarize and discuss next steps

Once the patient is ready to make a change, it is often useful to summarize your understanding of where things are now and plan for change: "So, if I understand things correctly, you would like to lower your blood sugar to prevent serious complications. In addition, you would like some help in considering what steps you need to take to do this." It is a good idea to use a summary to check in periodically and make sure you and the patient are on the same page. It saves a lot of misunderstandings.

We recommend providing the patient with options in planning for change: "There are three things you can do to lower your blood sugar: Change your eating habits by reducing sugars and carbohydrates; increase your physical activity, for example, by walking and taking the stairs instead of the elevator; and take your medication as prescribed. To lower your blood sugar, they work best together. Which of these would you like to work on first?" It would be great if the patient said, "All of them," but any steps the patient commits to are important and should be supported.

There are times when patients want to make changes because they want to lower their risks, but sometimes they feel overwhelmed. It is important to assure patients that you will help them break things down into doable steps. Also, it may be useful to make a suggestion rather than leaving things open-ended. Rather than saying, "There are three things you can do to lower your blood sugar; they are . . . ," you might say, "There are several things that you can do to lower your blood sugar. You're feeling somewhat overwhelmed, and if I were going to do one thing that would have the greatest impact, it would be taking the medicine once a day as prescribed. What do you think about that?" This response does more guiding than would a response that simply listed all the things that could be done. It is used because, although the patient wants to lower her blood sugar, she is overwhelmed and stuck. Notice that this approach still leaves the final decision to the patient, by saying, "What do you think about that?"

For many HCPs, this last step, involving planning for change, often is the starting point. That is, once a diagnosis is made, the patient is given instructions on how to treat the illness. But it really is folly to jump to this step without finding out how the patient is making sense of the diagnosis and treatment. The patient simply may not be ready to do anything or may need time to ask questions or express in her own words what any of this means to her. How important is it to her to treat the illness? Does she agree with the diagnosis and treatment? If not, why is she having doubts? Without this kind of understanding, a treatment plan can be imposed on a patient who may not be ready to take action.

## Conclusion

This chapter has presented the remaining steps in assisting a patient in the process of change through MI, starting with the simple, respectful act of asking permission to provide information or express a concern and ending in working with the patient on a negotiated plan.

### QUESTIONS FOR REFLECTION

1. In providing new information to the patient, what should you consider? How do you know what information to provide? What would make information irrelevant to the patient?
2. When should you use an analogy? How can you know if the analogy is effective? What should you do if it doesn't work?
3. What determines the appropriate time to do a summary? What elements should be part of the summary? What are the benefits of a summary?

# CHAPTER 9

# Special Considerations

I n this chapter we examine situations that sometimes cause problems for health care professionals (HCPs) attempting to use motivational interviewing (MI). We discuss ways to handle these situations without causing loss of face for the patient or the HCP.

MI cannot solve system problems or problems with bricks and mortar. For example, some health systems (and accrediting bodies) require that lengthy questionnaires be given to patients, some patient areas lack appropriate privacy, and some health systems have personnel resource issues that make spending time with patients problematic. MI—a systematic way of talking with patients about behavior change—should not be expected to solve these problems.

MI is useful, however, for some common problems that arise in communicating with patients. Some examples are discussed in the following paragraphs.

## Limiting time with talkative patients

HCPs, especially nurse case managers, often conduct patient interventions by telephone. Like other HCPs, they may have a limited amount of time to spend with the patient. Sometimes they deal with patients who want to talk about everything except their health. When time is limited, we recommend using one of two strategies:

- Take a preventive approach. At the start of the call, say, "I have about 20 minutes (or whatever is feasible) to talk with you about your diabetes. What questions do you have?" (Or "Last time we talked . . . ," or "There were three things we talked about that affect your diabetes. They are . . . . Which of these would you like to talk about first?") While engaging the patient, this sets the stage so the patient knows how much time you have for the discussion.

- If you forget to set the stage or if the patient still diverts the conversation to other subjects (e.g., local football, the fishing trip with the grandson), we suggest that you sincerely say, "The fishing trip with your grandson sounds like it was so much fun. I wish I had more time to hear about it. I have 10 minutes left on this call and then I need to talk with another patient who is important to me, just as you are. So, I would like to talk with you some more about your diabetes." The reality is that your time is limited, and gentle and caring boundaries sometimes have to be set. It's important to let the patient know you hear that the other subject is meaningful to him. It is also important to let the patient know that your time is limited.

A pharmacist described to us the following situation with a patient who had a chest cold. The patient's physician had directed him to the pharmacy for guaifenesin to help break up his congestion and make his cough more productive. At the pharmacy, the patient was surprised to see numerous products containing guaifenesin. He anxiously carried several of them to the counter and told the pharmacist he didn't know which one to take. The pharmacist started to explain the different products, but the patient's level of agitation didn't subside. Since other patients were waiting, the pharmacist needed to end the conversation soon. Thinking about this patient's distress, she said, "You came in expecting to see one guaifenesin product, and when you saw all these products you worried that you wouldn't pick the right one." In a calmer voice, the patient said, "Yes, exactly." Next the pharmacist said, "If you could briefly tell me about why you went to the doctor and what your symptoms are, I can help you pick the best one of these products for your situation." The patient was relieved, and the conversation was over in another two minutes. The pharmacist had realized that quickly going over each product would not address the patient's anxiety and sense making. When she accurately reflected the patient's worry, he relaxed and they were able to work toward a solution much more quickly. Being understood allowed the patient to trust that the pharmacist could help. With the use of MI, the interaction actually took less time, and the patient felt satisfied with the results. He had the product he needed, and the pharmacist had established a relationship that would be useful in the future.

But what would happen if, no matter what the pharmacist said, the patient continued to talk on and on while other patients were waiting? The pharmacist could say, after assessing the patient's reason for seeing the physician, "Based on what you have told me, I recommend this product. I have about two more minutes to answer any questions you may have, because other patients are waiting and they are important to me, too."

HCPs do have limited time, and they may worry that MI will take more time. We have listened to telephone conversations between HCPs and their patients before and after MI training. The amount of time spent on the calls went down significantly after MI training. The MI-trained HCP was able to focus on the patient's issues much more quickly, reflect that understanding, and address the specific issues with the needed information rather than with a long-winded "data dump." MI cannot give HCPs more time in their days, but it can make them far more effective in using whatever time they have. Although an MI-trained HCP may take a little more time up front with the patient, the downstream time drops dramatically, with far better outcomes—as we will discuss in Chapter 10.

## Encouraging nontalkative patients

We are often asked what to do about patients who aren't very talkative. It is important to sort out whether (1) the person is simply not very talkative in general or (2) the HCP is too practitioner centered and has thwarted communication. Loss of face can cause patients to become far less verbal. We believe that MI can encourage the patient to talk through developing rapport, empathic responding, open-ended questions, and so on.

Some people are just less talkative than others. When asked open-ended questions such as "How important is it to you to get your diabetes under control?" or "What's your understanding of what can happen if your diabetes is left untreated?" a patient may respond, "I don't know." It is important not to label such a patient as difficult or unmotivated. It is especially important to be patient and realize that you may have to carry more than your share of the conversation, as in the following dialogue:

HCP: Now that you've found out that you have diabetes, what does that mean to you?

Pt: *I don't know. I guess I have sugar.*

HCP: That's right. Your blood sugar is elevated. What did the doctor tell you about what can happen if you don't get your blood sugar down or under control?

Pt: *Not much.*

HCP: Would you mind if I share some information about your diabetes?

Pt: *OK.*

HCP: (HCP provides information about risks and complications.) So, after hearing this, how important is it to you to treat your diabetes?

Pt: *Well, I guess I need to.*

HCP: I'm glad to hear that you want to treat your diabetes. I want you to know that it really is your decision, and I want to help. I would hate to see you have any of those complications when you can prevent them. I'd like to work with you on that.

Pt: *OK.*

This HCP uses MI to elicit responses from the patient, yet the patient's responses remain brief. The HCP continues to ask open-ended questions, provides information, supports any change talk, and lets the patient know that even though these are her decisions, the HCP wants to help.

## Dealing with angry patients

People feel angry when they feel a sense of powerlessness. People can convert hurt, frustration, loss of control, or a sense of injustice into anger. Anger can be a very difficult emotion to deal with because we are often anxious and uncomfortable in the presence of others' anger. Empathy is especially important in responding to angry patients. Empathizing effectively requires being able to first listen for what the patient is feeling powerless about and then reflect that understanding. Here is a sample dialogue from a nurse case manager. The nurse is following up on the phone with a patent who has diabetes and whose A1c is still very high (nearly 9).

Nurse: Hi, Mr. Smith. This is Nancy from your health plan. How are you today?

Pt: (matter of fact) *Fine.*

Nurse: Mr. Smith, the reason I'm calling is to follow up on your diabetes. I got your new A1c back, and it's nearly 9. What is your understanding about what that means?

Pt: (angrily) *You people kill me. You think it's so easy to get your diabetes under control. You want me to take my medicine, exercise, change what I eat. . . . You should try it sometime! So, no, I don't need the lecture. I already got one at the doctor's office.*

Nurse: You feel that people haven't understood how hard it is to control your blood sugar. They've minimized how hard it is and instead told you that you need to do a better job.

Pt: *Damn right! I don't like it. I'm not some stupid kid, and I don't need a lecture.*

Nurse: Mr. Smith, I don't want to treat you that way. I really want to understand any difficulties you may be having and work with you on your diabetes. Would that be OK?

Pt: *I suppose. I just don't need a lecture.*

Nurse: I promise I won't do that. Tell me a little bit about what you have done so far and what has been the most difficult.

This nurse does not take the patient's anger and accusation ("You people . . .") personally. She is able to stay separate and available to the patient. She empathizes with his frustration and loss of face in being lectured to and treated like a "stupid kid." She recognizes that his anger stems from the sense of injustice he feels about how hard it is to control diabetes and how he received a lecture from his physician rather than compassion and understanding. The nurse lets him know that she won't treat him that way and that she wants to work with him and better understand where he is having difficulties. As a result, he is able to re-engage and talk with her about his diabetes, because he does not feel threatened.

When people are angry and feeling powerless, empathy and understanding are critical. It is difficult to be empathic when one is feeling threatened. Responding with empathy requires clarity and focus on the source of powerlessness. There are times, however, when despite being empathic and caring, the HCP has to deal with a patient who remains angry and continues to yell and swear. It is appropriate to set a boundary with that patient, such as "Mr. Smith, I hear how angry you are and I would like to help. I don't want to be yelled at and I don't want to be sworn at. Could we please talk about this?" If the patient continues to yell or swear, let the patient know you are going to get off the phone, walk away, or call security if necessary.

In addition to setting boundaries regarding the amount of time you have and patients' anger, it is appropriate to reset a boundary when it is violated. On occasion, patients can be inappropriate in a relationship with an HCP. A patient may be inappropriately flirtatious, sexist, vulgar, or racist, for example. According to Peterson, "Boundaries are the limits that allow for a safe connection based on the client's needs. When these limits are altered, what is allowed in the relationship becomes ambiguous. Such ambiguity is often experienced as an intrusion into the sphere of safety."[1] When patients are inappropriate, the safety of the HCP may be at risk. It is appropriate for the HCP to say to the patient, "Mr. Jones, I would like to discuss your diabetes with you and I want to help you get it under control. I want you to know that I am offended by your remarks (language, sexual innuendo) concerning (my sex, race). I would like us to focus on your diabetes. If you cannot do that, we need to stop and you will need to leave." If you are concerned about the emotional stability of the patient, you may decide to report the patient to the appropriate authorities. This should be a decision made with care and introspection. For more thorough coverage of this topic, we refer readers to Peterson's excellent book on boundary violations in professional–client relationships.[1]

# Patients with psychological problems

The topic of working with patients with psychoses or other severe psychological problems is too broad and complex for the scope of this book. However, we will touch on a few important points.

**Expertise.** Although we don't have to be mental health professionals to discuss drug therapy or psychotherapy with a patient, HCPs need to be clear about the limits of their expertise. When the HCP does not have the appropriate expertise to guide and assist a patient, referral to a psychiatrist, psychotherapist, or pharmacotherapy specialist (pharmacist) is important.

**Comfort and anxiety.** MI can be very helpful in discussing patients' treatment or nonadherence to drug therapy, especially when patients complain of side effects, costs, or other factors. HCPs need to be aware of their own responses to patients with psychoses or other severe psychological problems. For example, one patient with obsessive-compulsive disorder (OCD) constantly used hand sanitizer during a medication consultation with a community pharmacist and refused to shake the pharmacist's hand at the end of the consultation. He looked at the pharmacist and said abruptly, "I don't want your germs." Despite having had some training in school on OCD, the pharmacist said he had been very anxious the whole time he was with the patient and he thought the patient knew it. With such a patient it would be especially important to be calm, centered, respectful, and caring, even in the presence of behavior that is unfamiliar and uncomfortable. HCPs might consider receiving outside assistance from a psychologist if they work with such patients and are consistently anxious and uncomfortable.

**Patient's ability to make connections.** Some patients with psychoses or other psychological problems may have difficulty making sense of what is being communicated by the HCP or may be disconnected from reality. The HCP should not assume that this is the case; many patients are perfectly capable of understanding what is being discussed and what their options are. However, if such problems are present, working with a caregiver, friend, or relative of the patient can be useful.

# Telephone versus face-to-face communication

Many HCPs communicate with patients almost exclusively by telephone. We are often asked about the use and the effectiveness of MI in telephone interventions.

We cite two studies (and there are many more) that have examined the efficacy of telephone interventions using MI.[2,3] In a study of interventions to encourage weight loss,[2] the percentage of participants who lost 5% or more of their initial weight was not significantly different between the remote (telephone, e-mail, website) intervention group (38.2%) and the group receiving in-person support (41.4%). Weight loss was sustained throughout the study period in both intervention groups.

In Chapter 4 we described a randomized, controlled clinical trial involving patients who were receiving the injectable interferon beta-1a product Avonex (Biogen Idec) for multiple sclerosis.[3] A significantly lower percentage of patients in the MI telephone intervention group (1.2%) than in the standard care group (8.7%) discontinued their use of the drug. In addition, movement toward continuation of therapy was significantly higher in the intervention group. Given that the drug was a weekly injection that at the time of the study cost approximately $200 a dose, 9000 fewer dropouts from treatment with the drug represented a $93,600,000 cost recovery per year (9000 patients × $200/dose × 52 weeks/year = $93,600,000).

We have come to believe that MI is even more essential in telephone communication, since no information is available from visual and nonverbal cues such as facial expressions. It is especially important to be explicit in empathic responding and reflection in telephone communication. Saying "right" or "uh huh" or "I understand" does little more than tell the patient that you are still there. Such responses don't let the patient know what it is that you understand. The same problems that exist in face-to-face everyday conversation are exaggerated on the telephone. Explicit communication in MI can overcome these problems.

## Required patient questionnaires

To maintain accreditation by the National Committee for Quality Assurance or other accrediting bodies, health plans are required to interview patients and collect information such as family history, current conditions, demographics, and patient satisfaction with care. The requirement for data collection may be above and beyond what the patient's health plan requires. Usually a case manager collects the data in the initial telephone contact with the patient. This often takes at least 45 minutes. In our training programs we hear complaints from case managers that it takes so long. Patients don't like answering 45 minutes worth of questions, especially since much of this information has been provided to other HCPs already. We have been asked if MI can help alleviate this problem.

Although the collection of this information cannot be circumvented, it does not have to be done all at once. In conversation to develop rapport with the patient and discuss current conditions, a lot of the required information will come out through appropriate reflection, open-ended questions, and explanations by the patient. For example, the HCP might be making an initial call to a patient with high blood pressure and high cholesterol. During the call, the HCP would ask the patient to discuss what these two conditions mean to him and how important it is to him to treat them. Questions about family history would be a natural line of inquiry.

We believe it is of utmost importance to develop rapport with the patient before jumping into the list of questions required for accreditation. Unfortunately, these questions often are prefaced by the case manager saying something like "Well, I hate to do this, but I am required to ask you a bunch of questions and it's going take about 45 minutes." Not only does this convey to the patient that this is drudgery for the case manager, it also does not convey anything about the importance of the information being collected. It certainly does not convey how collecting this information may benefit the patient. In addition to breaking up the task, when some of this information needs to be collected it would be better to genuinely say to the patient something like "You have given me a lot of useful information already. In order to get to know you and your situation even better so that I can be as useful to you as possible, I need to ask some additional questions. This will take about 15 minutes now, and then I will need to ask some more questions in a later call. Is this a good time?" This conveys the message that the information is important in helping the case manager serve the needs of the patient.

We have also recommended to health plans that it would be beneficial to start the introduction to the call with a patient-centered message. We have listened to recordings of patient de-identified calls in which the case manager essentially said, "Hi. Is this Mr. Jones? This is Sally Brown from Allied Health Plan calling to talk with you about your diabetes. I need to ask you some questions before we start." A patient-centered approach would sound something like this: "Hi. Is this Mr. Jones? This is Sally Brown from Allied Health Plan calling to talk with you about your diabetes. Mr. Jones, I would like to be a resource for you in answering any questions or concerns you may have about your diabetes or your plan. I'm here to help you achieve your health goals. What questions or concerns do you have at this point that I might help with?"

# The HCP is a hypocrite

Every now and then a patient working on weight loss will look at the HCP and say, somewhat indignantly, "How can you talk to me about losing weight when you're overweight yourself?" This can also come up in phone conversations if the patient asks whether the HCP is overweight. Using what we have discussed about genuineness and respect for the patient, an appropriate response would be to directly address and acknowledge the patient's sense making (that is, the HCP is a hypocrite). Here is a brief dialogue:

> Pt:   *How can you talk to me about losing weight when you are overweight yourself?*
>
> HCP:   It seems hypocritical for me to be talking to you about weight loss when I am overweight myself.
>
> Pt:   *Darn right.*
>
> HCP:   I want you to know that I struggle with weight loss. I know that being overweight can have serious health consequences for me, but I also know that it's not easy to make changes in eating habits and get more physical activity. So I'm certainly not here to judge you. I would like to work with you on losing weight to improve your health, if that would be OK.

In this dialogue, the HCP genuinely addresses the assertion of the patient, briefly talks about her own struggles with weight loss and her understanding of the health consequences, and then focuses the conversation back on the issue at hand. It would be inappropriate to have simply responded, "We're here to talk about you, not me." That would have caused loss of face and defensiveness and would not have addressed the patient's issue.

Generally speaking, it is not appropriate for HCPs to talk about themselves in order to relate to a patient. For example, if the patient said, "It has been really difficult for me to quit smoking," it would not be appropriate for the HCP to say, "I used to smoke myself and I never thought I would be able to quit either, but I did." Although this HCP is trying to empathize with the patient and offer hope, his response changes the focus of the conversation to him, not the patient. The same would be true of an

HCP with high blood pressure who is trying to comfort a patient with high blood pressure. In addition, even though the HCP may have been a smoker (or may have high blood pressure or diabetes, for example), each situation is unique. The motivations and methods for quitting smoking, managing diabetes, or any other set of health behavior changes are different for each patient and need to be viewed from the patient's perspective, not the HCP's. How this patient decides to quit smoking may be very different from how this HCP quit. A better response from the HCP would have been "You know it's important to quit, yet it has been really difficult to quit and stay quit." After the patient affirms, the HCP could inquire about what kind of quit attempts the patient has made, what has worked (even briefly), and what has made it difficult to stay quit.

The same guidelines are valid for comparing patients to other patients. For example, a patient says, "I can't believe I have high blood pressure." The HCP then responds, "You know, a lot of my patients have high blood pressure, and it is very treatable." The problems with this comparison are that (1) it does not directly reflect and empathize with the patient's concern, (2) it runs the risk of diminishing the uniqueness of this patient's problem, and (3) it does not explore the reason for the patient's distress. While the information is not wrong, the response does run the risk that the patient will say, "Well, I'm not your other patients," indicating relational resistance. A better response, using MI, would be, "You weren't expecting to find out you have high blood pressure. What concerns you the most about knowing you have high blood pressure?" The HCP does not have to compare the patient to any other patient to show care and concern.

There is one situation in which it is appropriate to talk about other patients. That is when the patient is asking for a comparison in order to feel comforted. For example, if the patient says, "Did other patients feel this way when they found out they had high blood pressure?" the patient is really asking, "Is my response normal?" In this case, it is appropriate to say, "Other patients have been surprised to find out. Because they didn't have any symptoms, they didn't know their blood pressure was elevated, either."

## How can you help me?

Several HCPs have conveyed to us a concern about how to respond to a patient who says something like "How can you talk to me about losing weight? You don't look like you've ever had a weight problem" or "How can you talk to me about quitting smoking when you don't smoke?" or "How can you understand when you don't have high blood pressure?" In all cases, the patient is saying, "How can you help or relate to my problem when you don't have this problem?" The patient is questioning whether you can really help. An effective MI response starts with acknowledging the concern: "You're wondering how I can help you quit smoking when I don't smoke. How can I understand how difficult it is to quit?" After this is affirmed, the HCP would say, "I do know that quitting is different for everyone. And this is where I really need your help. I need to know how important it is to you to quit. Also, what have you tried, and what makes quitting and staying quit difficult for you?" This response addresses the patient's concerns and lets the patient know that his "expertise" is needed for the HCP to be able to help.

When patients ask the HCP, "Do you have high blood pressure?" or "Do you smoke?" it may be unavoidable to deflect the question, especially if the answer is yes. If the HCP answers in the affirmative, this can become problematic because the next question might be "How did you feel when you found out you had high blood pressure?" or "How did you quit smoking?" Self-disclosure here is not particularly useful or appropriate, and it can create problems. How the HCP felt about her blood pressure or how the HCP quit smoking may be very different from the patient's experience and needs. We know an HCP who quit smoking "cold turkey." This is not the recommended way to quit, and it does not have a high rate of success. Yet a patient might try quitting this way because the HCP said he had done so. An appropriate response to such a question from patients would be "Since we are all so different, rather than focusing on me, I would like to better understand how high blood pressure affects you and how important it is to you to treat it" or "I do smoke, but since we are all so different, rather than focusing on me, I would like to better understand how smoking affects you and how important it is to you to try to quit." The guiding principle must be that any self-disclosure on the part of the HCP should be for the benefit of the patient and not based on the needs of the HCP.

## Conclusion

In this chapter we have presented a number of special circumstances that challenge the ability to use MI. In all cases, using aspects of MI can improve a difficult or challenging situation. The principles of MI are useful in addressing the issues presented in each circumstance.

## QUESTIONS FOR REFLECTION

1. In setting a boundary with a patient, whether it concerns time, anger, or boundary violations, what should you consider in formulating your response to the patient? What would be appropriate and what might be inappropriate?
2. In what ways do the principles of MI have the ability to enhance telephone communication, given that some information (e.g., visual cues) is lost?
3. Since a certain amount of information must be collected from patients to meet both medical and accreditation standards, how can this information be collected in a patient-centered manner?

### REFERENCES

1. Peterson MR. *At Personal Risk: Boundary Violations in Professional–Client Relationships.* New York: Norton; 1992:74.
2. Appel LJ, Clark JM, Yeh H-C, et al. Comparative effectiveness of weight-loss interventions in clinical practice. *N Engl J Med.* 2011;365:1959–68.
3. Berger BA, Hudmon KS, Liang H. Predicting discontinuation of treatment among patients with multiple sclerosis: an application of the transtheoretical model of change. *J Am Pharm Assoc.* 2004;45:1–7.

# CHAPTER 10

# Putting It All Together

In this chapter we present three cases, each followed by a comprehensive dialogue and analysis. For each case we first present a dialogue between a health care professional (HCP) and a patient that does not use motivational interviewing (MI). We then present an analysis of this dialogue, exploring the problems that occur and why they occur. Next, we present the same case with a dialogue that uses MI and an analysis of that dialogue, identifying the skills and MI strategies that were used and why they were used.

The first case focuses on problems that occur because the patient (patient's mother) does not believe it is important to change the behaviors she presents. In the second case, a newly diagnosed patient believes that treating his diabetes is very important, but he is not at all confident that he can do what is necessary to prevent serious complications. In the third case, the patient has an issue with side effects, but even after that issue is addressed he is not fully committed to taking the medication.

To get a much better sense of the nuances, emotions, and nonverbal communication involved in these cases, you can view them in video format at www.mihcp. com/3443.html (see QR code at end of chapter). By viewing the videos you will see the stark contrast between traditional interventions and MI.

# Case 1

This case is based on a real interaction between an HCP and a patient's mother. The case is presented first without the use of MI and then with MI. The MI example (the second dialogue) represents what actually happened between the HCP and the patient's mother.

Julie Thompson, a 37-year-old mother, has taken her 10-year-old daughter Sara to the emergency room five times in each of the past two years. Sara has not been using her chronic inhaler for her asthma. Julie has been in to pick up the rescue inhaler much more frequently than prescribed.

## Dialogue without MI

HCP: Hi. Are you Julie Thompson? (Julie nods) I'm Bruce Berger. I work in the clinic. I know you're here to pick up a prescription today. We noticed from your records that you've been coming in to get Sara's rescue inhaler for her asthma quite frequently. And you haven't gotten her chronic inhaler for quite some time. I also see that she's been in the emergency room several times this year. Can you tell me what's going on there?

Julie: *I did research on the chronic inhaler and I saw that there were steroids in it, and I do not want my daughter taking steroids. I read about all the side effects of steroids and all of the potential health problems, so I don't want her taking them. And I just want to tell you right up front that I do not want to hear anything about the fact that I do smoke. I smoke outside, I smoke away from her, I don't ever do it around her, so I do not want to hear about that.*

HCP: (very matter of fact and condescending) Well, I need to tell you that the medicine she is taking, the chronic inhaler, which is really essential for controlling her asthma, is not a steroid like you're thinking. It's much safer. It's very safe, and she needs to take it to get her asthma under control. And I also want to tell you that your smoking does affect her asthma. Even if it's outside, it gets on your clothes, and to be honest, I'd like to see you quit smoking for you anyway. But, if you want to keep her out of the emergency room, she needs to use that chronic inhaler every day and you need to watch your smoking.

Julie: (insistent) *I am not going to allow her to take any kind of steroid. I am not going to allow that to happen. She's my daughter, she's my responsibility, and I'm not going to allow that to happen. And I absolutely make sure that the smoking does not affect her.*

HCP: OK, I don't want to argue with you about this. If you want to keep Sara out of the emergency room, I just wish you'd heed what I'm saying. She needs to use that chronic inhaler every day to get her asthma under control, and the smoke on your clothes flares her asthma up. So, she needs to use the chronic inhaler and you really need to think about quitting smoking.

Julie: (abruptly) *Fine. I'm in a really big hurry and I need to get those prescriptions filled as soon as possible, please.*

HCP: (matter of fact and firm) OK. Well, I hope you really listen to what I'm telling you about using that chronic inhaler, and I hope you consider quitting smoking.

Julie: (abruptly) *Fine. I just need to get my prescriptions.*

HCP: OK.

## Analysis

It would be tempting to label Julie Thompson as a difficult person. It would also be easy for some HCPs to label her as a "bad" or irresponsible mother, causing her child to suffer by not allowing Sara to use the chronic inhaler for her asthma and by smoking around Sara (smoke on her clothes) and causing flare-up of her unprotected lungs, resulting in trips to the emergency room. Julie certainly is resistant to Sara using the chronic inhaler and to quitting smoking. Julie's sense making is that the chronic inhaler is an anabolic steroid that can harm her daughter, and that she smokes outside and away from Sara so the smoking should not affect Sara. From her perspective, Julie is protecting her child from harm in regard to the chronic inhaler and her smoking.

The HCP gives Julie factual information about the chronic inhaler and about the possible impact of Julie's smoking on Sara. This information is provided in a very matter-of-fact way. Despite the fact that the information is valid, Julie rejects it and repeats her insistence that she will not give Sara a harmful anabolic steroid and that she makes sure the smoking doesn't harm Sara. Julie insists on not talking about her smoking, but the HCP brings it up anyway. The HCP repeats his claims several times, insisting that Julie needs to listen to him and that, essentially, she is wrong. Julie is tired of listening to the HCP and says she needs to leave. This exchange is a prime example of "yes, but" communication. Both parties are starting their sentences with "yes, but," even if they are not using those words. This is wrestling, not dancing; the goal is to win, to take the other down.

Remember that sense making on the part of the patient is not only about the health care situation (the chronic inhaler and smoking) but also about how the patient (here, the patient's mother) is making sense of the relationship. The HCP provides factual information to Julie, but he does this in a way that causes her to lose both competency face and autonomy face. The HCP's message is "You need to listen to me. I am the expert here, and you are wrong. Sara needs to take the medicine, and you need to quit smoking if you don't want to keep harming her." To Julie, this does not sound understanding, caring, or safe. Now, in addition to issue resistance, we have relational resistance. There is a complete lack of rapport. At no time does the HCP acknowledge that Julie's actions are because she cares about Sara and is trying to protect her. Julie may be misguided in her sense making, but she does care about her daughter. The HCP's message comes across as arrogant, uncooperative, and scolding. Not surprisingly, Julie cannot hear it, and she digs in even more. The chance that anything will change as a result of this interaction is very small. It could be said that the HCP is difficult.

## Dialogue with MI

Let's look now at how this interaction might have gone if the HCP had used MI.

> HCP: Hi. Are you Julie Thompson? (Julie nods) I'm Bruce Berger. I work in the clinic. I noticed that you're here to pick up a prescription for Sara's rescue inhaler for her asthma. I also noticed that she's been in the emergency room five times in the last year for her asthma. What's that been like for you?

Julie: *It's been difficult. I hate to see her gasping for breath, and I'm really worried when she has to go, so it's really difficult when I have to take her.*

HCP: (compassionately) It sounds like you'd be willing to do whatever you can to prevent that from happening.

Julie: (nods) *Uh huh, yes.*

HCP: I also noticed you've picked up the rescue inhaler quite frequently and that it's been about three months or so since you picked up the prescription for the chronic inhaler. Are you having some difficulties with that?

Julie: *Well, I did research on the chronic inhaler and I found out that there were steroids in it and that . . . that . . . I don't want her taking steroids. I did research on some of the potential side effects and some of the health problems that can result from taking steroids, and I just don't want her to take those at all. I don't want her exposed to them at all. And then, um—let me just go ahead and lay this out right now because I am sure it will come up—I do smoke, but I make sure that I do not smoke around her so I make sure it does not affect her, so I just wanted to let you know that right off.*

HCP: It sounds like you care about Sara a great deal. You don't want her using steroids. You're worried about what kind of effects those would have on her, and you're working hard to keep your smoking away from her so it doesn't affect her asthma.

Julie: (almost surprised) *Uh huh, yeah.*

HCP: (calmly) Would you mind if we talk a little bit about the chronic inhaler and the medicine you're concerned about with the steroids? Because, you know, I certainly don't want her using a medicine that has steroids in it like the ones that you're worried about for athletes. Could we talk about that just a little bit?

Julie: *Yeah.*

HCP: Even though this medicine, the medicine that's in the chronic inhaler, is in the same broad family as the steroids you're worried about, and those are called anabolic steroids, which build people up and can have masculinizing effects, if I could draw an analogy. . . . A grape and a watermelon both are in the same family, fruits, but obviously a grape is much smaller. If you ate one grape you'd be fine, but eating an entire watermelon could make you sick. If we look at the grape as the medicine your daughter is taking, again, it's in the same broad family. The drug prescribed for your daughter is like the grape—the amount is very small. And even though it's in the same big family, it's not an anabolic steroid. What this drug does is actually reduce the inflammation in your daughter's lungs. Very little of it gets absorbed into the body; it only goes to her lungs. As I said, I don't want your daughter taking a medication that could have the impact of those anabolic steroids. This is really safe for your daughter to use. What are your thoughts about considering having her use it?

Julie:    *I guess I didn't realize that they weren't the same thing as the anabolic steroids, the ones that can cause all the problems. So, um, if you can assure me that it's not going to have the same side effects and health problems as those do . . .*

HCP:     Yeah, you probably saw the name, corticosteroids, and thought, uh oh. . . . So, yes, that does concern people. I do want to reassure you that this is medication that only goes to her lungs and won't get in her body. They're not the same kind of drugs as the ones you're worried about.

Julie:    *OK.*

HCP:     Do you mind if I talk to you about what your daughter's lungs are like when she's having these inflammations and needing to go to the emergency room?

Julie:    (very interested) *Yeah, OK.*

HCP:     OK, when someone has asthma, their lungs are hypersensitive. If I can use an analogy again, if someone brushed up against your arm accidentally, it probably wouldn't bother you at all. But if you'd had the skin burned off your arm very recently, you would react to it because your arm would be exquisitely sensitive. Sara's lungs are exquisitely sensitive, like your arm would be with the skin burned off. And what this drug can do, this chronic inhaler, is reduce the inflammation in her lungs so they are no longer exquisitely sensitive. Otherwise, everything in the air—dust, pollen, and the like—affects her in ways that it would not normally affect us.

Julie: *OK, I see what you're saying.*

HCP: So, this chronic inhaler can really prevent that from happening when used every day. The other thing I was going to tell you is that, unfortunately, even though you are smoking outside and keeping the smoke away from Sara, the smoke on your clothes, because her lungs are so sensitive, can affect her lungs and cause her to have a reaction. Something I would like you to think about is that if Sara uses the chronic inhaler every day, she may not be sensitive to the smoke on your clothes . . . but she still may be, because her lungs are just very different from ours. Honestly, I'd love to see you quit smoking for you, too, because, as you know, it's not real good for you and it would certainly help her.

Julie: (calm and resigned) *Yeah, I know.*

HCP: I would like you to keep an eye on what happens when Sara uses the chronic inhaler daily and if she's still flaring up when you're around her.

Julie: *Even when the smoke is just on my clothes, she can still flare up? She's that sensitive. I didn't realize that.*

HCP: It may not happen when she uses the chronic inhaler. Keep an eye on it.

Julie: *The thought of quitting smoking is pretty daunting right now. I've tried to quit and it's very hard.*

HCP: It is very hard to quit. It's very relaxing, and it's hard to replace it with something. Any thoughts on what you might do if you aren't ready to quit right now?

Julie: *Since it affects her that it's on my clothes, if I only smoked while she was at school, and then changed clothes before she came home, would that help?*

HCP: That sounds like it would be great if you were able to do that. If you are willing to do that, it would certainly help. If you do get to the point somewhere down the road where you are willing to quit for both you and her, we would be more than happy to help you with that, because you're right, it's not an easy thing to do.

Julie: *Yeah, it's really difficult.*

HCP: So it sounds like right now, where we are is that you are willing to have Sara use the chronic inhaler every day to try to get the inflammation down so she won't have to go to the emergency room and willing to do whatever you can to keep the smoke off your clothes, and I think you're going to see big changes in terms of her not needing to go to the emergency room. Probably you will hardly need to use the rescue inhaler at all.

Julie: *Oh really?*

HCP: Yes.

Julie: *Good, because it's scary when she has to use that.*

HCP: Yes. We'll go ahead and get both prescriptions ready. Use the chronic inhaler every day, and keep the rescue inhaler around in case she needs it, and let's see how that works.

Julie: (hopeful) *OK. It sounds good.*

HCP: Good!

## Analysis

Julie Thompson was very resistant to the idea of Sara using her chronic asthma inhaler. From the research she did, her sense was that it contained anabolic steroids and could harm her daughter. She also believed that because she smoked outside, her smoking did not affect Sara's asthma.

By the end of this dialogue, she is willing to have Sara use the chronic inhaler, and she will work on not exposing Sara to smoke from her clothes. She might even consider quitting smoking. This is a great deal of change, much different from the outcome in the first dialogue. Let's take a look at what actually happened. Is Julie a difficult patient, or was it simply a difficult situation? When a well-trained HCP, using MI, interacts with Julie, she is not seen as difficult at all; in this encounter, there is no relational resistance. When a patient has issue resistance, that does not make the patient difficult. It just means that an expression of care, concern, and respect by the HCP becomes even more critical.

Here, the HCP first notes that Sara has been in the emergency room five times in the past year. He then says to Julie, "What's that been like for you?" This question begins the process of building rapport. Julie is Sara's mother. Watching her daughter suffer as she goes to the emergency room must be excruciating for her. The HCP realizes that this trauma is happening to Sara *and* to Julie, and he exhibits caring by asking about how this has affected Julie; he cares about her, too. Julie responds, "It's been difficult. I hate to see her gasping for breath, and I'm really worried when she has to go, so it's really difficult when I have to take her." The HCP listens carefully to Julie and then responds that he senses she would be willing to do whatever she can to prevent this from happening; Julie concurs. The HCP formulates Julie's goal in a very broad and inclusive way. He hears and reflects her care and concern for her child.

Next, the HCP relays to Julie that he has noticed that the prescription for the rescue inhaler has been filled frequently and that it has been over three months since the chronic inhaler prescription has been filled. In a nonjudgmental manner, he asks Julie if she has had any difficulty with the chronic inhaler. Julie tells the HCP that she looked up the ingredients in the chronic inhaler and believes it contains an anabolic steroid, which she does not want her daughter to use. She also brings up that she smokes but says that she smokes outside so it doesn't affect Sara. The HCP hears that the mother is concerned about the chronic medication harming her daughter and that she knows her smoking would also harm her but tries to protect Sara from that. Her statements indicate her care and concern for her daughter. The HCP then responds, "It sounds like you care about Sara a great deal. You don't want her using steroids. You're worried about what kind of effects those would have on her, and you're working hard to keep your smoking away from her so it doesn't affect her asthma."

If you watch the video of this interaction (see www.mihcp.com/3443.html or QR code at end of chapter), you will see the look of surprise and relief on Julie's face when she hears this statement: surprise because she expects to be corrected in some way, and relief because she knows that she is truly understood. The HCP is quite explicit in what he says. He does not just say, "You care about Sara" and move on. He tells Julie exactly how he knows that she cares. This lets Julie know that he really does understand her motives. This is a very important part of rapport building.

On the basis of Julie's sense making about the chronic medication and the impact of her smoking on Sara, any information the HCP provides must address two things if Julie is going to consider any kind of changes: (1) that the chronic inhaler is not an anabolic steroid and is, in fact, essential for Sara to control her asthma and (2) that Julie's smoking can affect Sara's asthma even though Julie smokes outside. This information must be presented in a way that does not cause defensiveness and loss of face. The rapport building that has taken place thus far will go a long way in helping to present this new information.

Because Julie seems to be most sensitive about her smoking, the HCP starts by asking permission to talk to Julie a little more about the chronic inhaler. The HCP basically tells Julie that he is on her side and that he does not want Sara taking an anabolic steroid either. He does this to reassure Julie that he is not there to "wrestle" with her. The HCP then uses the analogy that a grape and a watermelon are very different yet still part of the fruit family. He does this to make the point that even though Julie saw the word corticosteroid and that alarmed her, corticosteroids are part of the same family as anabolic steroids but are very different—like the grape and watermelon. The HCP reassures Julie that corticosteroids do not have the same side effects as anabolic steroids and that very little of the medication is absorbed. He lets Julie know that the prescribed medication is essential to reduce the inflammation in Sara's lungs.

He then asks Julie what her current thoughts are about Sara using the chronic inhaler. He does not draw any conclusions for Julie about what she should do. He presents his expertise and asks where this leaves her now. This is the only way he can know how the new information he has presented has affected her sense making. Julie responds that she is willing to have Sara use the chronic inhaler if he can assure her that it is not an anabolic steroid. The HCP actually does some face saving for Julie and reassures her by saying, "Yeah, you probably saw the name, corticosteroids, and thought, uh oh. . . . So, yes, that does concern people. I do want to reassure you that this is medication that only goes to her lungs and won't get in her body. They're not the same kind of drugs as the ones you're worried about."

Next, the HCP asks permission to talk about Sara's lungs in general and what they are like when she is having an attack. Julie is quite interested in this new information. Part of the reason for this information is to help Julie understand that Sara's lungs are really different and far more sensitive than most people's. This new information should also help Julie understand how smoke on her clothes, even though she smokes outside, can still affect Sara's asthma. The HCP uses an analogy again, about burned skin, to help Julie understand how exquisitely sensitive Sara's lungs are. The HCP then explains in a straightforward, nonjudgmental way that ". . . unfortunately, even though you are smoking outside and keeping the smoke away from Sara, the smoke on your clothes, because her lungs are so sensitive, can affect her lungs and cause her to have a reaction. Something I would like you to think about is that if Sara uses the chronic inhaler every day, she may not be sensitive to the smoke on your clothes . . . but she still may be, because her lungs are just very different from ours." Again, the HCP does not tell Julie what to do. He does tell Julie he would like to see her quit smoking for herself. Because of the amount of rapport that has been built, Julie can hear this and not feel defensive. It is heard as an extension of the caring she has experienced in regard to Sara. Again the HCP asks Julie how this new information affects her thinking about smoke on her clothes. Julie says that she is not ready to quit smoking but would be willing to smoke only when Sara is at school and change clothes before she comes home. The HCP lets Julie know that quitting smoking can be very difficult and that anything she can do to reduce Sara's exposure to smoke will help. The new information provided has affected Julie's sense making about smoking outside and having smoke on her clothes. Finally, the HCP summarizes what has taken place. This forms a kind of verbal contract, and Julie agrees. The HCP lets Julie know that if and when she is ready to quit smoking, he would like to help.

This was an actual encounter that occurred two years ago. Since then, Sara has not been in the emergency room for her asthma. Many HCPs are concerned about the amount of time MI might take. The first dialogue we presented, which did not use MI, took around two minutes. The probability that it would result in change was zero. The MI encounter took 6.50 minutes. This 4.50 minute increase saved 10 emergency room visits over two years and countless time spent by other HCPs scolding Julie about her smoking. Overall, it did not take longer to use MI, and the cost savings (and face saving) were substantial.

## Case 2

Jack Snow is a 63-year-old man newly diagnosed with type 2 diabetes. He is at the clinic to discuss his new diagnosis with a case manager from his health plan. He has been prescribed a once-daily oral medication for his diabetes.

## Dialogue without MI

HCP: (matter of fact) Hi. Are you, uh, Jack Snow? (shakes hands)

Pt: *Yeah.*

HCP: What brings you in?

Pt: (anxiously) *I'm supposed to come and learn about how to manage my diabetes. I just got diagnosed.*

HCP: I see that your A1c or your blood glucose is very high.

Pt: (worried) *That's what the doctor said. She really laid into me about that. She said it was . . . I guess this is really serious stuff. She was talking to me about my eyesight, my feet, problems with a lot of other stuff. Really scared me. So . . . (deep exhalation), how to manage all of this, I guess, is what I've gotta learn, but it just sounds massive.*

HCP: (matter of fact) Well, you do need to take your medicine. You'll need to start dieting, lose some weight, change your eating habits, and get some exercise to get your diabetes under control, because your doctor's right—it is very serious.

Pt: *Wow. That's a huge amount of stuff to do. I'm not certain I can do all that. And on top of that if I don't get it all done, all that stuff can happen to me?*

HCP: Sure can.

Pt: (upset) *Aggh.*

HCP: So, we need to start looking at doing all these different things to get your diabetes under control, because your number is very high.

Pt: (overwhelmed and dejected) *Well, I guess so.*

## Analysis

Jack Snow is feeling very worried and overwhelmed. He is worried about the complications of untreated diabetes, and he feels overwhelmed at all the things the physician has said he needs to do to prevent those complications. His sense is that his illness is very serious, especially if it is allowed to progress, yet he does not feel at all confident that he can do all that's needed to prevent having the serious complications. This patient understands the *importance* of treating his diabetes; he simply is not *confident* that he can do what is necessary. He feels hopeless and doomed, and his motivation for change is very low. He truly feels overwhelmed and stuck.

What does this patient need from the HCP? First, he needs some compassion and understanding. He needs to know that his concerns are being heard and honored. None of this is happening. After Mr. Snow expresses his concern about the seriousness of the diagnosis and the consequences if it's left undertreated, the HCP, in a very matter of fact manner, reels off everything Mr. Snow needs to do and reiterates the seriousness of the diagnosis. The patient responds with even more worry and concern and expresses doubt about being able to do everything the HCP has listed. He asks, if he doesn't do all of these things, can bad things happen to him? The HCP simply responds, "Sure can." Mr. Snow is left feeling even more frightened and overwhelmed.

If change is going to take place for Mr. Snow, he first needs to feel safe and understood. He must feel that the HCP understands he is frightened and feeling overwhelmed. Next, his sense that he can't do what's needed has to be addressed in a way that says to him, "We are going to work together to break this down into doable pieces so you can get your diabetes under control and prevent those serious consequences." Mr. Snow must be given some hope that this is possible, and he must feel confident that he can do what is needed, or change is not going to take place. He needs compassionate guidance, not just an impersonal set of orders.

## Dialogue with MI

Let's look at how this situation might have been handled using MI.

HCP: Hi, Mr. Snow. How are you doing today (shakes hands)? I'm Bruce Berger. I'm a case manager with your health plan. I understand that you came in today to talk about your diabetes.

Pt: (very somber) *Yeah, I'm supposed to learn how to manage it. I just learned that I've got diabetes, and apparently it's pretty bad. She said my blood sugar was sky high, and then she laid all these huge consequences on, things that can happen that just sound so disastrous. And then she told me you've gotta do all this stuff, and man, I'm just sorta swimmin' right now.*

HCP: So you just saw the doctor, and you sound like you got blindsided with not only how frightening this seems that you have diabetes . . . and she told you a whole lot of things that can happen to your eyes, your circulation (patient nodding in agreement), and all of those kinds of things.

Pt: *She mentioned my legs having troubles . . . I mean, it's bad.*

HCP: So you're sort of reeling right now from all that, and you sound a little bit . . . pretty scared, actually.

Pt: *Well that's . . . yeah . . . it's not just being scared, ya know. I don't want that to happen to me, but then when she counts off all these things I've gotta do, I'm sorta going waaaaa (gestures and rolls head and eyes). I'm not certain I can get it done. It's sorta like, I'm sitting here thinking, oh my god, this is what's gonna happen to me. And, it's discouraging. It's plain discouraging.*

HCP: So on top of the fact that you've got something that you're really scared about, and its consequences in terms of everything that can happen, it sounds like what worries you, also, is all the things she said you'll need to do to get it under control. You can't imagine doing all of those things, so you feel like all that bad stuff is almost bound to happen.

Pt: *Yeah, it looks like a massive task that I may not be able to handle and then, yeah, all this horrible stuff happens to me. It's a bleak-looking situation in a lot of ways.*

HCP: (nodding) OK. What I want to do is help you break this up into doable chunks so that we can get your blood sugar down. On the one hand, your doctor's right. Your blood sugar is very high and we do want to get it down so that those consequences don't happen, and there are a number of things you can do to get your blood sugar down. On the other hand, we can take this a step at a time so it's not so overwhelming. I'd like you to be able to tell me what kinds of things you can do right now. For example, there are basically three things that need to be worked on with diabetes: taking your medicine as prescribed—and honestly, if I were going to work on one thing right away—since everything seems so overwhelming, that would probably be first because it would have the biggest impact. How does that sound so far?

Pt: *I don't think I would have too much trouble taking the medicine, especially since I understand that my blood sugar's really high.*

HCP: So that sounds doable.

Pt: *Yeah, I can do that. I'm pretty good at taking medicine.*

HCP: Great. It looks like you need to just take your medicine once a day, from the prescription, so that sounds doable right now.

Pt: (calmly) *Yeah, I think I can probably do that.*

HCP: OK, and the other things that can be worked on over time are changing your eating habits—not necessarily to eat less, but to eat healthier foods—and getting more physical activity. And by the way, that doesn't mean you have to go to the gym; it means things like more walking, maybe using stairs instead of an elevator or escalator, things like that.

Pt: *Uh, she also mentioned monitoring my blood sugar with all of this, and that just seemed like . . . uh . . . a bunch of mumbo jumbo to me.*

HCP: Yeah. The reason for that is to give you feedback about how those other things are going, so that it keeps you on task. It helps you know that when you're taking your medication and changing your eating habits, it's really having an impact on your blood sugar, and getting your blood sugar down is going to keep you from having all those other problems.

Pt: *OK.*

HCP: Where does this leave you in terms of how you're feeling now?

Pt: *I like that we can do this a step at a time. That relieves some pressure. Being able to talk with you and doing this as we go along . . . rather than . . . I wasn't sure that I could just, wham, put this huge program into effect. But doing this a step at a time . . . getting on the medicine . . . I don't think that's any big problem. That I can do.*

HCP: Sounds like you're very committed to that.

Pt: (enthusiastic) *Yeah, I can do that . . . as long as there's no big-time side effects.*

HCP: People usually do very well on these medications. It sounds like you are going to take the medication and then add other changes as we go along.

Pt: *Right.*

HCP: OK. Let's see how things go, and if it's all right, I will call to check in with you in about two or three weeks.

Pt: *Sounds great.*

## Analysis

Jack Snow is feeling very worried and overwhelmed. He is worried about the complications of untreated diabetes, and he feels overwhelmed at all the things the physician has said he needs to do to prevent those complications. His sense is that his illness is very serious, especially if it is allowed to progress, yet he does not feel at all confident that he can do all that's needed to prevent having the serious complications. This patient understands the *importance* of treating his diabetes; he simply is not *confident* that he can do what is necessary. He feels hopeless and doomed, and his motivation for change is very low. He truly feels overwhelmed and stuck.

The HCP recognizes that Mr. Snow feels overwhelmed and that he didn't expect to be diagnosed with such a serious condition. The HCP says to Mr. Snow, "So you just saw the doctor, and you sound like you got blindsided with not only how frightening this seems that you have diabetes . . . and she told you a whole lot of things that can happen to your eyes, your circulation (patient nodding in agreement), and all of those kinds of things." Next, he says to Mr. Snow, "So you're sort of reeling right now from all that, and you sound a little bit . . . pretty scared, actually." The HCP reflects back these statements to let Mr. Snow know that he recognizes his concerns and that he is listening. Mr. Snow tells the HCP that he is not just scared about the consequences of his diabetes progressing, he also is not sure he can do what is needed to prevent that. He is feeling overwhelmed. Mr. Snow has actually corrected the HCP to let him know that it's more than just being scared. The HCP listens carefully and now reflects this new information back to Mr. Snow in a way that lets him know he has really been listening. The result is that Mr. Snow nods and then says, "Yeah, it looks like a massive task that I may not be able to handle and then, yeah, all this horrible stuff happens to me. It's a bleak-looking situation in a lot of ways."

An important point here is that the HCP has worked hard to develop rapport with Mr. Snow. He was genuinely listening and reflecting his understanding, and even though Mr. Snow corrected him, rapport was developed. The HCP listened to Mr. Snow's new information, reformulated his understanding, and reflected it back. It is far more important to make a genuine effort to understand patients than to always be perfectly accurate. Patients sense a genuine effort to understand. When patients correct a reflection by the HCP, they appreciate it when the HCP respects the patient and the relationship enough to reflect back this reformulation.

It is clear to this HCP that if Mr. Snow is going to "get unstuck" and manage his diabetes, he has to believe he is capable of taking the necessary steps to be successful. The HCP tells Mr. Snow that he wants "to help you break this up into doable chunks so that we can get your blood sugar down." The HCP gives Mr. Snow hope that this can be done so that he won't suffer the consequences he is worried about. Because this patient is feeling overwhelmed, the HCP suggests that the first step might be taking the medication as prescribed, since this will have the biggest impact right away; the HCP also mentions that the medication has to be taken only once a day. When asked what he thinks of the HCP's suggestion, Mr. Snow responds, in a noticeably calmer manner, that he thinks he can do that. Notice that even though the HCP suggests taking the medication, he still leaves the decision up to the patient. In a situation in which the patient isn't so overwhelmed, the HCP might provide a menu of options for treating diabetes and ask the patient which items he would like to work on.

Next, the HCP describes other lifestyle changes that Mr. Snow can make over time. At this point, the patient feels comfortable enough to mention that the physician said something about monitoring his blood sugar and that sounded like "a bunch of mumbo jumbo to me." The HCP explains the purpose of monitoring and how that relates to Mr. Snow's goals of getting his diabetes under control to reduce his risks. Mr. Snow is very satisfied with this response because it continues to address his sense making. Notice also that the HCP does not discount or argue with the comment about "mumbo jumbo."

Mr. Snow's comment about monitoring raises a question we often hear about empathy, reflection, and developing rapport: "Do you always have to reflect back what the patient is telling you?" We believe that early in the relationship it is crucial to empathize with the patient and reflect back your understanding explicitly and consistently. At that point patients are still making sense of the relationship, still trying to figure out if it is safe and if they can trust you. Once trust is established, it generally is still important to reflect or empathize with statements that have strong emotional content. However, since Mr. Snow is simply expressing a passing concern, the HCP addresses the question without empathizing or reflecting because rapport has already been established.

Finally, after all of the new information about immediate (taking the medication) and long-term changes, the HCP asks Mr. Snow how he is feeling now. The HCP and the patient have been over a great deal of information, and the HCP is checking on how the patient is feeling about it all. Mr. Snow responds that he feels good that he can talk with the HCP, take things a step at a time, and not try to put everything into place at once. He says, ". . . doing this a step at a time . . . getting on the medicine . . . I don't think that's any big problem. That I can do." The HCP reinforces and supports Mr. Snow's commitment and change talk by saying, "Sounds like you're very committed to that." Because he is feeling comfortable with the HCP, Mr. Snow raises a new concern by saying, "Yeah, I can do that . . . as long as there's no big-time side effects." The HCP addresses his concern and asks Mr. Snow if he can check in on him in a few weeks.

This patient was overwhelmed and frightened. In a relatively short time, through the use of MI, he becomes committed to taking his medication for his diabetes. He is in a far better position now to be willing to take additional steps to get his diabetes under control.

## Case 3

Jack Johnson, a 61-year-old man newly diagnosed with high cholesterol, presents a new prescription at the pharmacy. He is very concerned about the side effect of muscle weakness, which this medication can cause.

# Dialogue without MI

HCP:   Mr. Johnson?

Pt:   *Yeah?*

HCP:   I'm here to talk to you about your cholesterol and the medicine your doctor prescribed.

Pt:   *I talked to my doctor about my medicine. That's his job.*

HCP:   Well, it's my job, too, to help you understand how to use your medicine and give you information about getting the most benefit from it.

Pt:   *Well, to be honest with you, I'm not even certain I'm going to take the medicine. I know I've got high cholesterol and I've got to get that down, but on the other hand this medicine can cause some severe muscle weakness and I just can't afford that. I'm a truck driver and I haul those heavy boxes in on the dollies, and I just can't afford that, so you know . . .*

HCP:   So, your doctor told you that if your cholesterol remains elevated you're at risk of stroke or heart attack?

Pt:   *Yeah, down the line, but . . .*

HCP:   OK. Well, the side effect is something that's very, very rare. It's not really something you need to worry about, and the risk of stroke or heart attack is much worse.

Pt:   *Well, right now it's the muscle weakness that I'm concerned about. That's the present. I've gotta do my job.*

HCP:   I understand that, but, like I said, it's very rare. If you feel some muscle weakness you let your doctor know. It's not permanent. It won't get to the point where it affects your job . . .

Pt:   (interrupts) *Well, why don't you just give me the medicine and I'll take it home and I'll think about it. But, you know, I'm worried about my job.*

HCP:   You really need to take it. And, like I said, the muscle weakness is rare. If you feel some weakness, just let your doctor know. He can take you off it, switch you . . . it's not permanent.

Pt:     *Sure, fine.*

HCP:    It's not permanent.

Pt:     *Whatever.*

HCP:    OK. Stroke or heart attack is much worse. Make sure you go ahead and pick up your medicine on your way out. One every day to get your cholesterol down.

Pt:     *OK. Sure, fine.*

## Analysis

What happened here? What would you say is the probability that Mr. Johnson is going to take the cholesterol medication as prescribed? Probably very low. Why did this happen? Mr. Johnson was aware that he had high cholesterol and that this put him at risk for stroke or heart attack. But he was more concerned about the potential for muscle weakness that his physician had mentioned. Several things should be noted. When he greeted Mr. Johnson, the HCP did not shake hands with the patient (see video at www.mihcp.com/3443.html or QR code at end of chapter) or introduce himself. He only told Mr. Johnson that he was there to discuss his cholesterol and medication. When Mr. Johnson said that was his doctor's job, the HCP basically corrected him and told him that it was his job, too. A lot of relational resistance and loss of face was occurring from the very beginning of the encounter. When Mr. Johnson tells the HCP that he isn't sure if he is going to take the medication because he is a truck driver and has to lift heavy boxes and he can't afford to suffer from the side effect of muscle weakness, the HCP tells him that the side effect is rare and should not affect his job. The HCP does not acknowledge Mr. Johnson's legitimate concern; this creates more relational resistance and fails to create rapport. As a result, Mr. Johnson says he will take the medication home but isn't sure he will use it. The HCP then scolds Mr. Johnson, tells him he needs to take it, and repeats that the muscle weakness is rare and reversible. Although this information about muscle weakness is valid, Mr. Johnson cannot hear it because of his loss of face. He simply does not trust the HCP at this point, because his concern was not respected. The HCP seems to think that if he repeats himself enough times, Mr. Johnson will agree to take the medicine. Of course, this does not happen. Mr. Johnson says, "OK. Sure, fine" because at this point he is tired of "wrestling" and wants to end the conversation.

# Dialogue with MI

Let's take a look at how this interaction might go if the HCP uses MI.

HCP: (shakes hands) Hi, Mr. Johnson.

Pt: *Hey.*

HCP: I'm Tom Browning. I'm a pharmacist here, and I was wanting to spend just a little time with you talking about your cholesterol— I found out you were newly diagnosed—and your medicine for your cholesterol.

Pt: *Yeah, my doctor talked to me about my cholesterol. That's his job.*

HCP: OK, I'm certainly glad to hear that your doctor did spend some time with you. I see myself as somebody who works with your doctor to help you get the most benefit from your medicine; because you are going to spend money on it we want to make sure that you get the most benefit from it. Also, sometimes it may be difficult to reach your doctor; we're also here. And so, we try to work together. Would that be OK?

Pt: *Yeah, that would be OK. I'm not so certain I'm even going to take the medicine 'cause he mentioned muscle weakness. I know I've got high cholesterol. And that I'm runnin' the risk of stroke or heart attack down the line. But, he mentioned muscle weakness, and I've been thinking about that and, you know, I'm a truck driver and I've gotta haul the heavy boxes out of the truck on a dolly, and I can't afford that right now. That muscle weakness . . . that bothers me.*

HCP: So on the one hand the doctor talked to you about high cholesterol down the line possibly causing a stroke or heart attack (Pt: *Oh yeah*) and that would be pretty serious. On the other hand, when you found out that this drug might cause muscle weakness, that really alarmed you.

Pt: *Yeah, that's the present. That's what I face now with my job.*

HCP: Especially with your job (Pt: *Yeah*) and preventing you from earning your livelihood.

Pt: *Uh huh.*

HCP: OK. Would you mind if I give you a little bit of information about the muscle weakness and you tell me what you think?

Pt: *That would be fine.*

HCP: The muscle weakness with this drug is very rare. Usually it doesn't even happen, OK? If it happens, it usually happens within the first month of taking the medicine. You'll notice it in terms of weakness in the arms or some muscle pain that's not usual. If this should happen, uh, if you let the doctor or me know right away, we can get you off the medicine. It's completely reversible; the muscle weakness will go away within a couple days.

Pt: *Oh.*

HCP: Now, you don't want to let that go on for months at a time. That's when it can become serious.

Pt: *Oh. OK.*

HCP: But otherwise, again, it's rare and it's completely reversible if you let us know.

Pt: *Well . . . (pauses for two seconds) You know, I guess it doesn't worry me quite as much if it's reversible like that. You know, I was thinking this was gonna be big time . . . but ah . . . yeah, it sounds manageable.*

HCP: OK. So talk to me a little bit more about what the doctor's told you about your risks of stroke or heart attack while you have high cholesterol.

Pt: *Oh, he just said that the risks are up. I think he called it elevated. But, uh, that I'm at a higher risk of having a stroke or heart attack down the line. (pauses for two seconds) You know . . . that's down the line.*

HCP: Well, how important would it be for you to do whatever you can to reduce your risk of stroke or heart attack down the line?

Pt: *Well . . . (pauses for three seconds) you know, my wife and I want to retire in four or five years and we want to be really active, visiting all sorts of places* (glancing at book in his hand) *. . . the fjords of Norway and things like that. So, uh, I guess having a stroke or heart attack would really be bad for that. So, uh . . . we want to live our dreams actively.*

HCP: And certainly one of the risks of stroke is paralysis, and if you want to be active that could be (Pt: *Whoa*) really a problem.

Pt: *Yep. No, no . . . we want to be able to be very active.*

HCP: OK. This medicine can really help lower your risks of having a stroke or heart attack, so that five years from now when you do retire you can enjoy it without any disability. What are your thoughts about that?

Pt: *Well, uh, I guess, uh, that's the way to go then 'cause I don't want to be, you know, crippled by a stroke or heart attack* (HCP: Sure) *so taking the medicine sounds like the name of the game right now.*

HCP: I think that would go a long way toward reducing those risks.

Pt: *Yeah.*

HCP: So where we are right now, if I understand, is that you're feeling more comfortable about your concern about muscle weakness (Pt: *Oh yeah*) and you seem fairly committed to taking the medicine to reduce your risks so that you can enjoy your retirement. (Pt: *Yeah*) And so at this point you're going to get the medication . . .

Pt: (interrupting) *And the medicine can get my cholesterol down?*

HCP: Definitely. It can lower your cholesterol by up to 50%.

Pt: *Whoa! OK!*

HCP: So it's pretty effective.

Pt: *Yeah, I'll take the medicine.*

HCP: OK, and at some other point we can talk about some other things you may be able to do, including diet—changes in your eating habits that can lower your cholesterol even more.

Pt: *OK. That'll be fine.*

HCP: Well, they have your medication ready, and if you have any questions, let us know.

Pt: *Fair enough. Hey, thanks. I appreciate that.*

HCP: (shakes hands) Good to meet you.

## Analysis

By the time this conversation is over, Mr. Johnson is not only committed to taking the medication to lower his cholesterol, he is also interested in learning additional ways to lower it, *and* he actually thanks the pharmacist, Tom Browning, for his help. How did this happen? First, when he greets Mr. Johnson, Tom extends his hand, introduces himself, and explains why he is there. Even when Mr. Johnson questions Tom's wanting to discuss his cholesterol and medication by saying, "That's my doctor's job," Tom, rather than becoming defensive, calmly explains that he sees himself working with Mr. Johnson's doctor to help Mr. Johnson get the most benefit from his medication. He also says that he can be an additional resource for Mr. Johnson if he cannot reach his doctor. He then asks Mr. Johnson if this will be all right with him and Mr. Johnson concurs. Tom respects Mr. Johnson's statement and, rather than become argumentative, he simply focuses on how he wants to help Mr. Johnson. As a result there is no additional relational resistance or loss of face. Next, Mr. Johnson expresses his concern about muscle weakness and his resulting ambivalence about taking the medication. In a caring and respectful manner, Tom then builds rapport by summarizing what Mr. Johnson has told him: Mr. Johnson understands that his medication is for reducing his cholesterol and therefore his risk of stroke or heart attack, but he is alarmed right now about the effect of muscle weakness on his ability to do his job. Mr. Johnson indicates that Tom's summary is accurate. It is evident that he feels respected and understood. Next, Tom asks permission to provide some additional information about the muscle weakness for Mr. Johnson to consider. After receiving the information, Mr. Johnson says he is relieved that the muscle weakness is rare and not permanent.

At this point, Tom does not assume that Mr. Johnson is ready to take the medication. Sometimes, after a primary issue is addressed, a new issue surfaces. Tom now asks Mr. Johnson what the physician has told him about the risks of his cholesterol staying elevated (stroke or heart attack). What comes out in this part of the conversation is that Mr. Johnson realizes that there are risks but they are "down the line." Mr. Johnson seems to be saying that the risks are not an immediate problem. Rather than being argumentative, Tom explores with Mr. Johnson how important is it for him to reduce these risks. Mr. Johnson talks about wanting to retire in a few years with his wife, be very active, and travel. Tom mentions possible paralysis from a stroke and connects it to interfering with Mr. Johnson's goal of traveling and being active. This makes things more real and "present" for Mr. Johnson. Tom has helped Mr. Johnson figure out the personal implications a stroke would have for his future retirement. As a result, Mr. Johnson is more motivated to start taking the medication now. Tom summarizes Mr. Johnson's reduced fears about muscle weakness and his commitment to taking the medication to lower his risks. Mr. Johnson concurs and then asks for reassurance that the medication will lower his risks. Tom provides that reassurance along with information about the effectiveness of the medication. Mr. Johnson responds very favorably, saying, "Whoa! OK!" and then "I'll take the medicine." Sensing the patient's commitment to lowering his cholesterol and his risks, Tom plants a seed for a future conversation by saying, "OK, at some other point we can talk about some other things you may be able to do, including diet—changes in your eating habits that can lower your cholesterol even more" and Mr. Johnson seems quite interested. In fact, at the end of the conversation he thanks Tom for all of his help. This conversation was less than three minutes longer than the non-MI version, but what a difference it made in regard to the relationship and the outcomes.

## Conclusion

These cases provide examples of the effectiveness of MI. They demonstrate the importance of first building rapport, by using the spirit of MI, and then addressing the sense making of the patient. The cases depict how importance and confidence can greatly affect motivation for change. They also demonstrate that we should not assume that because one primary issue is addressed there are not other issues present. Exploration can help uncover additional concerns.

### QUESTIONS FOR REFLECTION

1. Why would some HCPs label Julie Thompson (asthma case) a difficult patient? Would this be a valid label? Does she present the same concerns in

the inappropriate and appropriate (MI) dialogues? Why does she seem so different in the two?

2. When Jack Snow finds out he has diabetes, what is his sense about the illness and its treatment? What is keeping him from treating his diabetes, if he knows it is serious? What does he need from the HCP?

3. Did Jack Johnson still seem somewhat unresolved about taking the medication, even after his expressed concern was addressed? What reasons would you identify for why he wasn't fully committed at that point? What changed that?

4. What are the three to five most important things you can learn from these three cases?

Scan the QR code for video of the interactions in this chapter.

# CHAPTER 11

# Considerations for Putting MI into Use

f you are reading this book, you've shown an interest in motivational interviewing (MI). We believe there are at least four good reasons for using MI:

1. Patients feel more respected, cared for, and understood. As a result, they are far more likely to consider what you have to say.
2. Health systems are more likely to see improved patient satisfaction with care and better outcomes, along with decreased total health care costs.
3. Your sense of who you are as a provider of care is likely to improve. Not only will you learn to take healthy and appropriate responsibility for the decisions and care of your patients, you will find yourself more relaxed and at peace in interactions with your patients. You will also notice that your patients are more receptive. Who wouldn't like that?
4. If you find yourself using a lot of what you have learned in this book in daily life outside health care, you will discover that others like the way you respond to them. The respect, care, and understanding displayed when using MI are very comforting and attractive to people and help put them at ease. A word of caution, however. Sometimes when you start to talk with others using MI, they may be suspicious of your motives; they may like the way you are treating

them yet wonder whether they can trust that it is genuine. This initial reaction will subside quickly if you are genuine and consistent in using MI.

## When do you get good at this?

People often ask us how long it takes to get good at MI. Our answer is not a simple one. People are very different in their gifts and capacities. In addition, barriers to effective MI must be overcome. How often individuals use and practice MI (and are reflective and get good feedback) also affects how proficient they are at MI.

## Barriers

Barriers to becoming "good" at MI are discussed in the following paragraphs.

**Lacking the spirit of MI.** Some people have a difficult time developing a true spirit of MI, for reasons too numerous and too complex to explore here. Without the spirit of MI, we simply don't believe that MI is possible. One has to cultivate a genuine desire to care for (not fix or control) others if MI is to work. This spirit of MI must be present even when the other is provocative, angry, unwilling, ambivalent, resistant, or defensive. This is not easy.

**Objectification.** Whenever we reduce another human to an object (an "it"), being effective at MI becomes impossible. We may feel justified in reducing others to objects ("that idiot," "difficult patient," "angry jerk," "addict," "stubborn so and so"), but when this happens, it is impossible to be empathic and helpful to the patient. When we objectify others, for whatever reason, we can even feel justified in withholding care and concern. This is a dangerous place to be for someone who provides care. For more information on how this can happen, we highly recommend the book *Bonds that Make Us Free* by C. Terry Warner.[1]

**Everyday talk.** As we have discussed, everyday talk makes a lot of implicit assumptions. Others talk, and we nod or say, "Right," "Yes," "Uh huh," "I understand," or "Got it." Much is assumed about what all these abbreviated responses mean. Also, our training teaches us how to talk *to* or *at* patients, rather than *with* patients. We are taught that we are the expert, so our talk often is directed outward rather than being a two-way exchange of expertise and sense making. MI changes both of these dynamics. We have to learn to become more explicit in responding to patients. We have to learn to exchange information and expertise in order to influence sense making.

**Anxiety.** We have also discussed how our own anxiety can undermine our ability to effectively use MI. Often we are anxious because we feel responsible for fixing a patient or a situation, and this can cause us to try to persuade or direct a patient who is not ready. Ironically, this produces the opposite of what we are hoping for. We also may be anxious because of a need to get things done. Getting things done can be part of our identity, but patients often are not ready to get things done as rapidly as we would like. We must learn to give up this need and the illusion of control. Becoming increasingly aware of when these kinds of anxiety come up is an important step. Introspection is critical. It may be useful to seek professional help if this is a major issue.

**Systems or environmental problems.** Many HCPs work in environments that create a great deal of stress. Heavy workloads, lack of privacy, administrative tasks, legal requirements, system requirements, menial tasks, and the like can make it more difficult to use MI. Add to this a disgruntled patient who decides *you* are the reason for all of his problems within the organization or health plan, and you have a less-than-ideal situation for providing care, much less for being effective at MI. When you are extremely busy and a patient is angry at you for problems you did not even cause, it is very easy to objectify that patient, write him off, throw up your hands, dismiss the patient ("talk to your plan"), and feel justified. If you tell another stressed employee about your encounter with this unreasonable patient and how you abruptly referred him to his health plan, "because I don't need this crap," the chances are good that the other employee will say something like, "Good for you!" and you will feel even more justified in your anger.

Unfortunately, MI cannot solve your system or environmental problems. However, given your situation, MI can at least help you feel that you are doing the right thing. There is value in this. Even if the patient remains unsatisfied or angry, you won't have to second guess your intentions or motives. At the end of the day, there is something to be said for knowing you acted out of genuine kindness and caring, despite difficult and imperfect situations.

# Practice

In addition to recognizing and removing as many barriers as possible, another way to get better at MI is to practice. Keep in mind that not all practice is useful, however. At the golf course, we watched someone throw a bucket of golf balls into a practice sand trap. He then proceeded to hit the golf balls and practiced *not* getting out of the trap.

Every now and then a ball came out of the sand trap, but because he basically didn't know how to hit out of a sand trap, he wasn't able to get a ball out with any consistency. Moreover, no one who actually knew how to get out of sand traps was there to give him feedback. For practice to be effective, you need to (1) have a good sense of the skills and preparation necessary for success, (2) get good, constructive feedback, and (3) know what success looks like when it happens. Success cannot be a random, hit-or-miss event, especially when it comes to using MI with patients.

In addition to reading this book, we recommend that you receive training from an expert in MI. The training should allow you to practice your newly acquired MI skills in a safe environment. We recommend stepwise training in which you practice using exercises of increasing complexity, culminating in facilitated role playing. In addition to structured feedback from peers that includes what you are doing well and how to fine tune or where improvements can be made, you should also receive direct feedback from an expert trainer. Feedback from newly trained peers is not sufficient. Although peers can be very helpful in providing supportive feedback, an expert can provide feedback with much greater depth and insight.

If possible, we recommend that at least two people from an organization get training together, to allow an exchange of ideas and accomplishments and help with difficulties encountered. This can really speed up the learning process. Moreover, being able to observe the other with a patient (with permission from the patient) in order to provide feedback can be very helpful. In organizations that use telephone interventions, observing the calls (again, with permission from the patient) and giving feedback can be very helpful for training purposes.

Because MI is caring, genuine, and respectful, the skills and principles can be practiced anywhere and with anyone. Keep in mind that MI involves voluntary behavior change. Patients don't have to change their behaviors; it really is their decision. Although asking a child to do chores or an employee to come to work is not asking for voluntary behavior change, the skills and principles of MI still apply. As a health care professional (HCP) working with patients, you have unlimited opportunities to practice and refine your MI skills. By being observant, you can begin to assess whether you are being more effective through the use of MI. Being more effective does not always involve behavior change; it can mean better rapport and increased change talk even if behavior does not change.

Being reflective and introspective is very important in learning MI. Regardless of how much training or experience you have with MI, you still can lapse into provider-centered ways. For example, if you get off a phone call with a patient and realize that you tried to "fix" or persuade a patient who was reluctant or not ready to change, ask yourself what you would do if you could repeat the call. It is not particularly instructive or useful to shame or scold yourself at this point. It also is not useful to just forget about the call without reflecting on what you could have done differently by using MI. Actually say the words, out loud or in your head. This is practice. It helps to reinforce your progress. In addition, it is completely appropriate on the next call to let the patient know you are sorry that you pushed too hard or too fast.

Many people we have trained have found it useful to focus on MI a step at a time. For example, some trainees will start off working hard to "master" developing rapport and using rapport-building skills. We support this approach, but with a word of caution. Rapport building, like MI, is not just something to do. It is not just this skill or that set of skills. In the absence of a genuine and caring desire to understand the sense making of the patient, those skills are not rapport, nor are they MI.

## Final thoughts

When MI is fully activated by a caring practitioner, it has the ability to create a deep connection with the patient through empathy, rapport, and fully addressing the patient's issues. Empathy can create hope for patients and relieve their despair and loneliness. When people feel that their problems or issues are understood and respected at a deep level, they believe there is hope that the problems or issues can be resolved. Without this deep level of understanding, there is far less hope.

Interacting with patients is a privilege. Patients often let us in on their private worlds and their joys and suffering. These privileged interactions, when held with the care afforded by MI, offer opportunities for mutual growth. Caring, safe, and respectful communication offers each person in the relationship the opportunity to learn more about himself. We humans feel best when we are engaged in this kind of growth.

### QUESTIONS FOR REFLECTION

1. Now that you have finished the book, what are the three most important things you'll take with you concerning MI for HCPs?

2. Discuss what is meant by objectification and what you will do to avoid objectifying others. What are the problematic and possibly dangerous results of objectification?
3. What will you do to practice introspection and develop a better understanding of yourself and what you bring (both positive and problematic) to your interactions with patients?

## REFERENCE

1. Warner CT. *Bonds That Make Us Free: Healing Our Relationships, Coming to Ourselves.* Salt Lake City: Shadow Mountain; 2001.

# Index